A US PIVOT AWAY FROM THE MIDDLE EAST
FACT OR FICTION?

Arab Center Washington DC
المركز العربي واشنطن دي سي

Copyright © 2023 Arab Center Washington DC, Inc. All rights reserved.

No part of this publication may be reproduced, copied or distributed in any form or by any means, or stored in any database or retrieval system, without the express prior written permission of Arab Center Washington DC, Inc. No part of this publication shall be reproduced, modified, transmitted, distributed, disseminated, sold, published, sub-licensed, or have derivative work created or based upon it, without the express prior written permission of Arab Center Washington DC, Inc. If you wish to reproduce any part of this publication, please contact Arab Center Washington DC, Inc., at the address below, providing full details.

Arab Center Washington DC, Inc.
800 10th Street, NW, Suite 650
Washington, DC 20001
www.arabcenterdc.org
info@arabcenterdc.org

Ordering Information: Contact Arab Center Washington DC, Inc. at the address above for additional copies or for quantity ordering by corporations, associations, and others.

An electronic copy of this publication is available online at www.arabcenterdc.org

Edited by Imad K. Harb and David J. Kanbergs

Book design by Sally Boylan

Cover Photo by Tech. Sgt. Erik Gudmundson, United States Air Force, taken in Balad, Iraq, on 11.18.2008.

Printed in the United States of America
First Edition

ISBN-13: 978-1-947772-05-2

Arab Center Washington DC, Inc. does not take institutional positions on public policy issues; the views represented herein are the authors' own and do not necessarily reflect the views of ACW, its staff, or board members. All materials found in this publication have been prepared for informational purposes only. The information herein is provided without any representations or warranties, express or implied, regarding the completeness, accuracy, reliability, suitability or availability with respect to the publication or the information, products, services, or related graphics contained in the publication for any purpose. In no event will Arab Center Washington DC, Inc. be liable for any loss or damage including without limitation, indirect or consequential loss or damage; or any loss or damage whatsoever arising from loss of data or profits arising out of, or in connection with, the use of this publication.

Table of Contents

Preface   5
Khalil E. Jahshan

1. THE ORIGIN AND FACETS OF A PIVOT AWAY FROM THE MIDDLE EAST

The Past and Future of the American "Pivot to Asia"   9
Charles W. Dunne

US Military Strategy in the Middle East and the Challenge of Demilitarization   23
Waleed Hazbun

The Economic Dimension of a Pivot Away from the Middle East   33
Mark Finley

Current US-China Relations and the Pivot to Asia   43
Yun Sun

**The US Pivot in the Context of Great Power Competition:
A New Multipolar Global Order?**   53
Patricia Karam

Arab Views on an American Pivot Away from the Middle East   65
Rami G. Khouri

The Greatly Exaggerated US Pivot and America's Failures on Human Rights   75
Sarah Leah Whitson

The US Pivot and Great Cyberpower Competition in the MENA Region   91
Tamara Kharroub

2. CURRENT US ENGAGEMENTS AND ENTANGLEMENTS

The US-Israel Nexus and the Question of a Pivot   105
Yousef Munayyer

The United States and the Arabian Peninsula   117
Kristian Coates Ulrichsen

Declining American Influence in the Middle East:
Afghanistan, Iraq, and Libya   127
Nabeel Khoury

The Syrian Conflict: A Turning Point in US Middle East Policy   139
Lina Khatib

The Mutual Pivot to Asia in US-Egypt Relations   151
Sahar Aziz

Iran and the Perceived US Pivot Away from the Middle East   163
Mahsa Rouhi

The US in the Middle East: Staying Put While Simultaneously Pivoting   175
Imad K. Harb

Biographies of Contributors   185

Preface

Khalil E. Jahshan

Arab Center Washington DC (ACW) is delighted to publish this edited volume, *A US Pivot Away from the Middle East: Fact or Fiction?* This compilation of short essays is primarily based on the proceedings of a conference that was convened by ACW on May 18, 2023 to discuss the widespread political impression, particularly in the Arab region, that the United States has been pivoting away from the Middle East to East Asia and consequently abandoning its security commitments to its regional allies and historical partners. Neither this recent conference nor this volume of essays were meant to advocate for or against such a shift in US foreign policy; rather, their goal is to explore the nature, intent, feasibility, and implications of such a step, should it indeed evolve into a formal tenet of US national security strategy.

Despite vehement denials by current US officials that such a change in US foreign policy has taken place under President Joe Biden (or under any of his recent predecessors for that matter), the perception of a shift has nonetheless taken root in the region. This perception has affected national narratives and official policy among Washington's closest allies and partners in the Arab world, including Saudi Arabia, the United Arab Emirates, and Egypt, not to mention America's challengers and detractors, such as Iran, Syria, China, and Russia.

Indeed, our main rationale for having convened this conference and published this volume stems from our interactions with Arab officials and opinion makers who insist that there is a growing pivot in US policy away from the region. This insistence is countered by equally vehement counterarguments from American officials and experts who stress that the shift is a figment of regional actors' imagination and argue that the United States is actually doing more, not less, in the region, and that the Biden administration intends to maintain its ties and presence there.

Needless to say, the divergent perspectives between American and Arab policymakers are real, and are currently having a detrimental impact on US-Arab bilateral relations, requiring serious attention on the part of think tank analysts and foreign policy practitioners concerned about the issue and its potential fallout. We are grateful for the diverse perspectives presented by our esteemed contributors in their analytical, forthright, and comprehensive handling of the issue, including its historical origins; its political, military, and economic dimensions; its regional and global elements; and its future prospects.

Typical of such collections, the credit for this volume goes to the contributors who were gracious enough to participate in our May conference and/or provide their thoughts and analyses for this publication. We are grateful to both speakers and writers for their invaluable input. It is our sincere hope that you will find these essays intellectually sound and stimulating, and that you will carry their insightful assertions and interpretations forward in your professional endeavors.

1

THE ORIGIN AND FACETS OF A PIVOT AWAY FROM THE MIDDLE EAST

The Past and Future of the American "Pivot to Asia"
Charles W. Dunne

US Military Strategy in the Middle East and the Challenge of Demilitarization
Waleed Hazbun

The Economic Dimension of a Pivot Away from the Middle East
Mark Finley

Current US-China Relations and the Pivot to Asia
Yun Sun

The US Pivot in the Context of Great Power Competition:
A New Multipolar Global Order?
Patricia Karam

Arab Views on an American Pivot Away from the Middle East
Rami G. Khouri

The Greatly Exaggerated US Pivot and America's Failures on Human Rights
Sarah Leah Whitson

The US Pivot and Great Cyberpower Competition in the MENA Region
Tamara Kharroub

The Past and Future of the American "Pivot to Asia"

Charles W. Dunne

Reducing US commitments in the Middle East and focusing strategic attention on Asia has been an attractive but elusive goal of successive US administrations for more than two decades. Former President Barack Obama was the concept's most visible proponent, putting considerable diplomatic effort into it during the third year of his first term, and his successors took up the idea as well. The time seemed right for a change, especially after the formal end of the US combat mission in Iraq in 2011. Since then, the defeat of the so-called Islamic State's "caliphate" in 2017 and the US withdrawal from Afghanistan in 2021 have meant that the United States is no longer actively engaged in major combat operations anywhere in the broader Middle East and North Africa. Meanwhile, the rise of a more aggressive China and the growing economic importance of the Indo-Pacific region have seemed to demand greater US involvement in that part of the world.

American weariness with the MENA region has played a major role too. The apparently intractable problems of the Middle East, from the Arab-Israeli conflict to the threat of Iran, have often seemed impervious to decades of US diplomatic and military interventions. Many expert observers and policy makers believe that the United States would be better off if it shifted its focus to more critical challenges elsewhere and left the Middle East to deal with its own problems, though with an occasional helping hand from Washington. However, the Russian invasion of Ukraine in February 2022 radically transformed the United States' diplomatic and security priorities, as did growing great power competition in the Middle East. As a result, President Joe Biden's initial impulse to reduce US involvement in the region while chastising its leaders for their egregious human rights abuses was quickly transformed into a new policy of outcompeting Russia and China while simultaneously countering Iran. This has meant, in part, taking on new and increasingly burdensome political and security commitments.

Today, the United States appears poised to assume even more responsibilities for its partners' defense, potentially including bilateral security guarantees that would have been unthinkable just a few years ago. These new obligations are anchored by a massive, long-standing American military presence in the region that shows every indication of being permanent. As Washington's latest moves to protect its interests in the Middle East take shape, it seems that if there was ever a moment when the United States could draw back from the region, that moment has passed.

The History of an Idea

During the first year of President Biden's term, discussion within both the administration and Washington's foreign policy establishment centered on the decreasing importance of the Middle East to US strategic calculations and the rising necessity of shifting resources away from the region to focus more intently on the Indo-Pacific. The debate is not new, of course. The George W. Bush administration contemplated focusing more attention on the Indo-Pacific region (at the time referred to as Asia-Pacific) as early as 2001, but this policy largely flew under the radar due to the administration's wish to keep it as quiet as possible to avoid provoking China.[1] This early "pivot" notably did not include any substantial shifts in the global US force posture, which would in any case have proved difficult, if not impossible, after the US-led invasions of Afghanistan and Iraq.

Former President Barack Obama, convinced that Bush had not done enough to engage with the Indo-Pacific region, aired a proposal for his

---

1 Nina Silove, "The Pivot before the Pivot: U.S. Strategy to Preserve the Power Balance in Asia," *International Security* 40, no. 4 (Spring 2016): 45-88.

own "pivot to Asia" during a trip to Australia and Indonesia in November 2011.[2] Unlike Bush's concept, this strategy envisaged a real military and diplomatic retrenchment in the Middle East. As Obama stated in a speech to the Australian Parliament, "After a decade in which we fought two wars that cost us dearly, in blood and treasure, the United States is turning our attention to the vast potential of the Asia-Pacific region."[3] Then Secretary of State Hillary Clinton, meanwhile, termed it the dawn of "America's Pacific century."[4] As the American public increasingly soured on US involvement in the broader Middle East, it soon became clear that the political environment in the United States was aligning neatly with Obama's own foreign policy instincts.[5]

But Obama's pivot did not go as planned.[6] The president's signaling about reducing the US footprint in the region—along with his successful efforts at concluding a nuclear deal with Iran, against the wishes of Israel and key Gulf states—caused alarm among the United States' closest partners, particularly Saudi Arabia. Riyadh, along with others in the Gulf, concluded that the United States was downgrading the importance of their legitimate concerns in its foreign policy and abandoning them to their own devices.[7] It was no coincidence that the kingdom and other Arab states began to hedge their bets on Washington by building closer ties with Moscow and Beijing.

For all his vehement disagreements with his predecessor, former President Donald Trump shared Obama's aversion to entangling commitments in

---

2 Kenneth G. Lieberthal, "The American Pivot to Asia," Brookings Institution, December 21, 2011, https://www.brookings.edu/articles/the-american-pivot-to-asia/.
3 "Remarks By President Obama to the Australian Parliament," The White House, November 17, 2011, https://obamawhitehouse.archives.gov/the-press-office/2011/11/17/remarks-president-obama-australian-parliament.
4 Hillary Clinton, "America's Pacific Century," Foreign Policy, October 11, 2011, https://foreignpolicy.com/2011/10/11/americas-pacific-century/.
5 Stephen P. Cohen and Robert Ward, "Asia Pivot: Obama's Ticket out of Middle East?," Brookings Institution, August 21, 2013, https://www.brookings.edu/opinions/asia-pivot-obamas-ticket-out-of-middle-east/.
6 John Ford, "The Pivot to Asia Was Obama's Biggest Mistake," *The Diplomat*, January 21, 2017, https://thediplomat.com/2017/01/the-pivot-to-asia-was-obamas-biggest-mistake/.
7 The Iran nuclear deal of 2015 (officially the Joint Comprehensive Plan of Action) may have been the last straw for Saudi Arabia, other Gulf nations, and Israel, but it certainly was not the first. Obama's perceived failure to support Egyptian President Hosni Mubarak during the Arab Spring in 2011 and his real failure to enforce his own "red line" on the Syrian regime's use of chemical weapons against civilians in 2013 reinforced the sense among allies of a feckless president eager to abandon long-standing commitments on his way out of the region.

the region, but his attempts to express that in policy terms compounded the confusion and resentment among US partners. Trump floated plans to pull US troops out of the Middle East and Afghanistan several times, and his sudden announcement that he was withdrawing all US forces from Syria in 2018 surprised the military and precipitated the resignation of then Defense Secretary James Mattis.[8] Trump's repeated complaints about the cost to the United States of defending Saudi Arabia, as well as his administration's low-key response after a 2019 attack on key Saudi oil facilities (which was claimed by Yemen's Iran-backed Houthi forces) were proof enough in the eyes of Gulf Arab states that the United States was no longer strongly committed to their defense against Iran.[9] At the end of his term in office, Trump had succeeded in reducing the overall US force presence in Syria, Iraq, and Afghanistan, against the advice of military leadership.[10] But a substantial US presence nonetheless remained embedded throughout the region.

Policy Debate in Washington: Is Less Really More?

After the policy disarray and mixed messages of the Obama and Trump years, leading Middle East analysts began to make a strong case for a thorough reevaluation of the US presence in the region. Aaron David Miller and Richard Sokolsky, for example, argued that, "The turbulent Middle East—where more often than not American ideas go to die—has become

---

8 Uri Friedman, "The Consequences of Donald Trump Washing His Hands of the Middle East," *The Atlantic*, October 23, 2019, https://www.theatlantic.com/international/archive/2019/10/donald-trump-middle-east-consequences/600610/.; Paul Sonne et al., "Mattis Resigns after Clash with Trump over Troop Withdrawal from Syria and Afghanistan," *The Washington Post*, December 20, 2018, https://www.washingtonpost.com/world/national-security/trump-announces-mattis-will-leave-as-defense-secretary-at-the-end-of-february/2018/12/20/e1a846ee-e147-11e8-ab2c-b31dcd53ca6b_story.html.

9 "Trump Complains US Is 'Subsidising' Saudi Arabia's Military," *Middle East Eye*, October 3, 2018, https://www.middleeasteye.net/news/trump-complains-us-subsidising-saudi-arabias-military.; Joshua Keating, "Why Trump Is Playing the Tough Guy With the Saudis Now," *Slate*, April 29, 2019, https://slate.com/news-and-politics/2019/04/trump-saudis-opec-salman.html. On the 2019 attack, see: Patrick Wintour and Julian Borger, "Saudi Offers 'Proof' of Iran's Role in Oil Attack and Urges US Response," *The Guardian*, September 18, 2019, https://www.theguardian.com/world/2019/sep/18/saudi-oil-attack-rouhani-dismisses-us-claims-of-iran-role-as-slander.

10 Lolita C. Baldor, "AP Sources: Trump to Order Troop Cuts in Afghanistan, Iraq," *Associated Press*, November 16, 2020, https://apnews.com/article/trump-troop-reduction-afghanistan-iraq-92e43910a8822160ce45f950139ae048.

decidedly less important to American foreign policy and to our interests. [...] American leadership and exceptionalism cannot fix a broken Middle East or play a major role in leading it to a better future."[11] They advocated a much smaller US military presence, with special forces and over-the-horizon capabilities—often called "offshore balancing"—employed as needed to respond to terrorism and military contingencies.[12]

Some went further, arguing that the United States should withdraw its troops altogether. One observer claimed that "the importance of the Persian Gulf long has been [sic] exaggerated," and that the presence of US troops in the region has actually fed instability, leading partners to assume that they can act with impunity under the American protective umbrella, which in turn fuels the rise of violent non-state actors and hostile proxy forces.[13] Not only is the Middle East, as another analyst once argued, a "small, poor, weak region beset by an array of problems that mostly do not affect Americans—and that US forces cannot fix," it is incredibly expensive for the American taxpayer to conduct Washington's (largely irrelevant) missions in the region, from fighting terrorism—when the threat to Americans outside a war zone is vanishingly small—to maintaining the many military bases required to do so.[14] Despite pushback from many in the think tank, policy, and academic spheres who believe the Middle East remains of vital strategic interest, this line of thinking remains durable among some prominent Middle East experts. One former senior official recently made the case that the United States is already well on its way to the exit, and for good reason: "A net assessment suggests that the United States would have been better off today had it not been so eager to intervene in the Middle East. Fortunately, America's era there is drawing to a close, and probably not a moment too soon."[15]

---

11 Aaron David Miller and Richard Sokolsky, "The Middle East Just Doesn't Matter as Much Any Longer," *Politico*, September 3, 2020, https://carnegieendowment.org/2020/09/03/middle-east-just-doesn-t-matter-as-much-any-longer-pub-82653.

12 Christopher Mott, "The Case for U.S. Offshore Balancing in the Middle East," *The National Interest*, October 14, 2020, https://nationalinterest.org/blog/skeptics/case-us-offshore-balancing-middle-east-170704.

13 Doug Bandow, "A Blueprint for Getting Out of the Middle East," Cato Institute, July 8, 2021, https://www.cato.org/commentary/blueprint-getting-out-middle-east.

14 Justin Logan, "The Case For Withdrawing From The Middle East," Defense Priorities, September 30, 2020, https://www.defensepriorities.org/explainers/the-case-for-withdrawing-from-the-middle-east.

15 Steven Simon, *Grand Delusion: The Rise and Fall of American Ambition in the Middle East* (New York: Penguin Press, 2023), 414.

Others, however, continue to believe that while a reduction in forces and political capital is desirable, some sort of limited engagement will continue to be necessary. Jake Sullivan, a longtime foreign policy aide to Joe Biden and now the president's national security advisor, has advocated something of a middle ground. He and Daniel Benaim—now the deputy assistant secretary of state for Arabian Peninsula affairs in the Near East Bureau at the Department of State—recommended a policy that would be "less ambitious in terms of the military ends the United States seeks and in its efforts to remake nations from within, but more ambitious in using US leverage and diplomacy to press for a de-escalation in tensions and eventually a new modus vivendi among the key regional actors."[16] Vigorous diplomacy and resizing the US military presence to reflect a "more modest regional engagement," as Tamara Cofman Wittes puts it, were seen by Sullivan and others as the future of American regional policy.[17]

As president, Joe Biden was more than happy to adopt this approach. He revived Obama's concept of a pivot to the Indo-Pacific region, promising to redirect America's strategic efforts to meet the challenge of a more aggressive China while simultaneously de-emphasizing the Middle East.[18] With Sullivan in the national security advisor's office, the Biden administration presumed that creative US diplomacy could encourage regional actors to negotiate their differences and find new ways to cooperate, obviating the need for either a significant US military presence or frequent diplomatic intervention to deal with regional conflicts. Biden's enthusiastic embrace of the Trump administration's singular Middle East diplomatic triumph, the Abraham Accords—which normalized relations between Israel, the UAE, and Bahrain (soon followed by Morocco and Sudan)—became the foundation of his Middle East policy.[19]

---

16 Daniel Benaim and Jake Sullivan, "America's Opportunity in the Middle East," *Foreign Affairs*, May 22, 2020, https://www.foreignaffairs.com/articles/middle-east/2020-05-22/americas-opportunity-middle-east.

17 Tamara Cofman Wittes, "What to Do—And What Not to Do—In the Middle East," Brookings Institution, January 25, 2021, https://www.brookings.edu/research/what-to-do-and-what-not-to-do-in-the-middle-east/.

18 Carla Freeman et al., "A Closer Look at Biden's Indo-Pacific Strategy," United States Institute of Peace, March 7, 2022, https://www.usip.org/publications/2022/03/closer-look-bidens-indo-pacific-strategy.

19 "The Abraham Accords," U.S. Department of State, undated, https://www.state.gov/the-abraham-accords/.; Charles W. Dunne, "US Middle East Policy: The Trump-Biden Doctrine in Action," Arab Center Washington DC, March 22, 2023, https://arabcenterdc.org/resource/us-middle-east-policy-the-trump-biden-doctrine-in-action/.

New Strategies and New Security Commitments Take Shape

If any serious consideration of paring back US involvement in the Middle East was being contemplated, however, the Russian invasion of Ukraine in February 2022 changed both the narrative and the thinking in Washington. The ensuing disruption to global oil markets forced Biden to abandon his earlier hard line on both Saudi Arabia (even if it had been mostly rhetorical to begin with) and its controversial crown prince, Mohammed bin Salman Al Saud (MBS).[20] In July 2022 Biden found it necessary to visit the kingdom and importune MBS to increase oil production in an effort to curb energy prices.[21] While the effort was unsuccessful, the Biden visit was crucial for another reason: it marked the end of any immediate plans to extricate the United States from its commitments in the region and the start of a process to deepen American political and security ties to regional autocracies.

During this trip, Biden reaffirmed the American commitment to maintaining a strong presence in the Middle East, stating that Washington "will not walk away and leave a vacuum to be filled by China, Russia or Iran," and promising to assert "active, principled American leadership" to confront challenges to the existing regional order.[22] While this statement emerged naturally from the president's rhetoric about defending global democracy against autocratic advances, it was also an acknowledgment that the war in Ukraine and continually rising US-China tensions had

---

20 Jonathan Guyer, "Biden Promised a Harder Line on Saudi Arabia. Why Can't He Deliver?," *Vox*, Jan 23, 2022, https://www.vox.com/22881937/biden-saudi-arabia-mbs-khashoggi-yemen-human-rights.
21 Hesham Alghannam and Mohammad Yaghi, "Biden's Trip to Saudi Arabia: Successes and Failures," Carnegie Endowment for International Peace, August 11, 2022, https://carnegieendowment.org/sada/87662.
22 David E. Sanger and Peter Baker, "As Biden Reaches Out to Mideast Dictators, His Eyes Are on China and Russia," *New York Times*, July 16, 2022, https://www.nytimes.com/2022/07/16/world/middleeast/biden-saudi-arabia-china-russia.html. This sweeping pledge did not extend to Syria, which was welcomed back into the Arab League at its May 2023 summit without noticeable opposition from the United States. This constituted a significant diplomatic win for Russia and Iran, Syrian President Bashar al-Assad's two major foreign backers, and for Assad himself. The Syrian president took the opportunity to tell the assembled Arab leaders that Syria's readmittance was an occasion "to rearrange our affairs with the least amount of foreign interference," an obvious hint that it was time to abandon ties to the US in favor, presumably, of warming up to his own patrons. See: Raffi Berg and David Gritten, "Syria's Assad Tells Arab Leaders to Take 'Historic Opportunity' to Remake Middle East," *BBC News*, May 20, 2023, https://www.bbc.com/news/world-middle-east-65625742.

suddenly vaulted questions about the American role to the top of the US foreign policy agenda.[23] Biden carried this theme forward in Jeddah, Saudi Arabia, where he met with the leaders of the GCC+3 (Saudi Arabia, the United Arab Emirates, Kuwait, Bahrain, Qatar, and Oman, plus Egypt, Iraq, and Jordan). According to a White House fact sheet, Biden underscored the "centrality" of the Middle East to the United States and highlighted America's "enduring commitment to the security and territorial defense of US partners."[24]

Biden's remarks may have been the most public acknowledgment of America's shifting policy, but the new approach was becoming clear even before the president's regional tour. The United States, for example, indicated that it would back a "Middle East Air Defense Alliance" actively organized by Israel alongside its Abraham Accords partner, the United Arab Emirates, with potential Saudi involvement.[25] And legislation introduced in Congress would require the Pentagon to develop a plan for an "integrated air and missile defense system" that is primarily intended to protect the six members of the Gulf Cooperation Council, as well as Israel, Egypt, Jordan, and Iraq, from Iranian attacks.[26] The integrated air defense scheme might only be the tip of the iceberg; the United States may be considering formal commitments to

---

23 Philip Bump, "The Newly Important American Political Axis: Democracy vs. Autocracy," *Washington Post*, March 18, 2022, https://www.washingtonpost.com/politics/2022/03/18/newly-important-american-political-axis-democracy-vs-autocracy/. On US-China tensions, see: Vivian Salama and Michael R. Gordon, "Chinese Balloon Carried Antennas, Other Equipment to Gather Intelligence, U.S. Says," *Wall Street Journal*, February 9, 2023, https://www.wsj.com/articles/chinese-balloon-carried-antennas-other-equipment-to-gather-intelligence-u-s-says-11675953033?mod=article_inline.

24 "FACT SHEET: The United States Strengthens Cooperation with Middle East Partners to Address 21st Century Challenges," The White House, July 16, 2022, https://www.whitehouse.gov/briefing-room/statements-releases/2022/07/16/fact-sheet-the-united-states-strengthens-cooperation-with-middle-east-partners-to-address-21st-century-challenges/.

25 Lara Seligman and Alexander Ward, "Biden Wants a Middle East Air Defense 'Alliance.' But It's a Long Way Off," *Politico*, July 12, 2022, https://www.politico.com/news/2022/07/12/biden-middle-east-air-defense-alliance-00045423.; Dan Williams and Aziz El Yaakoubi, "Israel Says It's Building Regional Air Defence Alliance under U.S.," *Reuters*, June 20, 2022, https://www.reuters.com/world/middle-east/israel-says-building-regional-air-defence-alliance-under-us-2022-06-20/.

26 Nancy A. Youssef and Stephen Kalin, "U.S. Proposes Helping Israel, Arab States Harden Air Defenses Against Iran," *Wall Street Journal*, June 9, 2022, https://www.wsj.com/amp/articles/u-s-proposes-helping-israel-arab-states-coordinate-air-defenses-against-iran-11654779601.

defend the Gulf states—possibly starting with the UAE—against outside threats.[27] Meanwhile, Saudi Arabia has reportedly asked the United States for security guarantees of its own as part of a potential deal to normalize ties with Israel.[28]

In addition to this behind-the-scenes maneuvering to deepen regional security partnerships, Biden has been careful to show Saudi Arabia signs of respect. During his visit to the kingdom, the White House announced a "new bilateral framework for cooperation" on 5G/6G telecommunications networks that is intended to rival Chinese firm Huawei's investments in Saudi Arabia and the Gulf.[29] A separate communique reaffirmed Washington's "strategic partnership" with Saudi Arabia, touting bilateral cooperation in diverse fields.[30] In fact, the administration's 5G/6G cooperative framework is but one example of how, rather than compelling Washington to reposition US resources and attention to the Indo-Pacific the geopolitical competition with China has instead done the opposite: it has helped to convince decision-makers of the need to engage more deeply with the Middle East.

As the Biden administration has acknowledged—and as a recent United States Central Command (CENTCOM) posture statement affirms—the Middle East, by dint of its strategic location and economic significance, will remain a major arena in which geopolitical competition

---

27   Hussein Ibish, "Biden's Trip Aims at Resurrecting U.S. Leadership in the Middle East," Arab Gulf States Institute in Washington, June 17, 2022, https://agsiw.org/bidens-trip-aims-at-resurrecting-u-s-leadership-in-the-middle-east/.; Barak Ravid, "Scoop: U.S. and UAE Discuss Strategic Security Agreement," *Axios*, June 1, 2022, https://www.axios.com/2022/06/01/us-uae-discuss-strategic-security-agreement.
28   Dion Nissenbaum et al., "Saudi Arabia Seeks U.S. Security Pledges, Nuclear Help for Peace With Israel," *Wall Street Journal*, March 9, 2023, https://www.wsj.com/articles/saudi-arabia-seeks-u-s-security-pledges-nuclear-help-for-peace-with-israel-cd47baaf.
29   "FACT SHEET: Results of Bilateral Meeting Between the United States and the Kingdom of Saudi Arabia," The White House, July 15, 2022, https://www.whitehouse.gov/briefing-room/statements-releases/2022/07/15/fact-sheet-results-of-bilateral-meeting-between-the-united-states-and-the-kingdom-of-saudi-arabia/.; Aziz El Yaakoubi and Eduardo Baptista, "Saudi Arabia Signs Huawei Deal, Deepening China Ties on Xi Visit," *Reuters*, December 8, 2022, https://www.reuters.com/world/saudi-lays-lavish-welcome-chinas-xi-heralds-new-era-relations-2022-12-08/.
30   "The Jeddah Communique: A Joint Statement Between the United States of America and the Kingdom of Saudi Arabia," July 15, 2022, The White House, https://www.whitehouse.gov/briefing-room/statements-releases/2022/07/15/the-jeddah-communique-a-joint-statement-between-the-united-states-of-america-and-the-kingdom-of-saudi-arabia/.

will play out.[31] The administration's I2U2 initiative—a partnership among India, Israel, the United States, and the UAE—seems intended as a counter to China's Belt and Road initiative (BRI) in the region.[32] As Jake Sullivan has said of the initiative, much like the BRI, "The fundamental notion is to connect South Asia to the Middle East to the United States in ways that advance our economic technology and diplomacy."[33] In a similar vein, elements of the Partnership for Global Infrastructure and Investment, announced by Biden and other leaders at the 2022 G7 summit, are aimed at mobilizing Middle East partner investments to fund strategic infrastructure projects linking the Middle East, Africa, and Asia.[34]

The anchor of the US commitment to the Middle East remains the substantial American force presence, which, although it has fluctuated amid frequent disputes about "rightsizing" the US military footprint, has remained remarkably consistent over time. For the last few years, the United States has maintained between 40,000 and 60,000 troops in the 21 countries that comprise the US Central Command area of responsibility (CENTCOM AOR), a number that varies depending on regional exigencies and troop rotations.[35] These forces are mainly stationed at bases in Jordan, Iraq, and the Arabian Peninsula. US troop missions in the CENTCOM AOR are broadly focused on counterterrorism, as well

---

31 "Statement of General Michael 'Erik' Kurilla on the Posture of U.S. Central Command - SASC Hearing Mar 16, 2023," U.S. Central Command, March 16, 2023, https://www.centcom.mil/ABOUT-US/POSTURE-STATEMENT/.
32 "Expanding Regional Economic Integration through I2U2's Business-to-Business Cooperation," U.S. Department of State, February 22, 2023, https://www.state.gov/expanding-regional-economic-integration-through-i2u2s-business-to-business-cooperation/.
33 Jake Sullivan, "Keynote Address: 2023 Soref Symposium," Washington Institute for Near East Policy, May 4, 2023, https://www.washingtoninstitute.org/policy-analysis/keynote-address-national-security-advisor-jake-sullivan.
34 "FACT SHEET: President Biden and G7 Leaders Formally Launch the Partnership for Global Infrastructure and Investment," The White House, June 26, 2022, https://www.whitehouse.gov/briefing-room/statements-releases/2022/06/26/fact-sheet-president-biden-and-g7-leaders-formally-launch-the-partnership-for-global-infrastructure-and-investment/.; Sullivan, "Keynote Address."
35 Nicole Robinson, "2023 Index of U.S. Military Strength/Middle East," Heritage Foundation, October 18, 2022, https://www.heritage.org/military-strength/assessing-the-global-operating-environment/middle-east.; "United States Central Command," Congressional Research Service, updated December 16, 2022, https://sgp.fas.org/crs/natsec/IF11428.pdf.

as on what can be described as "regional security and stability" activities, including exercises, training, and other forms of cooperation to support "enduring US interests."[36] That description, however, belies the sweeping nature of the commitment to which the Biden administration has tied the United States. According to the administration's 2022 National Security Strategy, "The United States will not allow foreign or regional powers to jeopardize freedom of navigation through the Middle East's waterways, including the Strait of Hormuz and the Bab al Mandab [sic], nor tolerate efforts by any country to dominate another—or the region—through military buildups, incursions, or threats."[37]

All this has justified a massive and, to all appearances, permanent US military presence in the Middle East. As political scientist Marc Lynch has stated, "The United States' network of bases and deployments may be low when compared with the mid-2000s, but it is rather more extensive than it was during the peak of the 1990s US unipolar moment."[38] In fact, as Under Secretary of Defense for Policy Colin Kahl stated at the Manama Dialogue in November 2022, "The United States remains committed to the region. We're here and we're not going anywhere."[39]

The Ties That Bind

With these latest moves to strengthen ties to the Gulf and other regional partners and allies, the United States seems to be implicitly acknowledging that it sees no way out of the Middle East for now. The current international situation, as well as the gravitational pull of Washington's political and military infrastructure in the region, will not permit a

---

36 "Operations and Exercises," U.S. Central Command, undated, https://www.centcom.mil/OPERATIONS-AND-EXERCISES/.; "CENTCOM Mission and Command Priorities," U.S. Central Command, undated, https://www.centcom.mil/ABOUT-US/.

37 "National Security Strategy," The White House, October 12, 2022, p.42, https://www.whitehouse.gov/wp-content/uploads/2022/10/Biden-Harris-Administrations-National-Security-Strategy-10.2022.pdf.

38 Marc Lynch, "Does the Decline of U.S. Power Matter for the Middle East?," *Washington Post*, March 19, 2019, https://www.washingtonpost.com/politics/2019/03/19/does-decline-us-power-matter-middle-east/.

39 Colin Kahl, "Remarks by Under Secretary of Defense for Policy Dr. Colin Kahl at the IISS Manama Dialogue (As Delivered)," U.S. Department of Defense, November 18, 2022, https://www.defense.gov/News/Speeches/Speech/Article/3223837/remarks-by-under-secretary-of-defense-for-policy-dr-colin-kahl-at-the-iiss-mana/.

disentanglement for the foreseeable future.[40] This infrastructure of course includes the complicated diplomatic relationships that the United States has spent decades developing. But it also comprises a vast and lucrative web of business and consulting ties, often involving high-ranking former US diplomatic, intelligence, and military figures. These individuals and the economic interests that they front—particularly in energy and the defense industry—serve to bind the US and the Middle East together in ways that resist pragmatic cost-benefit considerations.[41] In addition, the network of military bases and basing rights that the United States enjoys not only furnishes it with an invaluable forward presence in a strategic region, but its very existence is vital to maintaining close political ties and the trust of host nations. Any major changes to this presence would not be easy, and perhaps are not possible without provoking a crisis of confidence.

Even the current American approach of strengthening the ability of regional states to settle their disputes and cooperate in their own defense—a strategy ostensibly intended to lessen the need for intensive US involvement—seems to be having the opposite effect, requiring a massive diplomatic effort to bring US partners together and keep cooperation on track, in effect deepening their dependence on Washington's leadership role. The need for active US leadership in this sphere is strongly, if quietly, encouraged by Israel, a fact that is influential whenever voices in

---

40   An argument has been made that the March 10, 2023 deal brokered by China between Saudi Arabia and Iran to reestablish full diplomatic relations between the two rivals will boost Beijing and obviate the need for a US-led coalition to counter Iran, thus transforming the region to Washington's strategic disadvantage. That very much remains to be seen. The agreement, for one thing, solves none of the fundamental disputes between Riyadh and Tehran, especially the decades-long struggle for supremacy in the region, Iran's support for terrorism, and its malign activities in Lebanon, Syria, and Iraq. It may, however, help with a resolution of the Yemen war. See, inter alia: Maria Fantappie and Vali Nasr, "A New Order in the Middle East? Iran and Saudi Arabia's Rapprochement Could Transform the Region," *Foreign Affairs*, March 22, 2023, https://www.foreignaffairs.com/china/iran-saudi-arabia-middle-east-relations.

41   The United States is the largest international weapons exporter. It holds a 40 percent share of the global trade in major arms, amounting to $205.6 billion in FY2022. Forty-one percent of the total goes to the Middle East. Four Gulf states (Saudi Arabia, Qatar, Kuwait and the UAE) are among the top ten purchasers of US-made weapons. See: Mike Stone, "U.S. Arms Exports Up 49% in Fiscal 2022," *Reuters*, January 25, 2023, https://www.reuters.com/world/us/us-arms-exports-up-11-fiscal-2022-official-says-2023-01-25/.; Pieter D. Wezeman et al., "SIPRI Fact Sheet: Trends In International Arms Transfers, 2022," Stockholm International Peace Research Institute, March 2023, https://www.sipri.org/sites/default/files/2023-03/2303_at_fact_sheet_2022_v2.pdf.

Congress or advisors in the White House consider backing away from the region. The United States can (as it has from time to time) shift military assets and policy emphasis back and forth between the Middle East and the Indo-Pacific.[42] But this seems unlikely to result in a major downgrading of the MENA region in any administration's list of global priorities anytime soon. For now, the United States seems to be more firmly tied to the region than ever before, and content to make the best of it while leveraging old ties to confront evolving threats. Any serious US retrenchment from the Middle East will have to wait.

---

42 Michael R. Gordon, "U.S. to Send Aging Attack Planes to Mideast and Shift Newer Jets to Asia, Europe," *Wall Street Journal*, March 23, 2023, https://www.wsj.com/articles/u-s-to-send-aging-attack-planes-to-mideast-and-shift-newer-jets-to-asia-europe-df72da15?mod=hp_lead_pos5.

US Military Strategy in the Middle East and the Challenge of Demilitarization

Waleed Hazbun

With its troop withdrawals from Iraq in 2011 and Afghanistan in 2021, the United States currently exhibits a much smaller military footprint in the Middle East than it did in the mid-to-late 2000s. US regional strategy, however, remains structured around the capacity to deploy military force as a means to maintain regional influence, contain Iran, and compete against China and Russia. For many analysts and political leaders, and for much of the American public, a reduced US military posture in the Middle East is very compelling. While some argue that the United States should completely withdraw its forces from the region since none of its vital security interests are currently threatened, even those taking the opposing position and calling for continued engagement recognize the value of rebalancing the US military posture in response to changing contexts and needs.

However, the challenge for any withdrawal or rebalancing is that US engagement in the Middle East has become so deeply entangled with military institutions and assets that uprooting it would further erode US influence in the region. At the same time, even as previous rationales for the strategic value of the region decline, the United States is increasingly approaching the Middle East as an arena for militarized great power competition. As a result, any sustained reduction in the US military posture there would require a broader demilitarization of US policy, the reduction of great power conflict, and the development of alternative means to address diverse sources of regional insecurity.

The Current US Military Posture and Strategy

Over the past few years there has been much debate in Washington about the need to reduce and rebalance the United States' military posture and security commitments in the Middle East.[1] Since its peak in 2008, the total number of US military personnel deployed to the region has been reduced by 85 percent.[2] And in recent years it has ranged between 40,000 and 60,000 troops.[3] The Biden administration, however, has sought to maintain a robust posture. As US Secretary of Defense Lloyd J. Austin III has noted, "We have very real combat power in this theater. [...] And if needed, we will move in more."[4] US Central Command (CENTCOM) has spelled out its strategic priorities as deterring threats posed by Iran and its allies, and to a lesser degree continuing to contain violent extremist groups while also increasingly competing with China and Russia.[5] In response to past US policies that included high-profile troop drawdowns (in Iraq, Syria, and Afghanistan) and past refusals to use force in response

---

1 Mara Karlin and Tamara Cofman Wittes, "America's Middle East Purgatory: The Case for Doing Less," *Foreign Affairs*, December 11, 2018, https://www.foreignaffairs.com/articles/middle-east/2018-12-11/americas-middle-east-purgatory.
2 "Statement of General Michael 'Erik' Kurilla on the Posture of U.S. Central Command - SASC Hearing Mar 16, 2023," U.S. Central Command, March 16, 2023, https://www.centcom.mil/ABOUT-US/POSTURE-STATEMENT/.
3 Seth G. Jones and Seamus P. Daniels, "U.S. Defense Posture in the Middle East," Center for Strategic and International Studies, May 2022, p.2, https://csis-website-prod.s3.amazonaws.com/s3fs-public/publication/220519_Jones_USDefensePosture_MiddleEast_0.pdf?VersionId=60gG7N1_4FxFA6CNgJKAbr24zmsKXhwx.
4 Lloyd J. Austin III, "Remarks on Middle East Security at the Manama Dialogue," U.S. Department of Defense, November 20, 2021, https://www.defense.gov/News/Speeches/Speech/Article/2849921/remarks-by-secretary-of-defense-lloyd-j-austin-iii-on-middle-east-security-at-t/.
5 "Statement of General Michael 'Erik' Kurilla."; Micah Zenko, "US Military Policy in the Middle East: An Appraisal," Chatham House, October 2018, p.18, https://www.chathamhouse.org/sites/default/files/publications/research/2018-10-18-us-military-policy-middle-east-zenko.pdf.

to attacks on regional allies (most notably against the Abqaiq oil facility in Saudi Arabia in 2019), Biden administration officials have repeatedly told their longstanding regional partners that, "The US is not going anywhere. This region is too important, too volatile, too interwoven with American interests to contemplate otherwise."[6]

According to estimates published in the 2023 edition of *The Military Balance*, the US has around 40,000 military personnel deployed to the Middle East.[7] The bulk of these forces operate in the Arabian Gulf region from bases that were developed over years of intense combat focused on Iran and Iraq. Kuwait hosts the largest share of US ground forces, with over 10,000 military personnel and regional army headquarters. Another 10,000 are based in Qatar, now also a major non-NATO ally, which hosts the largest US Air Expeditionary Wing in the world, with heavy bombers and other aircraft. The US Air Force regional command and the regional forward headquarters of the US Special Operations Command are also located at Al Udeid Air Base in Qatar. Since its reactivation in 1995, the US Navy's Fifth Fleet has been based in Bahrain, which hosts a sprawling naval base with about 4,700 personnel, and from which the United States coordinates marine operations with allied forces and efforts such as Task Force 59 that uses artificial intelligence and unmanned craft to "secure the region's vital waterways."[8] The Fifth Fleet patrols the Arabian Gulf and the region's waterways, maintaining rotational deployments of Naval carrier strike groups (with about 7,500 personnel) and marine amphibious ready groups (with another 5,000).

The United Arab Emirates, another important US partner, has its own growing military capabilities and operates al-Dhafra Air Base that hosts 5,000 US military personnel, as well as surveillance and combat aircraft. And Dubai's Jebel Ali Port is a frequent port of call for US naval forces. The United States also maintains an air base and 2,000 personnel

---

6   Brett McGurk, "Remarks at the IISS Manama Dialogue," International Institute for Strategic Studies, November 21, 2021, https://www.iiss.org/Globalassets/Media-Library--Content--Migration/Files/Manama-Dialogue/2021/Plenary-Transcripts/Concluding/Brett-Mcgurk-Coordinator-For-The-Middle-East-And-North-Africa-Nsc-United-States---As-Delivered.pdf.
7   James Hackett, ed., *The Military Balance 2023* (London: Routledge, 2023) 47–49. All personnel figures are from *The Military Balance 2023*, unless otherwise noted.
8   Jake Sullivan, "Keynote Address: 2023 Soref Symposium," Washington Institute for Near East Policy, May 4, 2023, https://www.washingtoninstitute.org/policy-analysis/keynote-address-national-security-advisor-jake-sullivan.

in Saudi Arabia. The US-led campaign against the so-called Islamic State (IS), meanwhile, draws on military personnel based in Jordan, where 3,000 troops are stationed, and where the United States maintains a drone operating base. Another 900 remain in northeast Syria, where they work with local Kurdish militias to contain IS, and about another 2,000 remain at bases across Iraq, though now mainly in an advise-and-assist role. There are small numbers of US military personnel in other locations around the Middle East, such as those who help operate Israel's Iron Dome missile defense system and those involved in training and supporting the Lebanese Armed Forces.[9] In addition, as of December 2022, the US military employed about 22,000 contractors across the region, of whom about one-third were US citizens.[10]

The US military engagement in the region is extended by its miliary aid programs and arms sales. Following the 1978 Camp David Accords, the United States has been granting Israel about $3 billion annually in military aid designed to maintain its "qualitative military edge," while Egypt receives over $1 billion annually, despite occasional congressional efforts to withhold aid due to human rights violations by the Egyptian government.[11] Meanwhile, the Foreign Military Sales program helps the United States maintain long-term strategic ties with the region. Between 2018 and 2022, the US has facilitated almost $18 billion in sales to Saudi Arabia, $6 billon to the UAE, $5 billion to Egypt, $3 billion to Kuwait, $2 billion to Jordan, and over $1 billion to Qatar.[12] These sales in fighter jets and other hardware, together with related training and joint excises to increase cooperation, allow the US to sustain and deepen close military-to-military ties.

Apart from the 2021 withdrawal from Afghanistan, there has been little sign of major redeployments, though force structures and missions are being adjusted. As White House Coordinator for the Middle East and

---

9   Zenko, "US Military Policy in the Middle East," pp.13–14.
10 Andrea Mazzarino, "The Army We Don't See: The Private Soldiers Who Fight in America's Name," Tom Dispatch, May 9, 2023, https://tomdispatch.com/the-army-we-dont-see/.
11 Jeremy M. Sharp, "U.S. Foreign Aid to Israel," Congressional Research Service, updated March 1, 2023, https://sgp.fas.org/crs/mideast/RL33222.pdf. On Egypt, see: Jeremy M. Sharp, "Egypt: Background and U.S. Relations," Congressional Research Service, updated May 2, 2023, https://sgp.fas.org/crs/mideast/RL33003.pdf.
12 "Historical Sales Book Fiscal Years 1950–2022," Defense Security Cooperation Agency, 2022, https://www.dsca.mil/sites/default/files/2023-01/FY%202022%20Historical%20Sales%20Book.pdf.

North Africa Brett McGurk has explained, the United States is no longer seeking "maximalist" goals in the Middle East, such as regional political transformation or regime change in Iran.[13] Although the United States is committed to preventing Iran from obtaining nuclear weapons capabilities, it is currently seeking to avoid confrontation with Iran-backed militias in Iraq. Meanwhile, it has sought to address the concerns of partners like Saudi Arabia and the UAE. What McGurk refers to as a "back to basics" approach is focused on "rebalancing" by rebuilding traditional alliances and strengthening the military capacity of allies through their integration with US forces and regional partners.[14] At the center of this effort is the building of "an integrated air and maritime defense architecture in the region."[15]

This integration has been advanced in the political realm through agreements such as the so-called Abraham Accords and the Negev Forum, which have accelerated Israeli cooperation with other US partners, such as the UAE. Military cooperation has also been developed through joint exercises, efforts to promote interoperability, and collaborative operations such as the Combined Maritime Forces. More broadly, McGurk has stated that the US envisions an "interconnected, prosperous, and stable region over the medium and longer term."[16]

A Military Pivot Away from the Middle East?

Broad swaths of the US public and a diverse range of security and Middle East analysts have long called for a reduction in the US military posture in the Middle East. Most adamantly, advocates of a grand strategy of "restraint" propose that the US embrace a very narrow conception of its security interests in the Middle East, one that could justify a near total withdrawal from the region.[17] Defining the central US security concern

---

13   McGurk, "Remarks at the IISS Manama Dialogue."
14   Ibid.
15   Brett McGurk, "Remarks at the Atlantic Council Rafik Hariri Awards," Atlantic Council, February 14, 2023, https://www.atlanticcouncil.org/commentary/transcript/brett-mcgurk-sets-out-the-biden-doctrine-for-the-middle-east/.
16   Ibid.
17   Barry R. Posen, *Restraint: A New Foundation for U.S. Grand Strategy* (Ithaca, NY: Cornell University Press, 2015).; Eugene Gholz, "Nothing Much To Do: Why America Can Bring All Troops Home From The Middle East," Quincy Institute for Responsible Statecraft, June 24, 2021, https://quincyinst.org/report/nothing-much-to-do-why-america-can-bring-all-troops-home-from-the-middle-east/.

as preventing the rise of a hostile hegemon in the oil-rich Arabian Gulf, they argue that no regional power has the military capacity to dominate the region, that external powers like China have no interest in doing so, and that the fragmented multipolar geopolitics of the region mean that any rising power will be balanced by rivals. There is no strategic rationale, they argue, to justify the massive costs of the US presence in the Gulf. They note that there is little evidence that the United States has made the region more stable or made US territory more secure, and they question the logic of so-called "energy security."[18] Even hostile powers would sell oil on international markets, these proponents argue, and thus the US military is not needed to secure global "access" to Middle East energy sources. At the same time, these analysts, as well as many other observers and policy makers, have argued that in recent years the strategic value of the region and the threats the United States faces from it have diminished; the United States has become energy independent, Israel is regionally powerful and now has close ties with several Arab states, and terrorism is best viewed as a regional theat.[19]

Advocates of restraint call for the United States to evacuate most of its bases in the region over a five-to-ten-year period, leaving less than 5,000 personnel.[20] This drawdown would include most ground forces and leave limited air and maritime assets to support an offshore presence. The United States would end its practice of keeping a naval carrier strike group and marine amphibious ready group in theater, as it would only need a small maritime capability to patrol the seas. To safeguard the capacity to project force from over the horizon, the United States would maintain the option of access to bases in the region and the deployment of remote vehicles and surveillance technologies. Those promoting this position also argue that such a military disengagement from the region would reduce the threats the United States faces, such as being the target

---

18 Robert Vitalis, *Oilcraft: The Myths of Scarcity and Security That Haunt U.S. Energy Policy* (Stanford, CA: Stanford University Press, 2020).
19 Martin Indyk, "The Middle East Isn't Worth It Anymore," *Wall Street Journal*, January 17, 2020, https://www.wsj.com/articles/the-middle-east-isnt-worth-it-anymore-11579277317.; Sean Yom, "US Foreign Policy in the Middle East: The Logic of Hegemonic Retreat," *Global Policy* 11, no. 1 (February 28, 2020): 75–83.
20 Mike Sweeney, "A Plan for U.S. Withdrawal from the Middle East," Defense Priorities, December 21, 2020, https://www.defensepriorities.org/explainers/a-plan-for-us-withdrawal-from-the-middle-east.; Eugene Gholz, "Nothing Much To Do," 54.; Jones and Daniels, "U.S. Defense Posture in the Middle East," 22–28.

of terrorist attacks or assaults from pro-Iran militias, and would also incentivize regional actors to develop their own capacities for self-defense and to work toward both the de-escalation of conflicts and regional accommodation. Some observers point to the end of the blockade of Qatar in 2021, an ongoing cease-fire in the war in Yemen, and the recent normalization of Saudi-Iran ties as effects of the US adjusting its security commitments. Others simply suggest that the United States should seek to insulate itself from the geopolitical instability of the region.

Aside from those advocating for a US withdrawal from the region, there is an ongoing debate in Washington about the need for a limited rebalancing of the American military posture. Several members of the Biden administration, before entering their current posts, advocated for the need to shift away from a reliance on military tools to more active diplomacy instead. At the heart of this debate is the evolution of conceptions about core US interests and means. Many analysts call for the United States to reduce its posture in the region, leaving between 10,000 and 20,000 personnel to sustain a strategy of "limited engagement."[21] This approach recognizes that, in the words of researcher Becca Wasser, "The U.S. footprint at larger operating bases—particularly those within range of Iranian weapons—should be reduced."[22] Wasser advocates a more "distributed basing structure" that would shift assets from larger bases in the Arabian Gulf toward a "constellation of smaller bases located throughout the region," such as in Jordan and Saudi Arabia.[23]

This approach would also include converting current "hot" bases to "warm" ones that are maintained by host nations, but with the United States retaining contingency access and pre-positioning equipment. Under such an approach, the US Navy would limit the presence of a carrier strike group in the region, placing one in the Indian Ocean that could be deployed if needed, while keeping an amphibious ready group in rotation no closer than the Arabian Sea.[24] The purpose would be to

---

21 Jones and Daniels, "U.S. Defense Posture in the Middle East, 28–33."; Melissa Dalton and Mara Karlin, "Adapting U.S. Defense Posture in the Middle East for New Priorities," in *Re-Engaging the Middle East: A New Vision for U.S. Policy*, Dafna H. Rand and Andrew P. Miller, eds. (Washington, DC: Brookings Institution Press, 2020), 225–38.
22 Becca Wasser, "Drawing Down the U.S. Military Responsibly," Carnegie Endowment for International Peace, May 18, 2021, https://carnegieendowment.org/2021/05/18/drawing-down-u.s.-military-responsibly-pub-84527.
23 Ibid.
24 Jones and Daniels, "U.S. Defense Posture in the Middle East," 32.

reduce the firepower held close to Iran and move US forces away from possible conflict with pro-Iran militias in Iraq and from positions in range of Iranian missiles while retaining capabilities to deter threats to US partners. Additionally, others call for the US to try to redirect its arms sales and military support toward equipment and capabilities that are more clearly defensive, such as anti-missile technologies and intelligence, surveillance, and reconnaissance (ISR) capabilities, or to more carefully define the criteria for using US equipment.[25]

The likely regional geopolitical consequences of a US withdrawal or rebalancing that limits US security commitments are hard to assess. When former President Barack Obama sought to restructure US security commitments and suggested that America's Arab partners would need to accommodate a regional role for Iran, Gulf states reacted by escalating conflicts and resorting to force as a response to their fears about insecurity, thereby further eroding American leverage in the region. While most US partners have since dialed down their revisionist strategies and sought some regional accommodations, the United States continues to be the largest supplier of arms. For their part, critics of restraint who instead advocate a more robust military posture of "forward engagement" fear that such a withdrawal would leave current US allies and partners insecure in an increasingly unstable multipolar region and "shift the balance of power" in favor of rivals such as Iran, Russia, and China.[26] Absent the US capacity to promote "deterrence by denial" against Iran, Israel might go to war with the Islamic Republic, while Saudi Arabia and the UAE might want to develop their own nuclear programs.

In any case, a significant reduction of the United States' military posture or security commitments seems unlikely at this time. While such shifts might serve American security interests in rebalancing the US posture, avoiding conflict, and restraining allies, they would likely only further diminish US regional leverage. Put simply, the United States lacks the political leverage to sustain a transition from a focus on military impact to an emphasis on diplomatic influence at a time when regional actors are seeking more strategic autonomy in a multipolar system. Moreover,

---

25 Emile Hokayem, "Reassuring Gulf Partners While Recalibrating U.S. Security Policy," Carnegie Endowment for International Peace, May 18, 2021, https://carnegieendowment.org/2021/05/18/reassuring-gulf-partners-while-recalibrating-u.s.-security-policy-pub-84522.

26 Jones and Daniels, "U.S. Defense Posture in the Middle East," 26.

suggestions that regional states would be able to develop their own capacities for defense ignore how deeply interdependent regional states are on the US military infrastructure. For its part, US security assistance has too often been defined by local political needs and private sector economic interests than by operational requirements.[27] And even if regional states did seek to establish a stable regional balance of power, regional stability is by no means assured, as many of the sources of insecurity faced by regional states are due to internal factors, such as autocratic decision-making, political divisions, and states failing to address the needs and security of their societies.[28]

In addition, the challenge of a withdrawal from the Middle East is no longer a regional question. The rise of great power competition with China and Russia have come to redefine the United States' global strategy and goals in the Middle East. While the United States can organize efforts to promote regional security integration around shared security interests such as the need to contain Iran and protect the free flow of commerce, it faces challenges due to some interests and perspectives that diverge from those of its partners. For example, the United States' regional partners view economic ties with China as a means to advance their broader goals of economic transformation and global integration; but the US views China's efforts to build economic ties and infrastructure under its Belt and Road Initiative as "a strategic lever to supplant US leadership in the region under the guise of benign economic initiatives and broadening security relationships."[29] As a result, CENTCOM Commander Michael 'Erik' Kurilla argues, "We are in a race to integrate our partners before China and Russia can deeply penetrate the region."[30]

The Challenge of Demilitarization

The challenge for any major reduction of the US military posture in the Middle East is that US engagement has become so deeply entangled with military institutions and assets that disconnecting from them would only

---

27   Robert Springborg, "Retooling U.S. Security Assistance," Carnegie Endowment for International Peace, May 18, 2021, https://carnegieendowment.org/2021/05/18/Retooling-U.S.-Security-Assistance-Pub-84525.
28   Waleed Hazbun, "A History of Insecurity: From the Arab Uprisings to ISIS," *Middle East Policy* 22, no. 3 (2015): 55-65.; F. Gregory Gause III, "The Price of Order: Settling for Less in the Middle East," *Foreign Affairs* 101, no. 2 (March/April 2022): 10–21.
29   "Statement of General Michael 'Erik' Kurilla."
30   Ibid.

further erode American influence in the region. Military affairs analyst Micah Zenko notes that CENTCOM is "the most powerful and substantial US government actor in the Middle East."[31] This dynamic is reinforced by the economic linkages of arms sales, private contractors, and logistics firms, and by the circulation of former military officers as formal and informal advisors to governments and militaries in the region. Moreover, the militarized nature of US Middle East policy is sustained by the interest regional states have in US security commitments, which also help protect their regimes from domestic threats. These states often work to sustain US security commitments by maintaining political pressure and influence in Washington through direct lobbying, support for think tanks, and indirect economic leverage through arms purchases.

Against this self-reinforcing dynamic, any sustained reduction in the US military posture in the Middle East would likely require a reimagining of US foreign policy and a demilitarization of the institutions of strategic development and policy formation.[32] More broadly, it would also require some sort of great power detente, the development of a new and inclusive regional security architecture less dependent on US military force, and alternative means to address sources of regional and domestic insecurity, many of which US military force is ill-suited to address.[33] Within such a context, the United States could seek to replace its reliance on miliary power projection with policies and resources directed to negotiating regional security agreements, assisting states to promote economic development, addressing the sources of human insecurity faced by societies across the region, and working collectively with states in the Middle East and elsewhere to address global challenges like climate change, autonomous weapons proliferation, and great power conflict.

---

31 Zenko, "US Military Policy in the Middle East," 6.
32 Dalia Dassa Kaye, "America's Role in a Post-American Middle East," *The Washington Quarterly* 45, no. 1 (2022): 7–24.; Waleed Hazbun "Reimagining US Engagement with a Turbulent Middle East," *Middle East Report* 294 (Spring 2020), https://merip.org/2020/06/reimagining-us-engagement-with-a-turbulent-middle-east/.
33 Paul R. Pillar et al., "A New U.S. Paradigm for the Middle East," Quincy Institute for Responsible Statecraft, July 17, 2020, https://quincyinst.org/2020/07/17/ending-americas-misguided-policy-of-middle-east-domination/.; "The Middle East between Collective Security and Collective Breakdown," International Crisis Group, April 27, 2020, https://www.crisisgroup.org/middle-east-north-africa/gulf-and-arabian-peninsula/212-middle-east-between-collective-security-and-collective-breakdown.; Dalia Dassa Kaye, et. al, *Reimagining U.S. Strategy in the Middle East: Sustainable Partnerships, Strategic Investments* (Santa Monica, CA: RAND Corporation, 2021).

The Economic Dimension of a Pivot Away from the Middle East

Mark Finley

In many aspects, the direct linkages between the economies of the Middle East and the United States are small—at least in relation to the size of the US economy. But the centrality of oil to the US (and the global) economy, combined with the outsized influence the Middle East region has on the global oil market, makes the region a critical factor in the United States' economic well-being. While an eventual transition away from oil and other fossil fuels is likely to change this dynamic, this transition is expected to be slow, meaning the Middle East will loom large for US economic security interests for decades to come.

The countries of the Arabian/Persian Gulf have, to different degrees, long been central to the production and export of hydrocarbon products to the United States and the rest of the world. For this reason, the following data and analysis will focus, where possible, on these nations, although other producers in North Africa—Libya and Algeria, for example—also play an important role in the supply of oil and natural gas to the international economy.

The Big Picture: Direct Economic Connections Are Limited

The countries bordering the Arabian/Persian Gulf (hereafter, the Gulf states: Bahrain, Iran, Iraq, Kuwait, Oman, Qatar, Saudi Arabia, and the United Arab Emirates) comprise a relatively small share of the global population and economy, 2 percent and 4 percent, respectively.[1] Additionally, these countries account for relatively small shares of key indicators of US economic and financial relationships: just 2 to 3 percent of US trade in goods and services (in dollar value). Indeed, none of these countries is a top-20 trading partner for the United States among importers or exporters.[2] One strategically important exception to this overall picture of a small role for the Gulf states in US trade is arms sales, where the Middle East accounted for roughly 40 percent of American global exports from 2018 to 2022.[3]

Similarly, the United States is not a large trading partner from the perspective of the Gulf states; the US is the largest exporter to only Qatar, ranking behind China for all other countries under discussion here.[4] For energy trade, nearly 80 percent of the region's oil and liquefied natural gas (LNG) exports are sold in Asia, compared with 3 percent of oil exports (and no LNG) being sold to the United States.[5] Moreover, the Gulf states are not large contributors to other dimensions of US international economic relations; they account for small shares of US foreign direct investment

---

1   "Global Population Data for 2021," World Bank, undated, https://data.worldbank.org/indicator/SP.POP.TOTL; "GDP Based on PPP, Share of World," International Monetary Fund, undated, https://www.imf.org/external/datamapper/PPPSH@WEO/OEMDC/ADVEC/WEOWORLD.
2   For trade rankings, see: "U.S. International Trade in Goods and Services, December and Annual 2022," U.S. Census Bureau and U.S. Bureau of Economic Analysis, February 7, 2023, https://www.census.gov/foreign-trade/Press-Release/ft900/ft900_2212.pdf. For shares of trade in goods in 2022, see: "U.S. Trade in Goods by Country," U.S. Census Bureau, undated, https://www.census.gov/foreign-trade/balance/. For shares in trade in services in 2021, see: "Table 2.2. U.S. Trade in Services, by Type of Service and by Country or Affiliation," U.S. Bureau of Economic Analysis, July 7, 2022, https://tinyurl.com/3f3du26m.
3   Pieter D. Wezeman et al., "Trends in International Arms Transfers, 2022," Stockholm International Peace Research Institute, March 2023, https://www.sipri.org/sites/default/files/2023-03/2303_at_fact_sheet_2022_v2.pdf.
4   "Saudi Arabia Trade," World Integrated Trade Solution Database, undated, https://wits.worldbank.org/countrysnapshot/en/SAU. Unfortunately, country-specific data on export destinations *from* the Gulf states is not widely available (for many Gulf states, "unspecified" is by far the largest export destination), so we report here only leading countries exporting *to* the Gulf states.
5   "Statistical Review of World Energy," BP, 2022, www.bp.com/statisticalreview.

(both inbound and outbound, at 6 percent and 1 percent, respectively), and hold just 4 percent of the total number of US Treasuries held abroad.[6]

The (Indirect) Importance of Oil

Like other direct indicators of US international economic relations, US oil imports from the Gulf states are relatively small.[7] The impact of the US "shale revolution" on both American oil import dependence and global oil markets has been well-documented. With the US now a small net oil exporter, a widespread impression in the US has developed, which sees the country as no longer vulnerable to Middle East regional developments. But the oil price spike of 2022 exposed the myth and reminded US policymakers and consumers that the oil policies of the Gulf states remain critical elements of the Unites States' economic well-being—at least for now. In the US (and elsewhere), soaring fuel prices have boosted inflation, damaged consumer and business confidence, and lowered the approval ratings of political leaders.[8]

In 2022, the US Department of Energy reported that the US imported about one million barrels per day (mbd) from the Gulf states—12 percent of total (gross) oil imports, sufficient to meet 5 percent of domestic demand. This is well below the peak of 2.8 mbd imported in 2001, which represented nearly a quarter of US imports and 15 percent of domestic demand.[9] These reductions are similar to those among most other US oil trading partners, and have been driven by the growth of domestic production (the shale revolution), which has made the United States the world's largest producer of oil (and natural gas), and has turned it from the world's biggest oil importer into a small net exporter. It is important to note that while the United States is a *net* oil exporter, it remains intricately connected with global markets for both crude oil and refined products due to

---

6 "Direct Investment by Country and Industry, 2021," U.S. Bureau of Economic Analysis, July 21, 2022, https://www.bea.gov/sites/default/files/2022-07/dici0722.pdf.
7 Note that this discussion includes both crude oil and refined products such as gasoline and diesel when referring to "oil."
8 Mark Finley and Anna Mikulska, "Energy Transition, Energy Security, and Affordable Fuel: How the Energy Crisis Can Help Policymakers 'Thread the Needle,'" Baker Institute for Public Policy, August 5, 2022, https://www.bakerinstitute.org/research/energy-transition-energy-security-and-affordable-fuel-how-the-energy-crisis-can-help-policymakers-th.
9 "Petroleum and Other Liquids: U.S. Imports by Country of Origin," U.S. Energy Information Administration, undated, https://www.eia.gov/dnav/pet/pet_move_impcus_a2_nus_ep00_im0_mbblpd_a.htm.

the complexities of managing a continent-wide marketplace and because of quality and regional mismatches between domestic oil production and refining capacity. In 2022, the US Energy Department reported that the United States *exported* 9.6 mbd of crude oil and refined products, while *importing* 8.3 mbd.[10]

But while the United States has achieved overall self-sufficiency and reduced its direct dependence on imports from the Gulf states, its economy remains vulnerable to oil price shocks because oil remains the US economy's largest energy source. And vulnerability in turn means that the Gulf states remain vital to US economic interests because of their central role in driving global oil markets. Within the US, oil last year accounted for 36 percent of total domestic energy consumption. This was followed by natural gas (33 percent of total energy use), renewable energy (13 percent), coal (10 percent), and nuclear energy (8 percent).[11] Moreover, oil is the world's largest energy source, in 2021 accounting for over 30 percent of global energy use (followed by coal and natural gas, at 27 percent and 24 percent, respectively).[12] And in the global context, the Gulf states remain central players. They account for nearly half the world's proven oil reserves, roughly 30 percent of global production, and one-third of global oil trade. Indeed, the US Energy Department estimates that roughly 20 mbd flow through the strategic Strait of Hormuz daily.[13]

The importance of the Gulf countries to the global oil market is further accentuated by their participation in OPEC and the larger "OPEC+" group, through which they seek to cooperatively manage oil supply and prices. The OPEC+ group was organized in 2016 in response to the dramatic growth in US shale production, which was taking global market share at the time, and which had caused OPEC countries to engage in a damaging price war with US producers a year prior. Bringing Russia and other cooperating countries into the group greatly increased the share

---

10 "Monthly Energy Review, Table 3.1 Petroleum Overview," U.S. Energy Information Administration, undated, https://www.eia.gov/totalenergy/data/browser/index.php?tbl=T03.01#/?f=A&start=1949&end=2022&charted=6-12-15.
11 "Monthly Energy Review, Table 1.3 Primary Energy Consumption by Source," U.S. Energy Information Administration, undated, https://www.eia.gov/totalenergy/data/browser/index.php?tbl=T01.03#/?f=A&start=1949&end=2022&charted=1-2-3-5-12.
12 "Statistical Review of World Energy."
13 "The Strait of Hormuz Is the World's Most Important Oil Transit Chokepoint," U.S. Energy Information Administration, June 20, 2019, https://www.eia.gov/todayinenergy/detail.php?id=39932.

of global oil production under active management, and has been a key element in the improvement of political ties between Russia and the Gulf states.[14] Finally, and critically, these countries account for virtually all of the world's spare production capacity—unused production facilities that can be quickly tapped to increase production in an emergency, currently estimated at about 3.5 mbd.[15] The region's spare capacity in particular commands significant influence in global oil markets in times of crisis.

The global nature of the oil market is what connects US vulnerability to the Gulf countries, even though direct US oil purchases from the region are small. Both crude oil and refined products are widely traded internationally, and the fact that shippers can divert cargoes to seek the highest profits means that changes in prices of both crude and refined products in the US are closely correlated with global price changes. In essence, the lesson for US policymakers and consumers is that when the price of oil increases anywhere in the world, it increases everywhere, and that developments in the Gulf states therefore matter for US "prices at the pump."

Recognition of this connection was evident in US President Joe Biden's July 2022 visit to Saudi Arabia, part of a (failed) attempt to convince the kingdom's leaders to increase production. With prices at the pump soaring in the run-up to that year's US midterm elections, Biden, who had earlier promised to make Saudi Arabia a pariah due to its human rights violations, was forced to seek assistance from a country that held the lion's share of global spare production capacity.[16] His request was rejected, and indeed Saudi Arabia followed up by working with Russia in October 2022 to announce large production cuts by the OPEC+ group.[17]

---

14   Kristian Coates Ulrichsen et al., "The OPEC+ Phenomenon of Saudi-Russian Cooperation and Implications for US-Saudi Relations," Baker Institute for Public Policy, October 18, 2022, https://www.bakerinstitute.org/research/opec-phenomenon-saudi-russian-cooperation-and-implications-us-saudi-relations.
15   "Short-Term Energy Outlook Data Browser, Table 3c.: OPEC Crude Oil (Excluding Condensates) Production," U.S. Energy Information Administration, May 9, 2023, https://www.eia.gov/outlooks/steo/data/browser/#/?v=7.
16   Steve Holland et al., "Biden Fails to Secure Major Security, Oil Commitments at Arab Summit," *Reuters*, July 16, 2022, https://www.reuters.com/world/middle-east/biden-hopes-more-oil-israeli-integration-arab-summit-saudi-2022-07-16/.
17   Hanna Ziady, "OPEC Announces the Biggest Cut to Oil Production since the Start of the Pandemic," *CNN Business*, updated October 5, 2022, https://www.cnn.com/2022/10/05/energy/opec-production-cuts/index.html.

Looking Ahead: Dependence or Independence?

Will US vulnerability to oil shocks—and with it the economic importance of the Gulf states to US strategic interests—ease in the future? Such an outcome is widely anticipated in both the United States and the region, as electric vehicles are expected to displace the internal combustion engine and more aggressive climate policies loom on the horizon. This has contributed to the discussion of a potential US pivot away from the region. But the pace of the "energy transition" is highly uncertain and is likely to play out over several decades. Uncertainty is a crucial dimension of this discussion; as the great American folk-philosopher and baseball player Yogi Berra is reported to have said, "It's tough to make predictions, especially about the future."

The US Energy Department's reference case projects that oil will remain the country's leading energy source in 2050 (at 34 percent of energy use), with consumption of about 20 mbd—close to current levels.[18] In contrast, in 2021 the International Energy Agency's (IEA) sustainable development scenario projected that US oil demand could fall by 70 percent by 2050, at which point it would account for only about 15 percent of total energy use.[19] To a certain degree, these outlooks differ because they serve different objectives: the US Energy Department seeks to show the most likely outcome based on current policies, while the IEA's outlook is a "what if" scenario showing the need for additional policies to achieve a sustainable outcome. Importantly, the IEA emphasizes that massive actions would be needed beyond existing policies or even current governmental commitments to achieve its scenario. But the massive range of potential oil demand outcomes across these analytic efforts highlights the tremendous uncertainty of future developments in public policy (especially regarding climate change), as well as the pace of technological innovation. And in turn, these uncertainties drive a similarly large range of potential future pathways for future US (and global) oil demand.

While acknowledging that the US and global long-term oil demand outlook is massively uncertain, one can confidently project that, on

---

18 "Annual Energy Outlook 2023, Table 11: Petroleum and Other Liquids Supply and Disposition (Reference Case)," U.S. Energy Information Administration, 2023, https://www.eia.gov/outlooks/aeo/data/browser/#/?id=11-AEO2023&cases=ref2023&sourcekey=0.

19 "World Energy Outlook 2021," International Energy Agency, October 2021, https://www.iea.org/reports/world-energy-outlook-2021. Note that the IEA's subsequent "World Energy Outlook 2022" included a net-zero scenario but did not include detailed country-specific oil consumption for 2050 in its public data release.

current trends, it appears likely that the US economy's dependence on oil will persist for decades to come, and that US strategic planning must act more aggressively to reduce that dependence, or to plan for how to address continued vulnerability.

The Gulf region's importance to global oil supplies and trade may grow in the medium term, with Saudi Arabia, the UAE, and Iraq all planning to increase oil production capacity within the next five years. And the easing of western sanctions against Iran—or increased sanctions-busting—could see additional supplies return to the market. Over the longer term, much will depend on the (highly uncertain) pathways for global oil demand and non-OPEC supply—but the region's large, low-cost base of oil reserves suggest that it will continue to play a leading role, even if the global market shrinks significantly. Indeed, the market share for OPEC countries (with Gulf states playing the leading role) is predicted to rise from now until 2050 in all of the IEA's scenarios.

From the perspective of regional oil producers, this same uncertainty regarding future oil demand trends looms large—though it is important to note that many oil producers believe that future oil demand prospects are relatively robust, and will be driven by emerging economies, even as the industrialized world's vehicle fleet electrifies rapidly. For example, OPEC's World Oil Outlook 2022 predicted that global oil demand will reach nearly 110 mbd by 2045, up from about 100 mbd currently.[20] The possibility that aggressive climate mitigation policies will cause a sharp reduction in global oil demand is nonetheless driving the urgency of regional efforts to diversify economic activity and government revenues away from oil production and export. For example, Saudi Arabia's Vision 2030 and its related National Transformation Program seek to diversify the Saudi economy and reduce its dependence on oil revenues, and to achieve a broader transformation of the Saudi government and society.[21] Additionally, the possibility that US oil dependence may decline is adding to concerns about the future of US oil security guarantees and driving (or at least contributing to) the region's efforts to steer a more neutral path on the global stage.

---

20 "World Oil Outlook 2022," Organization of the Petroleum Exporting Countries, 2022, https://www.opec.org/opec_web/en/publications/340.htm.
21 "Vision 2030," Kingdom of Saudi Arabia, undated, https://www.vision2030.gov.sa/.; "National Transformation Program," Kingdom of Saudi Arabia, undated, https://www.vision2030.gov.sa/v2030/vrps/ntp/.

The question of dependence also looms large for the Gulf states themselves, especially regarding their dependence on oil exports for both economic growth and government revenues. Much depends on the success of national economic diversification plans. Success in these efforts could allow the Gulf states to pursue long-term oil strategies aimed at maintaining low prices and growing market share as a means to monetize their large hydrocarbon resources without depending on high prices to sustain government revenues.[22] But note that the near-term revenue requirements of these diversification programs have ironically raised the importance of near-term oil revenues and increased the likelihood of efforts to boost short-term revenues by cutting production.[23] Moreover, the focus on sustaining high oil prices to boost revenues would be longer-lived if a failure to diversify leaves these states highly dependent on oil exports over the longer term.

What Would a Pivot Mean for Economic Interests?

With the shale revolution having made the United States a significant exporter of both oil and natural gas, there is a newly important additional dimension to the US-Middle East economic relationship, namely one of competing suppliers. A US "pivot" away from the region would risk raising the profile of the United States as a competing producer. As with oil demand, the outlook for oil supply is massively uncertain, but the US Energy Department's long-term outlook projects a small increase in domestic US oil production and exports between now and 2050, and a doubling of US LNG exports (with the United States already having surpassed Qatar as the world's largest LNG exporter).[24] For oil, Gulf producers led by Saudi Arabia engaged in a price war in 2014 and 2015 that sought to discipline US shale producers and

---

22　Spencer Dale and Bassam Fattouh, "Peak Oil Demand and Long-Run Oil Prices," Oxford Institute for Energy Studies, January 2018, https://a9w7k6q9.stackpathcdn.com/wpcms/wp-content/uploads/2018/01/Peak-Oil-Demand-and-Long-Run-Oil-Prices-Insight-25.pdf.

23　Summer Said and Stephen Kalin, "Saudi Arabia's Oil Production Cuts Reflect Cost of Reshaping Economy," *Wall Street Journal*, April 3, 2023, https://www.wsj.com/articles/saudi-arabias-oil-production-cuts-reflect-cost-of-reshaping-economy-7fb6e09c?mod=Searchresults_pos1&page=1.

24　"The United States Became the World's Largest LNG Exporter in the First Half of 2022," U.S. Energy Information Administration, July 25, 2022, https://www.eia.gov/todayinenergy/detail.php?id=53159.

investors.[25] While price wars are clearly damaging to the Gulf states' revenues as well, a US pivot away from the region could lead to more confrontational oil policies.

In addition to its potential impact on oil price volatility, a US pivot could also impact the reliability of Gulf state oil exports. Would the withdrawal of the US military/security umbrella embolden opponents of regional regimes? The potential interruption of oil flows through the Strait of Hormuz, as well as the actual disruption of Saudi production following the September 2019 attack on Eastern Province oil facilities (and subsequent attacks on facilities in the UAE), highlight the potential risks. Alternatively, would a US pivot (either real or prospective) drive the Gulf states to be more active in managing their regional conflicts in a way that would reduce risks to oil supplies?

Current trends suggest that the US is likely to remain vulnerable to oil price volatility, and that the Middle East is likely to remain a key driver of global (and therefore US) oil prices. And in turn, these trends suggest that the Gulf countries will remain important to US and global economic well-being. Accordingly, without a greater policy focus on accelerating the move away from oil within the US economy, a pivot away from the Middle East will remain challenging, at least economically.

---

25 A brief—and intense—price war in the early days of the global COVID-19 pandemic in 2020, meanwhile, was driven by Russia's reluctance to join OPEC in aggressive production cuts, and saw US oil prices dip briefly below zero. While US production fell sharply due to the price war, shale producers were not the immediate target.

Current US-China Relations and the Pivot to Asia

Yun Sun

Ever since the Obama administration first announced the US "pivot to Asia" in November 2011, the policy has never been free of controversy or debate. At the center of the questions raised by the matter lies the essential definition of what, precisely, constitutes the most significant and strategically consequential challenge to American national security. Indeed, 12 years later, observers can examine the record of three administrations—Barack Obama's, Donald Trump's, and Joe Biden's—and discern a clear reorientation of US geopolitical priorities, shifting away from the Middle East and toward East Asia. Despite the partisan differences between the Obama and Biden administrations on the one hand and the Trump administration on the other, the reorientation of US national security strategy from counterterrorism to great power competition has been confirmed as the United States' general foreign policy guideline, not only for the time being, but also likely for years to come.

One could certainly question the premise, implementation, and conclusion of the United States' shift away from the Middle East to East Asia, and especially to China. Most important to ask is whether China warrants being assigned the role of the most consequential long-term strategic threat to the United States, and whether it truly represents *the* fundamental challenge to US hegemony. If the answer to both questions is in the affirmative, the natural next question would be how to best adjust US strategy to accommodate the strategic requirements from both regions—the Middle East and East Asia—on issues that run the gamut from nuclear nonproliferation to energy security. Furthermore, as a region that is central to the global energy supply, the role of the Middle East in current great power competition also deserves more consideration.

A Brief Overview of the "Pivot to Asia"

The "pivot to Asia," also known as the "rebalance to Asia," was officially launched in then Secretary of State Hillary Clinton's article in *Foreign Policy*, "America's Pacific Century."[1] The article emphasized the key importance of the Asia-Pacific region for the global economy and geopolitics, and called for a "sustained commitment" to "forward-deployed" diplomacy, new partnerships, multilateral cooperation, and elevated economic statecraft. The strategy, according to Clinton, would proceed along six courses of action: strengthening bilateral security alliances; deepening America's relationships with rising powers, including China; engaging with regional multilateral institutions; expanding trade and investment; forging a broad-based military presence; and advancing democracy and human rights.[2]

The pivot to Asia strategy was framed from the very beginning as a strategic rebalancing of US priorities and resources toward the Asia-Pacific, the perceived epicenter of the global economy and geopolitics. An implied premise of the strategy lies in the recognition that the Middle East, and especially America's wars in Iraq and Afghanistan, absorbed the majority of the United States' attention and priorities for so long that it was lagging behind in other geopolitically consequential regions, especially in light of China's rapid development and muscle-flexing in the Asia-Pacific. For this reason, throughout his two terms, President Obama worked to reduce the US military footprint in the Middle East, with greater emphasis placed

---

1 Hillary Clinton, "America's Pacific Century," *Foreign Policy*, October 11, 2011, https://foreignpolicy.com/2011/10/11/americas-pacific-century/.
2 Ibid.

on diplomacy—even though he did not always succeed in achieving his goal.[3]

Critics of the pivot to Asia, meanwhile, have been loud and clear about what was seen as a fundamental flaw in the strategy's assumption, namely that the United States had never been absent from Asia to begin with. Considering the United States' global superpower status, some have argued that the pivot to Asia neglected the reality that the United States cannot afford to prioritize one single region at the expense of other regions and issues, with the recent Ukraine war serving as a perfect example.

Asian allies of the United States had complained that the pivot strategy began to drift during Obama's second term, despite the nominal propensity and direction it maintained. By the beginning of the Trump administration, the buzzword of US grand strategy shifted to become the "Indo-Pacific Strategy," which to a certain extent also reflects the continuation of the US prioritization of the Asia region, as Indo-Pacific is perceived by many as "Asia-Pacific plus India." More importantly, the Trump administration clearly continued the tectonic shifts in the focus of US grand strategy away from counterterrorism, for which the Middle East is the geographical center. In the 2017 National Security Strategy, the Trump administration summed up its understanding of the return of great power competition as "China and Russia began to reassert their influence regionally and globally."[4] Despite the Trump administration's perceived deviation from multilateralism and the American alliance system, Washington from 2017 to 2020 clearly followed a theme of a vigorously competitive and "no-concessions" approach to China. In this sense, although Trump's grand strategy was quite different in its approaches to its adversaries, allies, and the global system, his focus on the Indo-Pacific region, especially his prioritization of China as America's most consequential strategic threat, attests to a continued shift away from the counterterrorism campaign and the Middle East region.

---

3 Greg Myre, "Pledging To End Two Wars, Obama Finds Himself Entangled In Three," *National Public Radio*, October 15 2015, https://www.npr.org/sections/parallels/2015/10/15/448925947/pledging-to-end-two-wars-obama-finds-himself-entangled-in-three.
4 "National Security Strategy of the United States of America," The White House, December 2017, p. 27, https://trumpwhitehouse.archives.gov/wp-content/uploads/2017/12/NSS-Final-12-18-2017-0905.pdf.

President Biden, meanwhile, has envisioned a future that seeks to "more firmly anchor the United States in the Indo-Pacific."[5] In its national security strategy, released in October 2022, the Biden administration defined China as the US military's "pacing challenge" and "the only competitor with both the intent to reshape the international order and, increasingly, the economic, diplomatic, military, and technological power to do it."[6] It also sees Beijing as having "ambitions to create an enhanced sphere of influence in the Indo-Pacific and to become the world's leading power."[7] In the China strategy also announced by Secretary of State Antony Blinken in 2022, the United States put forth its strategy of investing at home and aligning with its allies in order to compete with China.[8] The Biden administration continued the Trump administration's commitment to the Indo-Pacific region by defining the United States as "an Indo-Pacific power" and recognizing the Indo-Pacific as "vital to our security and prosperity."[9] The Russian war in Ukraine has forced the United States to divide and focus a significant portion of its attention and resources on the European theater. However, throughout the process, the United States has neither abandoned nor shifted its competitive strategy on China. With the formal US withdrawal from Afghanistan in 2021 and the effort to minimize its footprint in the Middle East, the essence of the pivot to Asia has continued.

Is the "Pivot" Warranted?

A key question associated with the "pivot to Asia" strategy is whether the threat and risks posed by China warrant such a dramatic overhaul of US national security priorities. After all, the decision was not made in a vacuum; in fact, it reflects a fundamental reassessment of China, its future trajectory,

---

5 "FACT SHEET: Indo-Pacific Strategy of the United States," The White House, February 11, 2022, https://www.whitehouse.gov/briefing-room/speeches-remarks/2022/02/11/fact-sheet-indo-pacific-strategy-of-the-united-states/.
6 "National Security Strategy," The White House, October 2022, pp. 8, 20, https://www.whitehouse.gov/wp-content/uploads/2022/10/Biden-Harris-Administrations-National-Security-Strategy-10.2022.pdf.
7 Ibid., 23.
8 Antony J. Blinken, "The Administration's Approach to the People's Republic of China," U.S. Department of State, May 26 2022, https://www.state.gov/the-administrations-approach-to-the-peoples-republic-of-china/.
9 "Indo-Pacific Strategy of the United States," The White House, February 2022, p. 4, https://www.whitehouse.gov/wp-content/uploads/2022/02/US-Indo-Pacific-Strategy.pdf.

and the reality of US-China relations that began under the Obama administration and was consolidated under the Trump administration.

The most significant change that happened in China toward the end of the Hu Jintao administration and the beginning of the Xi Jinping era in the early 2010s was the fast accumulation of national wealth and the growing sense of empowerment that came along with it. After China's accession into the World Trade Organization, its foreign trade experienced explosive growth. Driven in part by tariff reductions, China's trade in goods rose from $516.4 billion in 2001 to $4.1 trillion in 2017.[10] Foreign trade, along with the vast inflow of foreign direct investment, boosted China's economic growth during the first ten years of the twenty-first century. Six out of those 10 years saw double-digit economic growth, which peaked in 2007 at an astounding 14.2 percent.[11] With vast wealth came China's growing sense of national pride. While the 2008 Beijing Olympics were seen as China's return to the center of the world stage, domestic public opinion became increasingly impatient and dissatisfied with deceased former leader Deng Xiaoping's foreign policy mantra: "Keep a low profile and bide our time."[12] The muscle-flexing first began in the South China Sea, which China declared as its "core national interest" in 2010, implying that Beijing would resort to the use of force to defend it if necessary.[13] This uncompromising maritime position and China's growing assertiveness in its foreign relations became an increasingly harsh and alarming reality for the United States and its allies in the region.

From a political leadership perspective, the assertive trajectory only accelerated after President Xi Jinping formally took power in 2013. Defining his mission as "the great rejuvenation of the Chinese nation," Xi formally abandoned China's "keeping a low profile" diplomatic path, and instead sought a proactive diplomacy and security policy to assert

---

10 "How Influential is China in the World Trade Organization?," Center for Strategic and International Studies, July 31, 2019, https://chinapower.csis.org/china-world-trade-organization-wto/.
11 "1961-2021 GDP Growth (annual %) - China," The World Bank, 2022, https://data.worldbank.org/indicator/NY.GDP.MKTP.KD.ZG?locations=CN.
12 "Should China continue to keep a low-profile attitude?," *The People's Daily*, December 13, 2012, http://en.people.cn/90883/8057776.html.
13 Nicola Casarini "A Sea at the Heart of Chinese National Interest," *Global Challenges*, no. 1 (February 2017), https://globalchallenges.ch/issue/1/a-sea-at-the-heart-of-chinese-national-interest/.

China's interests.[14] With China's Belt and Road Initiative representing its geoeconomic campaign for expansion, Beijing has actively sought to build up its military sector, especially in terms of the Chinese Navy's power projection capability.[15] With China now equipped with new wealth from a decade of rapid economic growth, economic resources and statecraft have become two of the most effective instruments in its foreign policy toolkit, and Beijing has begun to adeptly utilize economic rewards and sanctions to influence other countries' policy decisions. All these developments are perceived as a fundamental threat to the US-led liberal international order and the rules that anchor it.

A strong and increasingly assertive China is not only challenging the US-led international system from the outside; its distinct model of growth—earlier called the "Beijing consensus," which combined political authoritarianism with economic capitalism—forms a powerful challenge to the liberal democratic political system on which the United States and its allies place great emphasis. With its own distinct growth and governance model, China successfully chartered a course of high-speed growth without accompanying political liberalization, thereby presenting itself to the rest of the world as an alternative model of development, with political and economic appeal unparalleled by any previous experience. Under Xi Jinping, China further developed its agenda to replicate its "China wisdom" and "China model" in other developing countries, a mission that was emphasized in the official report of the 19th National Congress of the Chinese Communist Party.[16] At this point, China has emerged not only as the near-peer competitor of the United States in terms of material wealth and national power, but it has also entered the realm of ideological competition with the US. This more profound layer of ideological contest led to the argument that the United States and China have formally entered a new

---

14 Graham Allison, "What Xi Jinping Wants," *The Atlantic*, May 31, 2017, https://www.theatlantic.com/international/archive/2017/05/what-china-wants/528561/.

15 James McBride et al., "China's Massive Belt and Road Initiative," Council on Foreign Relations, February 2, 2023, https://www.cfr.org/backgrounder/chinas-massive-belt-and-road-initiative.; Timothy R. Heath, "Why Is China Strengthening Its Military? It's Not All About War," The Rand Blog, March 24, 2023, https://www.rand.org/blog/2023/03/why-is-china-strengthening-its-military-its-not-all.html.

16 "Full Text of Xi Jinping's Report at 19th CPC National Congress," *China Daily*, November 4, 2017, https://www.chinadaily.com.cn/china/19thcpcnationalcongress/2017-11/04/content_34115212.htm.

"cold war." Since then, the dichotomy of "democracy versus autocracy" has become an even more distinct feature in the strategic competition between the two great powers.

Despite the close economic cooperation and interdependence China has formed with the United States over the past decades, in the national security arena the US has always been seen as the most significant and consequential external threat to China's national security. In Beijing's view, US intervention in China's civil war in the late 1940s is the core reason that mainland China remains divided from Taiwan, preventing unification seven decades after the founding of the People's Republic of China. And the United States' mission to promote democracy and human rights is the core reason for the "color revolutions" that overthrew authoritarian leaders in former Soviet states. That same US mission continues to threaten the Chinese Communist Party's domestic legitimacy and regime security.

With Xi's leadership and vision for China's resumption of regional and global leadership in place, Beijing sees the United States as the hegemon that it will surpass and displace, first in its immediate neighborhood of Asia, and then potentially in other parts of the world. It remains up for debate whether China should really aim to replace the United States as the global hegemon. Especially in regions farther away from the Chinese border, such as the Middle East and Africa, there is a strong argument in China that the country should just enjoy the free ride in terms of the security provided by the United States, at America's expense.

Indeed, the Chinese challenge to US hegemony is certain. Even if China does not aim to completely replace the United States as the global hegemon, it is keen on revising the international system, the geopolitical reality, and the rules and norms that it perceives to be against its national interests. For example, when China's Global Security Initiative challenges the US-led alliance system, such as NATO, painting it as a source of instability and insecurity, and instead tries to present an alternative definition of security as "common, comprehensive, cooperative and sustainable," the global security order under American leadership comes under serious challenges, both conceptually and in practice.[17]

---

17 "The Global Security Initiative Concept Paper," People's Republic of China Ministry of Foreign Affairs, February 21, 2023, https://www.fmprc.gov.cn/mfa_eng/wjbxw/202302/t20230221_11028348.html.

Choosing between Two Critical Regions?

Both East Asia and the Middle East carry tremendous strategic importance for the United States as a global hegemon, but another important region is Europe. For many Asian observers, the transatlantic NATO alliance has always remained the cornerstone of the United States' security strategy, as was demonstrated by the US prioritization of Europe during the Cold War. The end of the war and the disintegration of the Soviet Union have not removed Russia from its position as a primary geopolitical and geostrategic threat to the United States. The Russian war in Ukraine, ongoing since February 2022, is a living reminder that even if the United States is trying to pivot toward Asia and prioritize China as its "pacing challenge," the geopolitical reality in other key regions of the world does not allow for the luxury of focusing on only one region, or on one challenge at a given time.

The same is also true when it comes to East Asia and the Middle East. East Asia, or the Asia-Pacific more broadly, commands vast potential in terms of human and economic resources. The rise of China for the first time in recent history poses a credible and long-term critical challenge to the United States, not only in terms of economic and military hard power, but also through its ideological and revisionist appeal. Effectively countering China's rise and outcompeting it are indispensable to the maintenance of US supremacy and the international order as the world has known it.

However, this by no means suggests that the Middle East region has lost its geopolitical significance. The Middle East is still the center of global energy security and will remain so for the foreseeable future. Any instability in the region will create unimaginable disruption and damage to the global supply chain and to economic well-being. The profound spillover effect of security threats from the region extends to both traditional and nontraditional security arenas, including nuclear nonproliferation, counterterrorism, and climate change. Instability in the Middle East, as well as the region's future economic and security trajectory, have the ability to critically impact the future of the world and the United States' leadership role in it.

Furthermore, in today's interconnected world, and with the global implications of US-China great power competition, the Middle East does not exist outside the scope of the US-China power contest. The recent Saudi-Iran rapprochement brokered by China is a good reminder for the United States that any US withdrawal of attention and influence in the region will create a vacuum that Beijing will be eager to fill, and the consequences will play against the US strategic priority of effectively competing with China.[18] Indeed, the strategic competition between the United States and China is not just about the two countries' respective national wealth and technological advantages; more importantly, it is also about the rest of the world. Which great power the rest of the world will identify with and support will eventually shape the outcome of this great power competition. If the United States relinquishes its leadership and its focus on the Middle East, it will only create opportunities for Beijing and vulnerabilities that will cost Washington dearly later. This message is resonating loud and clear throughout the US policy community today.

Conclusion

Regardless of debate surrounding the issue, the American pivot to Asia is a reality, rather than a myth. After starting with the Obama administration's rebalance to Asia strategy, the reorientation of the United States' strategic focus to Asia, especially to East Asia and China, has remained in place under the Trump and Biden administrations. And in fact, it has accelerated with the prioritization of the Indo-Pacific region, the prominence of great power competition as a main theme of the US national security strategy, and the identification of China as America's most consequential challenge in the long run. The US reorientation is anchored on the rise of China and the growing economic, political, security, and ideological challenges that it represents, and this trajectory is unlikely to falter or shift in the foreseeable future.

However, the Middle East remains a critical strategic center of the global system, not only because of its central position in global energy security, but also due to the tremendous impact from both traditional and nontraditional security threats in the region. The Middle East is also emerging as a new area of US-China strategic competition, which means that the region's future is intricately linked to the result of the strategic contest between the two great powers.

---

18 Peter Baker, "Chinese-Brokered Deal Upends Mideast Diplomacy and Challenges U.S.," *New York Times*, March 11, 2023, https://www.nytimes.com/2023/03/11/us/politics/saudi-arabia-iran-china-biden.html.

The US Pivot in the Context of Great Power Competition: A New Multipolar Global Order?

Patricia Karam

While the United States maintains important investments in the Middle East, the general tenor of its transactions has been perceived as faltering, and indeed as disengaging from certain parts of the region. An early manifestation of what the foreign policy community saw as a "pivot away" from the Middle East was former President Barack Obama's failure in 2013 to react to the Syrian regime's chemical attack on its own citizens that killed 1,400 people, a stunning about-face from his avowed "red line" that, if crossed, would trigger US military intervention.[1] The administration's motivations at the time were avoiding the collapse of nascent nuclear talks with Iran and the hope of creating an equilibrium that would enable states in the region to police their own matters, a goal that, perhaps inadvertently, involved the tacit recognition of Iran's investments and influence and the provision of greater maneuverability to newer regional actors like Russia.

---

1 Patrice Taddonio, "'The President Blinked': Why Obama Changed Course on the 'Red Line' in Syria," *PBS*, May 25, 2015, https://www.pbs.org/wgbh/frontline/article/the-president-blinked-why-obama-changed-course-on-the-red-line-in-syria/.

Since then, the narrative about a declining US role in the region has focused mainly on the United States' abdication of its security commitments and its abandonment of its partners in the context of greater energy independence and a "rebalance" to Asia that has increased the relative significance of other regions.[2] This view was reaffirmed by the underwhelming US reaction in the wake of drone attacks on Saudi Aramco facilities in 2019 that were alleged to have been sponsored by Iran.[3] If any event can explain why Riyadh has lost its faith in the United States, it is this one; and the Saudis have since taken matters into their own hands by recalibrating alliances. The recent Saudi-Iran rapprochement is a case in point, and can be traced to Riyadh's realization that if it cannot get more from the United States, it will look elsewhere.[4] Repeated missile attacks against Abu Dhabi—and especially a January 2022 attack on its national oil company—similarly brought into question the United States' resolve and reliability as a strategic partner.[5] But US allies in Asia—who are almost completely dependent on Middle Eastern oil—worry that this approach is futile and that a US abandonment of the Middle East will have the opposite effect of making China even stronger in Asia.

Meanwhile, the power vacuum occasioned by the United States' halting disengagement has enabled both Russia's entrenchment and China's extended reach and influence in the region, as well as regional competition for influence between an assertive Iran, a more confident Turkey, an increasingly eager Israel, and reactive Arab actors. The region is "there for the taking," with these trends intensifying in the aftermath of Russia's invasion of Ukraine, during which media efforts promoting anti-US and anti-western perspectives that are detrimental to universal norms and values have dealt America's image a serious blow. And although China, within this great power

---

2   Tania Branigan et al., "Obama's First Term: Pivot to Asia and Tweaks to Latin America," *The Guardian*, October 21, 2012, https://www.theguardian.com/world/2012/oct/21/obama-foreign-policy-pivots-asia.
3   Ben Hubbard et al., "Two Major Saudi Oil Installations Hit by Drone Strike, and U.S. Blames Iran," *New York Times*, September 14, 2019, https://www.nytimes.com/2019/09/14/world/middleeast/saudi-arabia-refineries-drone-attack.html.
4   "The Impact of the Saudi-Iranian Rapprochement on Middle East Conflicts," International Crisis Group, April 19, 2023, https://www.crisisgroup.org/middle-east-north-africa/gulf-and-arabian-peninsula/iran-saudi-arabia/impact-saudi-iranian.
5   Jon Gambrell, "Satellite Photos Show Aftermath of Abu Dhabi Oil Site Attack," *Reuters*, January 18, 2022, https://apnews.com/article/business-dubai-united-arab-emirates-only-on-ap-abu-dhabi-4a72597046dab910fbcbc1634bfa05b1.

competition, has chiefly sought to stabilize the region to protect its access to oil, Russia threatens to spoil its attempt to do so as it seeks to restore its own status in the region while undercutting US leadership. While the US approach to China needs to focus on neutralizing the latter's quiet dominance, it will also need to contain Russia so that its opportunistic interventions and predilections for superpower projections do not disrupt stability. The next decade is one that will surely be shaped by how these rivalries play out.

Questions about the United States' dedication to the region are often explained within US policy circles by referencing the need for a more pragmatic approach to Middle East entanglements, one that factors in the changing geopolitical environment (including Russia and China's forays), US interests, and the costly price tag—both in human lives and in dollars—of pursuing a more hard-hitting foreign policy. Primacy is also placed on newer and possibly grimmer threats, such as those posed by China's rise to power and its challenge to US global hegemony. Statements coming from US administration officials about reoriented priorities have emphasized, over and over, China's new centrality in foreign policy, above and beyond that of Russia. In the most recent US National Security Strategy, China is referred to as America's "most consequential geopolitical challenge," especially given what the Biden administration sees as the increasingly threatening China-Russia axis.[6] But there is also an understanding within these same circles that efforts to restrain China also need to include the Middle East.

Accordingly, despite frustration with lasting violence and instability in the region, US leadership is engaged in a strategic rethinking of the nation's foreign policy, taking into account the changed reality on the ground and the failures of prior interventions. This effort needs to make better use of the full range of diplomatic, economic/financial, and military tools. Therefore, any talk of a downgraded US involvement in the region has to be measured. The flurry of US administration trips to Saudi Arabia—the most recent by Secretary of State Antony Blinken in early June 2023—are seeking, if anything, to detract from talk of a pivot away from the Middle East and to reassure partners that the US remains committed to offsetting the overarching distrust of Washington that has taken hold in the region.[7]

---

6 "National Security Strategy," The White House, October 12, 2022, https://www.whitehouse.gov/wp-content/uploads/2022/10/Biden-Harris-Administrations-National-Security-Strategy-10.2022.pdf.

7 Humeyra Pamuk, "Blinken Heads to Saudi Arabia amid Strained Ties, Israel Normalization in Mind," *Reuters*, June 6, 2023, https://www.reuters.com/world/middle-east/blinken-heads-saudi-arabia-amid-strained-ties-israel-normalization-mind-2023-06-06/.

Push and Pull Factors of Russian and Chinese Power

Within the Middle Eastern theater of great power competition, Russia has sought to remain relevant by tenaciously shoring up allies like Syria's Bashar al-Assad, while simultaneously frustrating US ambitions. In the 1990s, Russia was a defeated adversary trying to find itself again on the world stage after the end of the Cold War. But since intervening to prevent both US-approved regime change in Syria and a transition to democracy in Libya, Moscow has been searching for conduits through which to amplify its sway. In part through deployments in Syria and Libya—failed states where it has made progress by taking advantage of the chaos—Russia has formed a complex partnership with Iran (on which it depends for artillery and drones in its Ukraine war) and has also expanded its interests and involvement in the Gulf to avoid destabilizing moves, especially given western sanctions that have wracked its energy industry.[8] And it has succeeded: Bashar al-Assad is still in power and Russia has gained military air and naval bases in Syria, in Humaymim and Tartus, and in the north at al-Jarrah.[9] In the process it is cozying up to Turkey, which itself is seeking to diversify its allies and move away from the United States to secure its own spheres of influence, namely in the Caucasus region and the Eastern Mediterranean—also areas of Russian involvement. And Turkey's competing involvement in Syria and Libya will eventually factor into the competition between the US and Russia. These Russian forays, mostly opportunistic and disruptive, have enabled Russian President Vladimir Putin to enhance both his country's global standing and his popularity at home by demonstrating the value of an assertive, hard-line foreign policy. By positioning itself as a powerful and effective player that is actively thwarting US interests, Russia is signaling that it can confront anyone who wishes to prevail in the region. As such, Moscow has also gained the esteem of countries—Egypt, for example—that, disillusioned by the United States' support for the anti-regime popular revolts that swept the

---

[8] "Iran's Deepening Strategic Relationship with Russia," United States Institute of Peace, April 25, 2023, http://iranprimer.usip.org/blog/2023/feb/24/iran%E2%80%99s-deepening-strategic-alliance-russia.; Darya Korsunskaya and Jake Cordell, "Western Sanctions Push Russia's Energy Revenues to Lowest since 2020," *Reuters*, February 3, 2023, https://www.reuters.com/business/energy/western-sanctions-push-russias-energy-revenues-lowest-level-since-2020-2023-02-03/.

[9] Guy Faulconbridge and Caleb Davis, "Syria's Assad Would Like More Russian Bases and Troops," *Reuters*, March 16, 2023, https://www.reuters.com/world/middle-east/syrias-assad-says-would-welcome-more-russian-troops-2023-03-16/.

region in 2011, are looking to be pulled into the Russian orbit, and that have deepened, as a result, their military and diplomatic ties with Moscow.

In the meantime, the Middle East is quickly becoming the cornerstone of China's Belt and Road Initiative (BRI), a colossal international infrastructure project that consists of a mix of development and investment initiatives seeking to link East Asia to the rest of the world.[10] At base, this is an economic development strategy aiming to improve regional connectivity and cooperation through free trade zones and to accelerate trade and investment by creating new export markets for China, all in the name of more sustainable growth. The BRI now includes well over 100 countries, and has thus come to signify a more dramatic expression of Chinese economic, cultural, and political influence.[11]

China's fast economic growth has been accompanied by a rising demand for oil, and China is expected to make up 60 percent of all oil demand growth in 2023.[12] As almost half of China's oil imports now come from the Middle East, oil remains at the core of its interests in the region, which have broadened to encompass investment and trade. And indeed, China reached $330 billion in trade with GCC countries in 2021, and US-Gulf trade is on the decline.[13] Chinese-Saudi bilateral trade, for example, stood at $3 billion in 2000, and reached $41.6 billion in 2010 before totaling $87.3 billion in 2021.[14] There are thus huge stakes in this and other regional partnerships, and they are growing exponentially.

---

10 James McBride et al., "Backgrounder: China's Massive Belt and Road Initiative," Council on Foreign Relations, February 2, 2023, https://www.cfr.org/backgrounder/chinas-massive-belt-and-road-initiative.
11 David Sacks, "Countries in China's Belt and Road Initiative: Who's In And Who's Out," Council on Foreign Relations, March 24, 2021, https://www.cfr.org/blog/countries-chinas-belt-and-road-initiative-whos-and-whos-out.
12 Will Horner, "China's Demand for Oil Hits Record as IEA Raises Global Forecasts," *Wall Street Journal*, May 16, 2023, https://www.wsj.com/articles/chinas-demand-for-oil-hits-record-as-iea-raises-global-forecasts-67daad8e.
13 Nurettin Akcay, "Beyond Oil, A New Phase in China-Middle East Engagement," *The Diplomat*, January 25, 2023, https://thediplomat.com/2023/01/beyond-oil-a-new-phase-in-china-middle-east-engagement/.
14 Jon B. Alterman, "Chinese and Russian Influence in the Middle East: Statement before the House Foreign Affairs Subcommittee on the Middle East, North Africa, and International Terrorism," U.S. Congress, May 9, 2019, https://www.congress.gov/116/meeting/house/109455/witnesses/HHRG-116-FA13-Wstate-AltermanJ-20190509.pdf.; Ruxandra Iordache, "Saudi Arabia Takes Step to Join China-Led Security Bloc, as Ties with Beijing Strengthen," *CNBC*, March 29, 2023, https://www.cnbc.com/2023/03/29/saudi-arabia-takes-step-to-join-china-led-security-bloc-as-ties-with-beijing-strengthen.html.

Amid changing regional dynamics, China is also establishing economic and strategic partnerships with an increasing number of countries in the region, thus creating a web of allies. Strategic cooperation agreements in a range of critical areas, including telecommunications, infrastructure, technology, and energy have been signed with Iran and with its rivals, including Saudi Arabia, the UAE, Oman, Bahrain, Kuwait, Egypt, and others. Many of these investments come with no human rights strings attached (as is, by contrast, sometimes the case with US agreements), making them especially enticing for leaders in the region who do not want to be held accountable for the repression that has become part and parcel of their mode of governance. Indeed, much of China's engagement has been guided by the principle of non-interference in domestic affairs, making sure not to unsettle prevalent autocratic and patriarchal political systems.

China's economic moves may, however, signal a more audacious form of diplomacy under President Xi Jinping in the form of deliberate peacemaking, most significantly epitomized by the recent China-brokered Iran-Saudi deal that could dramatically alter the geopolitical balance in the region. China's own approach in East Asia has consisted of patient and methodical moves, such as its militarization in the South China Sea, over which it has long claimed sovereignty. The PRC has accordingly been increasingly less timid about military engagement in the Middle East. It has, for example, steadily extended its naval footprint since launching its first regional base in Djibouti in 2017, which quickly expanded from a logistics facility to a "military support facility."[15] And it is also quietly searching for new bases in the Arabian/Persian Gulf. This search has included Khalifa Port in the UAE (a close partner of the United States), where Beijing is believed to be building a more permanent military presence as part of efforts to create a global network of military bases and logistical support sites by 2030, an initiative referred to by Chinese officials as Project 141.[16] Budding security ties between China and the UAE, with the concurrent establishment of a Chinese base in the country, will certainly complicate the United States' own ability to maneuver there.

---

15 Erica Downs et al., "China's Military Support Facility in Djibouti: The Economic and Security Dimensions of China's First Overseas Base," CNA, July 2017, https://www.cna.org/archive/CNA_Files/pdf/dim-2017-u-015308-final2.pdf.

16 John Hudson et al., "Buildup Resumed at Suspected Chinese Military Site in UAE," *Washington Post*, April 26, 2023, https://www.washingtonpost.com/national-security/2023/04/26/chinese-military-base-uae/.

China has further upped its soft power engagement in the region through an international media network, cultural centers, and educational investments that have been cautiously undertaken yet steadily effective. Surveys show that views of China in the Arab world tend to be positive, and that there appears to be an openness toward China among Arabs. By contrast, 81 percent of Arabs see the United States as a foreign threat, while only 32 percent perceive China as such.[17] The reality is that China has had little negative press in the region. Having stayed out of both conflicts and domestic affairs, it is increasingly perceived as a stabilizing force. But China is bound to become more conspicuous as it identifies opportunities to expand its influence in the region—and here the question becomes not if it will replace the US but how it is becoming a welcome player in a region looking to diversify its patrons.

Saudi Arabia's Realignment

At the regional level, Saudi Arabia's rapprochement with Iran and its alliance with Russia on oil cooperation—expanded significantly since the formation of OPEC+—have prompted questions as to the kingdom's motivations.[18] Riyadh's single most important concern has been that of protection provided by external actors. Despite having a large arsenal (provided by the US), Saudi Arabia's defense management and its ability to use and sustain these weapons remains weak, while the Saudi Ministry of Defense has "little ability to effectively identify, train, deploy, and retain a technically capable force."[19] The efficacy of a recent Saudi defense establishment overhaul—undertaken under Crown Prince Mohammed bin Salman Al Saud's leadership—is yet to be ascertained. This means that Saudi Arabia is essentially incapable of defending itself against external threats, at least in the short term.

Today, Riyadh is absorbed by the implementation of its Vision 2030 project, a "whole economy" strategic framework and development program

---

17 "The 2019-2020 Arab Opinion Index: Main Results in Brief," Arab Center for Research and Policy Studies, November 16, 2020, https://arabcenterdc.org/resource/the-2019-2020-arab-opinion-index-main-results-in-brief/#section6.

18 Sean Hill and Owen Comstock, "What Is OPEC+ and How Is It Different from OPEC?," U.S. Energy Information Administration, May 9, 2023, https://www.eia.gov/todayinenergy/detail.php?id=56420.

19 Bilal Y. Saab, "After Oil-for-Security: A Blueprint for Resetting US-Saudi Security Relations," Middle East Institute, February 17, 2023, https://www.mei.edu/publications/after-oil-security-blueprint-resetting-us-saudi-security-relations.

that seeks to diversify the kingdom's economy away from resource-dependence and to transform it into a regional business hub.[20] Around $3 trillion in investment opportunities for foreign companies have already been identified, and while plans are underway to enhance the country's internal business infrastructure, the broader regional investment climate will be the principal factor for attracting diverse and steady investments. Accordingly, although keen on becoming a bigger player in the region, Saudi Arabia is even more interested in keeping the region stable.

From the Saudi perspective, US policy failed to rein in Iran, which today is steps away from obtaining weapons-grade nuclear material.[21] Furthermore, Tehran has neither reduced its support to its proxy militias nor ceased its malign foreign interference outside its borders, thereby rendering the region more volatile. In the absence of security guarantees and a defense pact with the United States, the Chinese approach to stabilizing the region is almost irresistible.[22] Riyadh is thus recalibrating its approach and taking matters into its own hands to improve its regional standing, reduce its involvement in military confrontations, and alter the regional balance of power in its favor. The Middle East, in this instance, needs to be seen less as a region that has been conquered by China or Russia and more as one that is fundamentally displeased with the terms of its current arrangement with the United States, which is perceived to have not only taken the region for granted but effectively abandoned it.

The End of US Hegemony

The Middle East has changed in the last decade in ways that affect US national security interests. Existing troop levels in the region—which stand between 40,000 and 60,000—are at their lowest since the September 11 attacks, and the US is not involved in any active conflicts.[23] At the same

---

20 "Vision 2030," Kingdom of Saudi Arabia, undated, https://www.vision2030.gov.sa/.
21 Phil McCausland and Dan De Luce, "Iran Enriching Uranium to Near Weapons-Grade Levels, Nuclear Watchdog Warns," *NBC News*, March 8, 2023, https://www.nbcnews.com/news/world/iran-enriching-uranium-weapons-grade-nuclear-iaea-rcna72753.
22 Michael Crowley et al., "Saudi Arabia Offers Its Price to Normalize Relations With Israel," *New York Times*, March 11, 2023, https://www.nytimes.com/2023/03/09/us/politics/saudi-arabia-israel-united-states.html.
23 J.P. Lawrence, "US Troop Level Reduction in Middle East Likely as Focus Shifts Elsewhere," *Stars and Stripes*, January 14, 2022, https://www.stripes.com/theaters/middle_east/2022-01-14/centcom-central-command-drawdown-iraq-afghanistan-kuwait-saudi-arabia-4289137.html.

time, civil wars continue to rage in Libya, Syria, and Yemen, and have also given rise to instability. The region's outlook for stable democratic governance and consistent economic growth has regressed, with citizens having less and less of a say in their governments and being forced to live under corrupt, parasitic, or simply unresponsive political systems. Youth unemployment continues to stand at around double the world average as overly centralized public-sector-dominated economies have failed to create jobs for an ever-growing number of young people entering the workforce across the region.[24] Unaddressed youth resentment creates fertile ground for radicalization, giving illiberal actors leverage over liberal voices. Moreover, the threat of nuclear proliferation is rising, primarily from Iran, but also from powers like Saudi Arabia and Turkey, which are likely to follow in Iran's footsteps in developing their nuclear programs.

At the same time, the region houses nearly half of the world's oil reserves and accounts for 31 percent of global oil production.[25] Although the ongoing transition to renewable energy will certainly reduce the global significance of the Middle East eventually, this is not likely to happen anytime soon. And while the United States may no longer rely on Middle East oil as much as it has in the past, its allies still do, and the region is still crucial for the stability of global energy markets. Furthermore, the United States is hardly protected against disruptions in world energy supplies.

Today, US supremacy in the Middle East is finished. Though still an important actor, the US role is currently diminished, as it is no longer the only superpower in a region that is increasingly marked by a contest between those who are in the process of demarcating their roles and priorities. By projecting its might, Russia is seeking to reclaim its superpower status in order to offset its relatively weak domestic economic and political situation. China is playing the long game by trying to ensure a cheap inflow of oil and a steady outflow of goods to new markets in the region while also hoping, as the Middle East's main source of foreign investment, that economic influence will eventually translate into greater political and military significance. And here, Russia and China are actively positioning

---

24 "Young People Address Challenges and Explore Opportunities of Transition from Learning to Employment in the Middle East and North Africa/Arab States Region," UNICEF, May 23, 2022, https://www.unicef.org/mena/press-releases/young-people-address-challenges-and-explore-opportunities-transition-learning.

25 "Middle East's Energy Market in 2020," Statistical Review of World Energy 2021, undated, https://www.bp.com/content/dam/bp/business-sites/en/global/corporate/pdfs/energy-economics/statistical-review/bp-stats-review-2021-middle-east-insights.pdf.

themselves against the US, competing for economic, diplomatic, and military clout, so far without forming a united front. China is taking the lead in the ideological confrontation over democracy and human rights by presenting an autocratic alternative in a region where autocracy and paternalistic governance is rampant. This opposition to liberal and democratic values is resonating with local leaders who, themselves preempting and suppressing domestic calls for liberalization, are increasingly competing for China's attention.

The Developing Multipolar Order and the Rise of China

There now exists a burgeoning multipolar order in the Middle East, one in which a confident China could use the goodwill it has cultivated, alongside various economic and political tools, to more forcefully exert its influence with the region's autocratic elites. China has given precedence to promoting stability and shared economic interests, but any new hostilities or tensions could push it toward an enhanced military posture to protect its now extensive regional interests. It has already stepped up its military cooperation with Saudi Arabia, the UAE, and Iran in reaction to US sanctions against a China-based network of companies accused of supplying aerospace parts, including for drones, to Iran.[26] Russia, meanwhile, has actively used conflicts in the region to deepen its influence and establish an order that runs against US interests.

The firming up in the region of these great powers, who are brandishing quintessentially autocratic playbooks as their modus operandi against fast-waning liberal values while regional partners more forcefully pursue their self-interest, bodes ill for the region's trajectory and for US interests. China in particular, which is quietly exploiting openings and US detachment to expand its hegemony, is likely to become the most daunting of America's adversaries. The recent China-brokered peace deal between Saudi Arabia and Iran is one such opening, and it is upending traditional alliances.

This challenge needs to be factored into a reexamination of what is and is not working in current US policy, new approaches to proactively managing opportunities and threats, and a recognition of the need to deploy tools that are more effective in addressing the new brand of security threats

---

26 Daphne Psaledakis and Michelle Nichols, "US Sanctions China-Based Network Accused of Supplying Iran Drone-Maker," *Reuters*, March 9, 2023, https://www.reuters.com/world/us-targets-china-based-network-supporting-irans-drone-procurement-efforts-2023-03-09/.

emerging from the region. The US will need to pay more deliberate attention to helping address and contain socioeconomic challenges within the region, and must not succumb to the temptation of subcontracting out responsibility for the region's stability to the emerging authoritarian nexus and its clients. The less influence the US has, the more its illiberal and undemocratic competitors will fill the void. And while regional autocratic actors vie to expand their influence in a contested space, the region risks sliding into multipolar autocracy.

Even if the US wanted to withdraw from the Middle East, so long as China has stakes in the region, the US will have a role there. The United States' reading of the next few decades has to be less about great power competition more broadly than about a more specific US-China competition. Just this year, President Xi upped the ante by brazenly accusing the US—following restrictions on access to Chinese technology—of leading a campaign of "containment, encirclement and suppression" against China and challenging its economic development.[27] He then warned of the possibility of confrontation. While US policymakers certainly realize that divesting from the region is not a viable option, they have failed to present a steady, sober alternative for a realistic and responsible engagement that serves US interests. A fundamental component of the US strategy to contain China must be renewed attention to the Middle East, if only because the region is so important to China for oil, trade, and investment. The US also needs to counter China's new hegemony in the Middle East—and contain Russia's subversive rogue actions there—not just to bolster US strength in the region, but in other parts of the world as well.

---

27 Chun Han Wong et al., "China's Xi Jinping Takes Rare Direct Aim at U.S. in Speech," *Wall Street Journal*, March 6, 2023, https://www.wsj.com/articles/chinas-xi-jinping-takes-rare-direct-aim-at-u-s-in-speech-5d8fde1a/.

Arab Views on an American Pivot Away from the Middle East

Rami G. Khouri

The US government's "pivot" from the Middle East to focus on Asia, and especially on China, has been much debated but not well documented since President Barack Obama first proposed it a decade ago. The reality behind the notion of a pivot is much more complex than a unilateral American decision. It includes a dozen Middle Eastern and global actors who all at once are diversifying their international strategic and economic relations, in line with their national vulnerabilities and interests.

Americans and Arabs' perceptions of themselves and their global relationships are now evolving steadily and revealing new developments: Arab citizens and governments are converging in their desire to reduce but not end their reliance on the United States and to diversify ties with other powers. Meanwhile, foreign policy decisions by all actors downplay their previous black-and-white, friend-or-foe dichotomy between two ideological camps, in favor of flexible and nuanced relations with a wider network of partners.

Why and How Change Happens

Five critical dynamics occurring simultaneously across the Middle East clarify why so many states have been adjusting their foreign ties, and why most Arabs welcome a lower level of American engagement in the region.

First, half a dozen Middle Eastern states now actively project their power—money, military, trade, and technology—across the region, including by adjusting and even reversing long-standing policies if this serves their best interests (e.g., Saudi Arabia and the UAE's renewed ties with Iran, Turkish-Egyptian reconciliation, and Israel's formal agreements with four Arab governments). Activist and often wealthy or militarily powerful regional states—Iran, Saudi Arabia, Turkey, the United Arab Emirates, Qatar, and Israel, for example—can provide more vulnerable states some of the external support that they have long sought from global powers. Arab states have shown higher levels of independent action by resuming full diplomatic ties with Iran, hedging on strong and deep ties with Israel, avoiding taking sides in the Ukraine-Russia conflict, seeking to join the BRICS group of nations, and hesitating to join a regional network of militaries to confront Iran.

Second, the United States is adjusting some of its engagements in the Middle East as it experiences a great reckoning for its past policies during the bipolar and unipolar global eras that existed after 1945, when its power allowed it to dictate to weaker Arab states. But the United States' few political or military successes in the Middle East in recent decades, especially its heavy reliance on warfare and sanctions, have come at a heavy cost to citizens in the region.[1] Recent studies show that this includes the displacement of at least 37 million, and perhaps as many as 59 million people.[2] Not surprisingly, polls repeatedly indicate that Arab publics widely dislike or distrust American policies—though many Arab governments rely on American military and economic support to keep

---

1 Jennifer Kavanagh and Bryan Frederick, "Why Force Fails: The Dismal Track Record of U.S. Military Interventions," *Foreign Affairs*, March 30, 2023, https://www.foreignaffairs.com/united-states/us-military-why-force-fails.
2 David Vine et al., "Creating Refugees: Displacement Caused by the United States' Post-9/11 Wars," Watson Institute, September 21, 2020, https://watson.brown.edu/costsofwar/files/cow/imce/papers/2020/Displacement_Vine%20et%20al_Costs%20of%20War%202020%2009%2008.pdf.

themselves in power.³ Following its military and political withdrawal from Afghanistan, Iraq, and most of Syria, the United States could be reconsidering militarism and sanctions as its most effective foreign policy tools. It participates in sanctions on 27 percent of all countries in the world, which together account for 29 percent of the global economy, with very mixed results.⁴ And even where severe sanctions are applied, they often do not achieve their goals, as *Reuters* reported recently about Iran's growing oil output that reached 3 million barrels per day in May 2023, compared to 2.5 million before the Trump administration imposed oil export sanctions.⁵ The United States henceforth is likely to focus more on areas that directly impact its national interests, such as ensuring both energy flows and Israel's security, containing Iran, preventing nuclear proliferation, and limiting Russia and China's expanding regional links.

Third, Russia and China have been expanding their interactions with states across the region in multiple sectors (including military, economic, infrastructure, and energy arenas), often responding to requests by Arab states that want to diversify their global links. The American political elite feels its global reach and former dominance are threatened by a China that is more globally active and expanding its ties with Middle Eastern states of all ideological stripes.⁶

Fourth, fast-growing new coalitions across the Global South, such as BRICS (Brazil, Russia, India, China, South Africa) and the Shanghai Cooperation Organization, might provide alternatives to a US-dominated world economic order, including reserve and trade currencies that challenge the US dollar and development aid mechanisms that challenge

---

3 Merissa Khurma, "Ukraine, Russia and the Arabs," Wilson Center, February 18, 2022, https://www.wilsoncenter.org/article/ukraine-russia-and-arabs.; "15th Annual ASDA'A BCW Arab Youth Survey," BCW Global, June 20, 2023, https://arabyouthsurvey.com/wp-content/uploads/whitepaper/presentation-2023-en.pdf.; Mohamed Younis, "Muslim-Majority Countries Doubt U.S. Motives," Gallup, April 7, 2023, https://news.gallup.com/poll/473546/muslim-majority-countries-doubt-motives.aspx.

4 Francisco R. Rodriguez, "The Human Consequences of Economic Sanctions," Center for Economic and Policy Research, May 4, 2023, https://cepr.net/report/the-human-consequences-of-economic-sanctions/.

5 Alex Lawler, "Iran's Oil Exports Hit 5-Year Highs as US Holds Nuclear Talks," June 16, 2023, *Reuters*, https://www.reuters.com/markets/commodities/irans-oil-exports-output-hit-five-year-highs-us-holds-nuclear-talks-2023-06-16/.

6 "Americans See China as Biggest Security Threat," What's News: WSJ Podcasts, December 2, 2021, https://www.wsj.com/podcasts/whats-news/americans-see-china-as-biggest-security-threat/843ac88b-0384-4b9c-81b5-487faa6bb091.

the World Bank and the International Monetary Fund's roles. Half a dozen Middle Eastern states have already become associate members of these organizations or are seeking to join them.[7] As analyst James Durso recently noted, "The US is still the world's pre-eminent economic and military power, but BRICS countries will continue to grow their share of the world economy."[8]

Fifth, growing divides on key domestic and regional policies between pauperized, disgruntled, and powerless Arab citizens and their autocratic governing elites have sparked mass citizen rebellions and civil wars. In the short term these have led to brittle or fractured states, and have also increased and hardened autocratic rule. Yet this could also accelerate Arab leaders' perceptions that their long-term security relies more on addressing critical local human needs and environmental threats and reducing destructive confrontations than on maintaining "security guarantees" from global powers (mostly the United States in recent years) that have contributed to greater regional poverty, sectarianism, tensions, and strife.

As key regional and global actors make their policy adjustments, none are doing so in absolute terms; none are aiming to shape policy on a black-or-white basis, to pivot or remain static, to be in or out of the region, or to promote dynamics of war vs. peace, competition vs. cooperation, or economic and energy vs. military and ideological interests. Rather, most actors are pursuing more nuanced and flexible foreign policies that can be modified or totally and abruptly reversed if need be, as has been seen in the past year among Saudi Arabia, Iran, Turkey, Egypt, Qatar, and others.

Arab Self-Interest Drives Policy Changes

Middle Eastern states have taken the initiative to form more diversified networks of trade, finance, investment, and security partners while also seeking to have fewer conflicts in the region as a recipe for lasting national security and well-being. Time will tell if this will be more productive and sustainable than the political autocracy, economic inequality, and active conflicts that accompanied half a century of relying on foreign military alliances.

---

7 Tim O'Connor, "Why Saudi Arabia Is Following Iran to Join China and Russia's Security Bloc," *Newsweek*, March 29, 2023, https://www.newsweek.com/why-saudi-arabia-following-iran-join-china-russias-security-bloc-1791326.

8 James Durso, "Washington and a Changing Middle East: A Dramatically Shifting Narrative?," *Eurasia Review*, April 14, 2023, https://www.eurasiareview.com/14042023-washington-and-a-changing-middle-east-a-dramatically-shifting-narrative-analysis/.

Saudi Arabia is leading this adjustment among Arab states because it has both the motives and capabilities to change. These include its substantial financial assets, influence in global energy markets, trade and arms sales opportunities, infrastructural and developmental investment requirements, and—since the lack of any serious American response to a September 2019 attack on its Abqaiq petroleum facility, allegedly orchestrated by Iran—its abrupt realization that the long-standing American security commitment to the Gulf region is neither reliable nor comprehensive. As respected analyst Dina Esfandiary noted in a recent press interview, "It is very engraved in [Saudi and UAE leaders'] minds that, 'We can't count on Washington to defend us, so we have to do it ourselves.'"[9] And the recent China-brokered Saudi-Iran restoration of diplomatic relations could not have been negotiated by the US, a fact that is spurring Gulf Cooperation Council (GCC) states to diversity their political, economic, and military networks.

Riyadh's policies have affirmed Arab states' prioritization of their own national interests over the desires of their foreign allies and protectors. This has included pursuing oil production policies that defy American demands, not getting sucked into the Ukraine-Russia war on the side of NATO, and resuming relations with Iran. Such independence of mind was on vivid display in mid-June, when within a span of two days, Saudi Arabian Crown Prince and Prime Minister Mohammed bin Salman Al Saud met with US Secretary of State Antony Blinken, phoned Russian President Vladimir Putin, welcomed the visiting president of Venezuela, and hosted a major Chinese-Arab business conference whose aims and message to the West far transcended commercial contracts.[10]

Other examples of this repositioning are found in the UAE's expanding financial and energy ties with Russia, its independent-minded engagement in conflicts across the region (Yemen, Libya, Sudan, Ethiopia, and Syria, most notably), its expanded military cooperation with China—reportedly including allowing construction of a new Chinese military base

---

9   Ben Hubbard, "From 'Pariah' to Partner, Saudi Leader Defies Threats to Isolate Him," *New York Times*, June 10, 2023, https://www.nytimes.com/2023/06/10/world/middleeast/saudi-leader-prince-mohammed.html.
10 James M. Dorsey, "Rebalancing US-Saudi Relations," Substack, June 12, 2023, https://jamesmdorsey.substack.com/p/rebalancing-us-saudi-relations.

while ignoring American demands—and its withdrawal from a US-led multinational marine protection group in the Gulf.[11]

Security Ties Critical, But Less Flexible

The Arab uprisings of 2010–2011 and the lack of an American response to the 2019 attack on Saudi Arabia's Abqaiq oil facility were two important security-related factors that rattled Arab states' views of the United States as a reliable ally. But security ties are the most difficult to diversify quickly, and most Arab states still prefer American arms to other options due to their technical performance and the stubborn sense that only the United States has the capacity and the will to step in to protect threatened Arab or American interests. Key Arab states cannot and do not wish to quickly drop their primary security reliance on Washington given its global military dominance since WWII, its more than 40 military bases in the Middle East (out of 750 worldwide), and its proven will to go to war there.[12] China, Russia, Turkey, Israel, and Iran all continue to expand their military footprints across the region, including bases and port facilities, arms sales, and training schemes.

Analyst Mona Abu Shanif presciently noted last year that, "Relations between the US and its Gulf allies are now governed by mutual doubts over intentions, commitments, ongoing haggling over what each can offer the other, alternative options, and their respective bargaining chips. Undoubtedly, China's presence in the equation expands the Gulf states' room to maneuver in their relations with Washington and puts them in a stronger negotiating position. However, this position does not come without a cost, as the Gulf states also harbor their own suspicions regarding China's close strategic relationship with Iran."[13]

---

11 Matthew Hedges, "United States Cannot Stand Idly By as United Arab Emirates Sidles Up to China, Russia," *Washington Times*, June 6, 2023, https://www.washingtontimes.com/news/2023/jun/6/united-states-cannot-stand-idly-by-as-united-arab-/.
12 Mohammed Hussein and Mohammed Haddad, "Infographic: US Military Presence around the World," *Al Jazeera*, September 10, 2021, https://www.aljazeera.com/news/2021/9/10/infographic-us-military-presence-around-the-world-interactive.
13 Mona Abu Shanif, "Strategic Maneuvering: The Gulf States amid US-China Tensions," Middle East Institute, January 20, 2022, https://www.mei.edu/publications/strategic-maneuvering-gulf-states-amid-us-china-tensions.

Resisting American Hegemony, Arrogance, and Con Games

Arab states that enhance economic and security links with China, Russia, Iran, Turkey, and other powers expect to play a role in shaping evolving new orders, whether regional or global. Prominent analyst Fareed Zakaria has noted that Saudi Arabia and its GCC partners can create global networks to satisfy their own priorities while also influencing global trends due to their immense financial power, stating, "The [G]ulf states are all deepening their relations with China, which is now the region's largest customer. […] They want to be able to deal freely with everyone, including Russia. […] They have growing ties with India and are even building new links with Israel."[14] Former German Foreign Minister Joschka Fischer coined what is perhaps the best phrase to describe the evolving nature of the global and Middle Eastern systems: "the Great Revision." He notes that Russia's invasion of Ukraine "represented the global order's first major revision in the twenty-first century, and now China and Russia have entered a deeper (albeit unformalized) alliance to challenge the United States and the West's dominance."[15]

Arabs and others across the Global South widely resent the arrogance of big powers that feel they can act as they wish to pursue their own interests across the world, without acknowledging the views of local allies. The common talk in the United States of an American pivot away from the Middle East offers a classically colonial western view of a complex global issue with many actors across multiple arenas. It suggests that the United States can unilaterally move in and out of various regions of the world when it serves its interests, regardless of the material carnage or human ill will it leaves behind. This attitude sees the Middle East as a passive, inert actor that is acted upon by foreign powers and that lacks the agency to define its own priorities or shape its own regional and global policies. The United States pivots, in this picture, but the Middle East passively watches to learn its fate. Respected American diplomat and scholar Chas Freeman put this most starkly and accurately when he recently wrote, "We treat diplomatic dialogue as little more than the deceptive foreplay that precedes an intended assault. In fact, our 'diplomacy' now is mostly aimed at

---

14   Fareed Zakaria, "The Rise of the Persian Gulf Is Reshaping the World," *Washington Post*, June 16, 2023, https://www.washingtonpost.com/opinions/2023/06/16/saudi-arabia-gulf-reshaping-world/.
15   Joschka Fischer, "The Great Revision," Project Syndicate, March 31, 2023, https://www.project-syndicate.org/commentary/russia-war-means-europe-transforming-and-global-order-realigning-by-joschka-fischer-2023-03.

appeasing domestic opinion rather than persuading foreigners to see their interests as we do. This is diplomacy as transnational con-game."[16]

A 2023 Gallup poll identified another reason why citizens in Arab and other Muslim-majority societies dislike US foreign policies: Washington is not serious about promoting democracy in foreign societies and it does not allow them to shape their own future. This echoes persistently strong anti-colonial sentiments across the Arab region and much of the Global South. Gallup reported in April 2023: "Iraqis and residents of 12 other Muslim-majority nations [nine Arab states and Turkey, Iran, and Pakistan] do not view the US as serious about encouraging the development of democracy in the region, nor allowing people to fashion their own political future as they see fit."[17] A recent Cato Institute report captures widespread popular and official exasperation with American-led militarism and economic sanctions around the world. It notes that the US is always eager to attack and invade other countries when it serves its interests, and that it has recently begun using economic warfare against the Global South as well.[18]

Views of Arab Citizens and Their Governments Are Converging

Some leaders in the region have recognized since the 2010–2011 Arab uprisings that they should pay more attention to the opinions of their citizens, whose condition will ultimately drive national policies—though in the short run most states are resisting this and still rely on what they know best: using security measures to quell popular discontent. Citizens and leaders appear to converge on whether the United States should reduce its presence in the Middle East—one of the few arenas of such congruence. Polls and surveys such as the Arab Center for Research and Policy Studies' Arab Opinion Index, the Arab Youth Survey, the Arab Barometer, and Gallup polls reveal clear trends in citizen sentiments, alongside contradictions and inconsistencies.

First, the 2022 Arab Opinion Index confirmed Arab opposition to the United States in its continuing efforts to promote greater Arab-Israeli agreements and to harness Arab power to check Iran's regional links and

---

16 Chas Freeman, "Time to Try a Different Approach to Foreign Relations?," Chasfreeman.net, December 6, 2022, https://chasfreeman.net/time-to-try-a-different-approach-to-foreign-relations/.
17 Younis, "Muslim-Majority Countries."
18 Doug Bandow, "Western Sanctimony Drives Global South Away from Supporting Ukraine," Cato Institute, February 25, 2023, https://www.cato.org/commentary/western-sanctimony-drives-global-south-away-supporting-ukraine.

influence. According to the latest poll, 59 percent of Arabs see the United States and Israel as the greatest threat to their security and stability (followed by Iran and Russia). And 84 percent of Arabs disapprove of their countries recognizing Israel, even though the last two US presidents have pushed hard to secure more Arab recognition of it.[19] Arabs in general resent such American persistence, pressures, or financial and political inducements to get their governments to sign on to agreements (for example, on peace with Israel or confronting Iran) that Arab publics have repeatedly opposed.

Second, 61 percent of Arab youth support US disengagement from the region, and a sizeable majority ranks China, the UK, and Turkey (80 percent, 79 percent, and 82 percent, respectively) as their most important allies, with the United States coming in seventh, at 72 percent.[20]

Third, the Arab Barometer 2021-22 analysis notes that, "Across the region, China tends to be viewed somewhat more favorably than the US in the majority of countries surveyed. Roughly half or more say they have a very or somewhat favorable view of China in eight of the nine societies surveyed. […] By comparison, only in four of nine countries surveyed do half or more have a positive view of the US."[21] Yet this same survey reveals conflicting perceptions of Arabs' desire to improve economic ties with world powers, and also shows youth more favorable to the United States than to China when it comes to the economy: "When asked about closer economic ties between their country and the two global powers, in the majority of countries surveyed, citizens are significantly less likely to say they want stronger ties with China than they were in 2018-19. In no country is there an increased desire for stronger economic ties with China while in multiple cases there has been a 20-point shift against China. By comparison, in most countries the desire for closer economic ties with the US has increased or remained unchanged over the same period."[22]

Conclusion: Trends Set to Continue

For the first time since 1945, when American and Russian colonial interests with local partners and proxies shaped the contemporary Middle East,

---

19 "Arab Opinion Index 2022: Executive Summary," Arab Center Washington DC, January 19, 2023, https://arabcenterdc.org/resource/arab-opinion-index-2022-executive-summary/.
20 "15th Annual ASDA'A BCW Arab Youth Survey."
21 "Public Views of the U.S.-China Competition in MENA," Arab Barometer, July 2022, pp. 3-4, https://www.arabbarometer.org/wp-content/uploads/ABVII_US-China_Report-EN.pdf.
22 Ibid., 2.

Arab states today recognize that existing strategic links and rivalries are unsustainable and have ravaged both the well-being of citizenries and the security of regimes. As the US reduces some military engagements in the region and transitions in slow-motion to more pressing Chinese issues, more Arab states are in turn seeing the US as an unreliable security partner and as lacking conviction about genuine, sovereign, Arab national development. This has sparked an unprecedented Arab assertion of self-interest, autonomy, and options to diversify relations with mid- and large-level powers across the world in all key sectors (military, economic, political, energy, and infrastructure). Some governments are openly snubbing American demands regarding energy, participation in global economic organizations, and relations with China, Russia, Israel, and Iran. These trends are likely to continue for years to come, as Washington concentrates on military, terrorism, and energy issues in the region, and as Arabs recalibrate their dominant strategic links with NATO states into more balanced worldwide relations that better meet their needs and reduce their vulnerabilities.

In practice, most Arab states now experience the strange phenomenon of government and public opinion coinciding on the need to reduce their exaggerated dependence on former colonial patrons, expand their relations across the globe, and resolve active conflicts in the region. If this ultimately triggers reforms to temper autocracy and promote greater citizenship rights and public accountability, the region might finally see progress on key deficiencies in equitable economic growth, environmental challenges, and healthy citizen-state relations. Yet the Arabs proceed on this historic path with limited leverage and bargaining chips beyond the energy and financial assets of Saudi Arabia, the UAE, Qatar, and Kuwait. As economic links expand with China, India, Turkey, Iran, and others—especially BRICS states—security will remain skewed toward the United States due to its large troop presence across the region and its long-term training and spare parts responsibilities with Arab militaries.

A more stable, nonviolent Middle East that is linked more closely with global powers and trading states, and that prioritizes its own citizens' rights and well-being, can only augur better decades ahead—but only if powers like the United States, China, Russia, the United Kingdom, Israel, Turkey, and others allow the Arab people to enjoy greater prosperity, self-determination, and sovereignty, something that has not happened in the past half century.

The Greatly Exaggerated US Pivot and America's Failures on Human Rights

Sarah Leah Whitson

For the past several decades, one US administration after another has signaled big plans for a new foreign policy centered on a "pivot to Asia" made possible by a "withdrawal" from the Middle East.[1] With each new administration, Middle East governments and their partisan Washington analysts have interpreted every US move in the region as evidence of a withdrawal already underway, and have pushed back against such alleged efforts with furious, alarmist, and even emotional critiques, describing each move as an "abandonment" of friends that justifies expanded ties between Middle East governments and China or Russia as a natural reactionary hedge.[2]

In contrast to these tropes, the record amply demonstrates the failure of successive US administrations to carry out plans to withdraw from the Middle East, a failure that is matched only by their record of unkept

---

1 Kenneth G. Lieberthal, "The American Pivot to Asia," Brookings Institution, December 21, 2011, https://www.brookings.edu/articles/the-american-pivot-to-asia/.
2 Caroline B. Glick, "Biden Abandons Middle East Peace," *Israel Hayom*, March 5, 2021, https://www.israelhayom.com/2021/03/05/biden-abandons-middle-east-peace/.

promises to prioritize human rights in foreign policy for the region.[3] By any measure of security exposures and commitments, including the presence of military troops and bases, kinetic engagement in armed conflicts, arms transfers, and the provision of political, military, and security protection, the United States remains the unmatched goliath in the Middle East, exceeding the cumulative commitments of all other governments in the world combined.[4]

The Biden administration, like others before it, certainly may have believed that a reduction in these commitments would best serve the interests of the American people, and thus started its term with vigorous promises to end arms sales to Saudi Arabia, wrap up both America's "forever war" in Afghanistan and its continued support for the war in Yemen, reduce the exposure of US troops in the region, and even end "blank checks" for Middle East dictators.[5] The administration admirably took important steps in this direction, most notably withdrawing US forces from Afghanistan in August 2021, a move that the American public overwhelmingly supported despite withering criticism from those who were disappointed to see any war end.[6] It also moved to withdraw some US Patriot missiles that former President Donald Trump had moved into Saudi Arabia and suspended some arms transfers to the kingdom and the United Arab Emirates while announcing a plan to "recalibrate" its

---

3   Lana Baydas, "Rethinking U.S. Foreign Policy for the Middle East and North Africa," *Georgetown Journal of International Affairs*, October 28, 2021, https://gjia.georgetown.edu/2021/10/28/rethinking-u-s-foreign-policy-for-the-middle-east-and-north-africa/.
4   On US military presence, see: C. Todd Lopez, "Defense Official Says U.S. Remains Committed to Middle East," *U.S. Department of Defense News*, June 5, 2023, https://www.defense.gov/News/News-Stories/Article/Article/3417495/defense-official-says-us-remains-committed-to-middle-east/. On arms sales, see: Bruce Riedel, "It's Time to Stop US Arms Sales to Saudi Arabia," Brookings Institution, February 4, 2021, https://www.brookings.edu/blog/order-from-chaos/2021/02/04/its-time-to-stop-us-arms-sales-to-saudi-arabia/.
5   On arms sales, see: Riedel, "It's Time." On war, see: Missy Ryan, "As Biden Touts an End to America's 'Forever' Wars, Conflict Drags On Out of Sight," *Washington Post*, September 22, 2021, https://www.washingtonpost.com/national-security/biden-wars-afghanistan-iraq-syria/2021/09/22/cc090ff0-1b08-11ec-914a-99d701398e5a_story.html. On Biden's comments, see: Joe Biden, Twitter post, July 12, 2020, 4:59 p.m., https://twitter.com/JoeBiden/status/1282419453939113989.
6   Ted Van Green and Carroll Doherty, "Majority of U.S Public Favors Afghanistan Troop Withdrawal; Biden Criticized for His Handling of Situation," Pew Research Center, August 31, 2021, https://www.pewresearch.org/short-reads/2021/08/31/majority-of-u-s-public-favors-afghanistan-troop-withdrawal-biden-criticized-for-his-handling-of-situation/.

relationship with Gulf Arab governments.[7] The administration did this buttressed by strong disdain from the American public for these states' egregious abuses, from the relentless bombardment of civilians in Yemen to the persecution of journalists and activists at home, punctuated by Saudi Crown Prince Mohammed bin Salman Al Saud's (MBS) murder of US-based Saudi journalist Jamal Khashoggi.[8]

The most cited "evidence" of US disengagement, however, was the Biden administration's refusal to go to war against the Houthis (and Iran) following a January 17, 2022 drone attack on a UAE fuel depot that killed three migrant workers. Coming as it did on the heels of the Trump administration's refusal to go to war against Iran following a 2019 drone attack on Saudi oil facilities—which the Houthis claimed, but for which Saudi Arabia insisted Iran was responsible—President Joe Biden's inaction cemented a view among the Gulf states and their allies that the US was no longer a reliable partner.[9]

Sullivan's MENA Policy Pillars: No Real Accountability for Human Rights

Instead of any meaningful recalibration—and much less an actual withdrawal or pivot—we find the Biden administration rather desperately trying to amplify its relevance and influence in the region with expanded political, military, and economic support for autocratic regimes. National Security Advisor Jake Sullivan gave a speech to the Washington Institute for Near East Policy on May 4, 2023, clarifying the administration's updated priorities for the region by identifying the five pillars of a new framework for US engagement: "partnerships, deterrence, diplomacy and de-escalation,

---

7   On arms transfers, see: "Yemen: Biden Temporary Freeze of Arms Sales to Saudi Arabia and UAE Is Welcome," Amnesty International, January 28, 2021, https://www.amnesty.org/en/latest/press-release/2021/01/yemen-biden-temporary-freeze-of-arms-sales-to-saudi-arabia-and-U.A.E.-is-welcome/. On the US-Saudi relationship, see: Raf Sanchez, "Biden Looks to Recalibrate Relationship with Saudi Arabia and Crown Prince Mohammed bin Salman," *NBC News*, February 20, 2021, https://www.nbcnews.com/news/world/biden-looks-recalibrate-relationship-saudi-arabia-crown-prince-mohammed-bin-n1258354.
8   Stephanie Kirchgaessner, "US Finds Saudi Crown Prince Approved Khashoggi Murder but Does Not Sanction Him," *The Guardian*, February 26, 2021, https://www.theguardian.com/world/2021/feb/26/jamal-khashoggi-mohammed-bin-salman-us-report.
9   "Timeline: U.A.E. under Drone, Missile Attacks," *Al Jazeera*, February 3, 2022, https://www.aljazeera.com/news/2022/2/3/timeline-uae-drone-missile-attacks-houthis-yemen.; Geoff Brumfiel, "What We Know About The Attack On Saudi Oil Facilities," *National Public Radio*, September 19, 2019, https://www.npr.org/2019/09/19/762065119/what-we-know-about-the-attack-on-saudi-oil-facilities.

integration, and values," part of a full-throttle manifesto designed to put the last nail in the coffin of any talk of a Middle East pivot.[10]

The Sullivan pillars are, at best, tactics and strategies for the stated goal of a "stable," "integrated," and "prosperous" Middle East. The specific American interests underlying these goals remain largely unspoken and only obscurely hinted at. Omitted entirely from the pillars is even a mere mention of the Biden administration's claimed national security interest in preserving, promoting, and protecting democracies against authoritarianism, as was emphasized in the administration's two iterations of a much-ballyhooed "democracy summit."[11] The word "democracy" appears nowhere in the Sullivan pillars, other than to describe America's own imperfect government. As for human rights, Sullivan assures his listeners that the Biden administration will merely "raise concerns."[12]

Taken together, the pillars describe a coherent policy for the Middle East, but only if one excludes the last, and indeed the flimsiest of the five pillars: values. The interwoven pillars of partnerships, deterrence, and integration reflect a long-standing US approach of seeing the countries in the region as a single zone that must be influenced and integrated within Washington's orbit or be punished and deterred as enemies. Thankfully, Sullivan does not describe these partnerships as democracies or as countries with which the United States shares values. Nor does he, however, describe them as what they actually are: states headed by unelected tyrannical rulers in most cases, and by an apartheid government in the case of Israel.

Instead, Sullivan identifies the transactional basis of what the US wants from these partnerships: "diversified and resilient supply chains"; "clean energy" (which apparently includes cheap oil and natural gas, obliquely defined as "the stable supply of current energy"); and "solutions on everything from food security to water security" that are central "to the demand signal from countries that are getting entreaties from some of our great power competitors." This last point obscures US partners' demands for the "solutions" they really want—weapons and security—in return for

---

10 Jake Sullivan, "Keynote Address by National Security Advisor Jake Sullivan," Washington Institute for Near East Policy, May 4, 2023, https://www.washingtoninstitute.org/policy-analysis/keynote-address-national-security-advisor-jake-sullivan.
11 Ted Galen Carpenter, "The Truth of Biden's Fraudulent Democracy Summit," Cato Institute, December 10, 2021, https://www.cato.org/commentary/truth-bidens-fraudulent-democracy-summit.
12 Jake Sullivan, "Keynote Address."

keeping China and Russia out.[13] Excluded from Sullivan's accounting, as is usually the case when it comes to this and other US administrations, is what Israel provides in this transactional partnership framework.

Sullivan claims that expanding and enhancing the integration of the Biden administration's partners in the region "empowers our allies and partners, advances regional peace and prosperity, and reduces the resource demands on the United States."[14] Elements of this proposed integration not only include military, economic, and trade integration, but also the "ultimate, final, complete integration" of Israel into the region and the world via the Abraham Accords.[15] While it is true that expanding the military and economic integration of these abusive authoritarian governments will make them more powerful, Sullivan does not tell his listeners why the US should want to strengthen them, particularly in the context of the existential battle that the Biden administration has declared between democracies and autocracies.

What is far more debatable is the notion that empowering such an axis of authoritarian regimes will bring peace and prosperity. This is a problematic point of view given the Biden administration's argument that peace and prosperity can only result from liberal democracies; after all, if abusive authoritarian regimes can deliver these outcomes then what exactly can the US offer that China cannot? It is also problematic as a matter of fact, given that Biden's Middle East partners remain key sources of violence, war, corruption, and tyranny in the region—hardly a recipe for peace or prosperity.

Sullivan's emphasis on integration decreasing the region's "resource demands on the United States," which alludes to the notion that the increased military integration of America's Middle East partners will make them feel more secure, better protected, and therefore less reliant on US military resources, is no less contentious. The Biden administration may well wish to reduce the presence of human military resources (i.e., troops) in the region and to temper partner demands that the United States use its muscle to support them in their endless conflicts. But there is really no evidence that the US wishes to reduce its weapons sales to the region, which bring great benefit to the defense industry. It is hard not to see at least one outcome, if not the goal, of military integration under a US

---

13   Ibid.
14   Ibid.
15   Ibid.

umbrella being the deepened and expanded reliance of countries under its protection—particularly in terms of necessary US supervision, coordination, interoperable weapons, supplies, and training—making it harder for any of them to break away from America's influence and control.[16]

And while the record shows that Saudi Arabia, the UAE, and Egypt are indeed diversifying their weapons purchases and business deals—specifically partnering with China and Russia—they are not reducing their demands for US military protection, but are rather using this diversification to exercise reverse leverage on the United States.[17] Saudi Arabia and the UAE are demanding unprecedented bilateral security guarantees from the US in exchange for remaining loyal purchasers of American weapons, and in the case of Saudi Arabia, for normalizing with Israel.[18] An updated assessment on the state of bilateral influence and leverage in 2023 would recognize that the buyers are the ones calling the shots. Hence, we see Sullivan gently and cryptically citing "policy changes in arms sales" when extolling the Biden administration's early efforts to end the Yemen war.[19]

By far the most arrogant and patronizing of Sullivan's remarks is his faux humility for the administration's realpolitik framework. The administration's new "realistic and pragmatic" policies for the Middle East are the product of a "clear-eyed"—and almost sad—acceptance that the US has "been naive about what is possible to achieve in terms of transforming societies by force or by diktat," and they incorporate "hard lessons learned to eschew grand designs or unrealistic promises of transformational change."[20] What is so discombobulating about this argument is not just the halo it places on past administrations for their noble, if misguided, efforts to transform the region into democratic countries that respect

---

16 "U.S Power and Influence in the Middle East: Part One," Center for Strategic and International Studies, March 8, 2022, https://csis-website-prod.s3.amazonaws.com/s3fs-public/publication/220308_Babel_Power_Influence.pdf?VersionId=qfAaWzp6OEppfK4GMFshnrrHFIqe4OeN.

17 Paul Iddon, "China Emerges as an Arms Supplier of Choice for Many Middle East Countries, Say Analysts," *Middle East Eye*, July 22, 2022, https://www.middleeasteye.net/news/china-emerges-major-exporter-weapons-middle-east-north-africa.

18 Jon Hoffman and Sarah Leah Whitson, "Breaking Away From Secret Concessions in the Middle East," *The American Prospect*, March 28, 2023, https://prospect.org/world/2023-03-28-secret-concessions-middle-east/.; "Saudi Arabia Offers Its Price to Normalize Relations With Israel," *New York Times*, March 9, 2023, https://www.nytimes.com/2023/03/09/us/politics/saudi-arabia-israel-united-states.html.

19 Jake Sullivan, "Keynote Address."

20 Ibid.

human rights. Putting aside debating the sincerity or success of US Middle East policies over the past several decades to transform the region, it is worth noting that whatever the efforts, no country in the Middle East today—and certainly not the Biden administration's partners—governs democratically or with a modicum of respect for human rights.[21]

More egregious is Sullivan's absolute punt on responsibility for the harm that results because of the United States' partnerships with some of the world's most abusive governments. In Sullivan's view, replacing grand designs for democracy and human rights (and sweeping away any lingering remnants of Biden's earlier promises in that regard) with expanded partnerships and integration with Middle East despots—apparently the only two options on the table—is a win-win proposition. Sullivan sees no need to account for the costs of US military support and political protection for these governments, thereby enabling, protecting, contributing to, and even profiting from the very human rights abuses about which he assures the world the United States will continue to speak. The lives cut short, the children maimed, the journalists tortured, the schools bombarded, the lands stolen, the homes burned to ashes, the dignity destroyed, and the tens of millions of men and women subject to the tyranny of America's partners never show up in Sullivan's ledger.[22] While the United States is able to count its increased corporate profits from deepened economic and defense ties, there is no room in the balance sheet for the costs, because they are supposedly not America's own.

---

21 "Middle East and North Africa 2022," Amnesty International, undated, https://www.amnesty.org/en/location/middle-east-and-north-africa/report-middle-east-and-north-africa/.

22 On children, see: Emma Thomasson, "UNICEF Says 10,000 Children Killed or Maimed in Yemen since 2015," *Reuters*, October 19, 2021, https://www.reuters.com/world/middle-east/unicef-says-10000-children-killed-or-maimed-yemen-since-2015-2021-10-19/. On journalists, see: "The Safety of Journalists and the Issue of Impunity in Bahrain and Saudi Arabia," Americans for Democracy and Human Rights in Bahrain, undated, https://www.ohchr.org/sites/default/files/Documents/Issues/Journalists/GA72/AmericanDemocracyHumanRightsBahrain.pdf. On schools, see: "Bombing of Schools by Saudi Arabia-Led Coalition a Flagrant Attack on Future of Yemen's Children," Amnesty International, December 11, 2015, https://www.amnesty.org/en/latest/news/2015/12/bombing-of-schools-by-saudi-arabia-led-coalition-in-yemen/.

Sullivan also fails to even attempt to account for the costs of these deepened partnerships to Biden's national security strategy of protecting democracies to win against the United States' authoritarian rivals. That peoples and governments around the world believe less and less in American rhetoric about the value and importance of democracy and human rights can only be a product of US administrations having repeatedly proven that they do not believe it either, as US policies in the Middle East make clear.[23] We see the immediate costs of such disbelief in the wobbly global support for the war in Ukraine, as many nations are skeptical of the claim that it is principally about preserving international laws and norms, as the Biden administration has claimed.[24] Even America's Middle East partners are not persuaded, and are hedging their bets by simultaneously strengthening their ties with Russia, even laundering sanctioned Russian assets and deepening intelligence ties.[25] A truly clear-eyed, pragmatic, and realistic approach would take these costs into account.

US Hegemony: Oil, Weapons Sales, and Support for Israel

Not one purported change has happened under the Biden administration; not the pivot, not the withdrawal, not the recalibration, and certainly not the prioritization of human rights. The status quo continued because the administration was ultimately unwilling to demote the long-standing interests that would form the cost of pivoting away from support of powerful Middle East regimes: cheap oil, immunity for Israel, corporate weapons sales, and the broadest interest of all (the belief in which is an article of faith in Washington), US hegemony in the Middle East. There has been no effort by the Biden administration to scrutinize whether these interests serve the American people, despite the occasional concessionary

---

23 Richard Wike et al., "What People Around the World Like—and Dislike—About American Society and Politics," Pew Research Center, November 1, 2021, https://www.pewresearch.org/global/2021/11/01/what-people-around-the-world-like-and-dislike-about-american-society-and-politics/.
24 Ted Galen Carpenter, "Ukraine: A War to Save the Rules-Based International Order?," Cato Institute, October 20, 2022, https://www.cato.org/commentary/ukraine-war-save-rules-based-international-order.
25 Peter Hobson, "From Russia with Gold: U.A.E. Cashes In as Sanctions Bite," *Reuters*, May 25, 2023, https://www.reuters.com/markets/russia-with-gold-uae-cashes-sanctions-bite-2023-05-25/.; Nomaan Merchant et al., "Leaked US Intel: Russia Operatives Claimed New Ties with U.A.E.," *Associated Press*, April 11, 2023, https://apnews.com/article/intelligence-leak-russia-U.A.E.-pentagon-9941a3bb88b48d4dbb5218649ea67325.

nod to the need for clean energy, reduced US military entanglements, and "values" such as those mentioned in Sullivan's remarks.

The issue that comes closest to being at least a short-term interest of most Americans is cheap oil from the Gulf, in exchange for which the US has for decades provided weapons and protection for petro-rulers. While there have been many oil price skirmishes with Gulf states, the most recent showdown between the Biden administration and the Saudi government was particularly brutish. Faced with spiraling oil prices in the wake of the Ukraine war, Biden appeared in Jeddah on bended knee in July 2022 to reconcile (and exchange a much-mocked fist bump) with MBS, not long after his administration had identified the latter as having ordered the murder of Jamal Khashoggi and had promised to hold him accountable.[26] But MBS rebuffed Biden's pleas for increased oil output, instead hosting Chinese President Xi Jinping just days after Biden's visit and announcing new deals worth billions between the two nations.[27]

In October 2022, when the Biden administration grew more desperate to see oil prices come down ahead of the November midterm elections, MBS was able to secure another precious concession that he had been demanding from Biden: the recognition of his diplomatic immunity in lawsuits against him for both the murder of Khashoggi and the attempted murder of Saad al-Jabri and the kidnapping and detention of his children.[28] When MBS still refused to increase oil output after this humiliating capitulation, the Biden administration made some renewed noise about "recalibration," but ultimately did nothing. It was a checkmate for MBS, and was followed by trips to Riyadh by Biden's most senior officials to beg

---

26 Fred Ryan, "Biden's Trip to Saudi Arabia Erodes Our Moral Authority," *Washington Post*, July 11, 2022, https://www.washingtonpost.com/opinions/2022/07/11/biden-saudi-trip-post-publisher-fred-ryan/.

27 On oil, see: Ken Klippenstein, "Saudi Arabia Rejects Biden Plea to Increase Oil Production as Midterms Loom," *The Intercept*, February 15 2022, https://theintercept.com/2022/02/15/saudi-arabia-gas-price-oil/. On Xi's visit, see: Aaron David Miller, "Xi's Saudi Visit Shows Riyadh's Monogamous Marriage to Washington Is Over," *Foreign Policy*, December 7, 2022, https://foreignpolicy.com/2022/12/07/xi-jinping-saudi-arabia-trip-mbs-biden/.

28 "Khashoggi's Widow and DAWN Sue MBS and Co-Conspirators in US Court for WashPost Journalist's Murder," DAWN, October 20, 2020, https://dawnmena.org/khashoggis-widow-and-dawn-sue-mbs-and-co-conspirators-in-us-court-for-washpost-journalists-murder/.; "Saudi: Case against MBS in US Court 'Public Relations,'" *Middle East Monitor*, August 15, 2020, https://www.middleeastmonitor.com/20200815-saudi-case-against-mbs-in-us-court-public-relations/.

his favor, first White House Coordinator for the Middle East and North Africa Brett McGurk and Special Presidential Coordinator for Global Infrastructure and Energy Security Amos Hochstein, then Jake Sullivan, and most recently Secretary of State Antony Blinken.[29]

The Biden administration's prioritization of Israeli interests is another important factor impeding designs for a US pivot away from the Middle East, though there is never any explanation as to how Israeli interests serve US interests, and Israel remains excluded from any realpolitik evaluation like those to which America subjects its other global relationships. Instead, Americans are required to accept as an article of faith that the United States' "unconditional support" for and "unbreakable bond" with Israel are based on "shared values" that justify providing the latter with billions in weapons and invaluable political protection from global scrutiny and accountability.

Despite the growing erosion of popular and international support for Israel, US support remains an untouchable anomaly, one that sees the US take on massive liabilities while gaining nothing, not even good will from the Israeli government, in return.[30] Although the Biden administration identifies securing Israel's integration in the Middle East by expanding the Abraham Accords as one of its top priorities (based on an argument that doing so will enhance regional peace), it does not bother to explain to the American public why the US must be the one to pay the price for it.[31] This price not only includes damaging political and economic concessions to Arab states but also a proposed security guarantee and a nuclear power plant for Saudi Arabia. The short-term political interests here—namely continued support from pro-Israel lobbying groups that dictate the continued prioritization of Israeli interests and that ensure the maintenance of Israel's apartheid governance, military occupation, and global

---

29 Edward Wong and Vivian Nereim, "Blinken's Visit to Saudi Arabia Caps U.S. Effort to Rebuild Ties," *New York Times*, June 8, 2023, https://www.nytimes.com/2023/06/08/us/politics/blinken-saudi-arabia-crown-prince-biden.html.

30 Taylor Orth and Kathy Frankovic, "The Share of Americans Who Say the U.S. Favors Israel over Palestine Has Fallen since 2017," YouGov, March 17, 2023, https://today.yougov.com/topics/international/articles-reports/2023/03/17/who-americans-favor-israel-vs-palestine-poll.

31 Sanam Vakil and Neil Quilliam, "The Abraham Accords and Israel-U.A.E. Normalization," Chatham House, March 28, 2023, https://www.chathamhouse.org/2023/03/abraham-accords-and-israel-U.A.E.-normalization.

immunity—are well-established and well-understood.[32] The costs, including keeping America tethered to abusive dictatorships in the Middle East, remain ignored.

Similarly, the baked-in influence of weapons manufacturers has made it difficult for any administration that has talked the talk of curbing weapons transfers to abusive Middle East regimes or decreasing the United States' matchless militarization of the region to walk the walk.[33] Saudi Arabia, the UAE, and Egypt are not only the largest weapons purchasers in the world; they are also the largest purchasers of US weapons. And Israel is the world's largest recipient of US military assistance.[34] Cutting weapons transfers to these regimes would mean cutting profits to weapons manufacturers, who in turn would cut their campaign donations and their provision of jobs to the officials in the administration doing the cutting. Coupled with the lobbying and financial influence of Middle East governments, the current system of carrots and sticks demands relentless and expanded weapons transfers. And while such an approach well serves corporate profits, no explanation or justification is proffered for how this serves the interests of the American people.

The non-partisan and often unspoken ideology that undergirds each of these interests is a belief in US hegemony as a positive value in and of itself, one that needs no justification, despite the sizeable cost of its maintenance, which is estimated to be between $65 and $70 billion annually, not to mention the trillions of dollars spent on US wars.[35] America "winning" against China and Russia is defined not merely as containing their bad actions but as maintaining US dominance, even harmful dominance. In this context, it makes perfect sense to maintain military and political support for abusive regimes and to expand their dependence on US

---

32 "Israel's Apartheid Against Palestinians," Amnesty International, undated, https://www.amnesty.org/en/latest/campaigns/2022/02/israels-system-of-apartheid/.
33 Clayton Thomas et al., "Arms Sales in the Middle East: Trends and Analytical Perspective for U.S Policy," Congressional Research Service, updated November 23, 2020, https://sgp.fas.org/crs/mideast/R44984.pdf.
34 Irina Ivanova, "Saudi Arabia is America's No. 1 Weapons Customer," *CBS News*, October 12, 2018, https://www.cbsnews.com/news/saudi-arabia-is-the-top-buyer-of-u-s-weapons/.; Jeremy M. Sharp, "US Foreign Aid to Israel," Congressional Research Service, updated March 1, 2023, https://sgp.fas.org/crs/mideast/RL33222.pdf.
35 Justin Logan, "The Case for Withdrawing from the Middle East," Defense Priorities, September 30, 2020, https://www.defensepriorities.org/explainers/the-case-for-withdrawing-from-the-middle-east.

security in the Middle East because, the thinking goes, doing so deters China and Russia from expanding their spheres of influence.

Saudi and Emirati Influence in Washington

The Biden administration's efforts to win its great power competition with China and Russia have contributed to the emergence of a new power axis in the Middle East, including Saudi Arabia, the UAE, and their junior partner, Egypt. The very efforts the US has made to maintain its hegemony in the Middle East have ironically encouraged the development of unprecedented Saudi and Emirati independence and influence in the United States.[36] The risks of such influence remain underappreciated.

Measurements of polarity are typically based on "measurable" power in the form of resources, military strength, and economic pull.[37] Saudi Arabia's GDP exceeded $1 trillion for the first time in 2022, and the UAE's reached nearly $500 billion in 2023, both ahead of many European states.[38] Emirati GDP per capita, meanwhile, stands at $49,450, also ahead of most European nations.[39] The unprecedented increase in the wealth of the Gulf states over the past decade, driven by record-high oil prices, has created an apparently bottomless pit of wealth for Gulf economies, and that wealth is expected to grow, even if more slowly than it has previously. Oil still represents one-third of all energy consumed globally, while natural gas accounts for another 24 percent.[40] With somewhere between 20 and 30 percent of global oil passing through the Strait of Hormuz and the vast majority of spare production capacity held by OPEC states, we can

---

36 Ben Freeman, "How the U.A.E. Turns Its Interests into US Policy," *Responsible Statecraft*, December 6, 2022, https://responsiblestatecraft.org/2022/12/06/how-the-U.A.E.-turns-its-interests-into-us-policy/.
37 Stephen G. Brooks and William C. Wohlforth, "The Myth of Multipolarity: American Power's Staying Power," *Foreign Affairs*, April 18, 2023, https://www.foreignaffairs.com/united-states/china-multipolarity-myth.
38 Salim A. Essaid, "Saudi Arabia's 2022 GDP Breaks Record, Exceeds $1 Trillion," *Al-Monitor*, March 10, 2023, https://www.al-monitor.com/originals/2023/03/saudi-arabias-2022-gdp-breaks-record-exceeds-1-trillion.; "Countries by GDP," PopulationU, undated, https://www.populationu.com/gen/countries-by-gdp.
39 "GDP per Capita, Current Prices," International Monetary Fund, undated, https://www.imf.org/external/datamapper/NGDPDPC@WEO/OEMDC/ADVEC/WEOWORLD.
40 Robert Rapier, "Fossil Fuels Still Supply 84 Percent of World Energy—and Other Eye Openers from BP's Annual Review," *Forbes*, June 20, 2020, https://www.forbes.com/sites/rrapier/2020/06/20/bp-review-new-highs-in-global-energy-consumption-and-carbon-emissions-in-2019/.

expect to see the Gulf Arab states' purchasing power and influence grow in the foreseeable future.

While these countries are far from acting as a unified EU- or NATO-level bloc, and at times work against each other's interests, their reconciliation with Iran, Turkey, and Qatar, and their negotiations to end the war in Yemen serve the smart and important goal of reducing their conflicts while also shoring up their influence and standing in the region and creating the space to focus on exporting their influence and power. Nevertheless, both the UAE and Saudi Arabia have demonstrated uncommon independence and regional maneuvering in the past few years, particularly in their resistance to US pressure on various issues, including, for example, oil prices and the war in Yemen. The UAE has for several years now pursued its own pugilistic foreign policy, at times aligned with the United States, as in Afghanistan, where it actively supported the US war, and at other times at odds with it, as in Libya.[41] More significantly, it has deliberately and openly rebuffed US complaints about expanded Chinese and Russian influence, instead flaunting its developing ties with these countries as another show of its independence.[42] And both Saudi Arabia and the UAE have become independent sources of influence in military conflicts to whom the US can and does appeal for help, as it is currently doing to quell the conflict in Sudan.

While the UAE has pursued policies of economic diversification, political independence, and regional influence for over a decade, the same approach in Saudi Arabia is new, and should appropriately be attributed to MBS's new, and it must be said, revolutionary and change-driven leadership.[43] There is no denying that there is a domestic revolution of sorts underway, one that, but for the brute repression and authoritarian diktat that accompanies it, is quite positive, with reformed laws and an altered judicial system, increased freedom for women, and an unprecedented

---

[41] Bilal Y. Saab, "In Afghanistan, the Gulf Arab States Stepped Up," Middle East Institute, September 1, 2021, https://www.mei.edu/publications/afghanistan-gulf-arab-states-stepped.; Ali Bakir, "The UAE's Disruptive Policy in Libya," *Insight Turkey* 22, no. 4 (Fall 2020): 157–177, https://www.insightturkey.com/articles/the-uaes-disruptive-policy-in-libya.

[42] Alvaro Escalonilla, "Saudi Arabia in the Orbit of China and Russia: Towards a New Strategic Alliance?," *Atalayar*, March 27, 2023, https://www.atalayar.com/en/articulo/politics/saudi-arabia-orbit-china-and-russia-towards-new-strategic-alliance/20230327170255182347.html.

[43] Nader Kabbani and Nejla Ben Mimoune, "Economic Diversification in the Gulf: Time to Redouble Efforts," Brookings Institution, January 31, 2021, https://www.brookings.edu/research/economic-diversification-in-the-gulf-time-to-redouble-efforts/.

openness to foreign art, culture, and business.[44] As quick studies, the Saudi and UAE governments have absorbed lessons regarding political influence in the United States from the Israel and defense lobbies, but have one-upped them both with exponentially greater spending to infiltrate and influence broad swaths of the American government, economy, and cultural sphere. While there is nothing unique about their efforts, their far greater wealth means that they can buy a lot more influence than anyone else.

Saudi Arabia's spending on American technology, sports, entertainment, gaming, news, film, and the arts has reached unprecedented new levels, not just in purchases for domestic consumption, but in ownership of businesses themselves.[45] These expanded investments will naturally expand the kingdom's influence on and control over the American economy, making it less likely that a falling-out would occur in the wake of another grave crime, as happened after the Khashoggi murder, when investors pulled more than $1 billion from the Saudi stock market.[46]

More dangerous is the outright purchase of American government officials. While the defense industry has been renowned for its revolving-door employment of former government officials, who make up a large percentage of defense industry lobbyists, they are no match for the

---

44 Natasha Turak, "Saudi Arabia Announces Major Legal Reforms, Paving the Way for Codified Law," *CNBC*, February 9, 2021, https://www.cnbc.com/2021/02/09/saudi-arabia-announces-legal-reforms-paving-the-way-for-codified-law.html.; Megan K. Stack, "The West is Kidding Itself about Women's Freedom in Saudi Arabia," *New York Times*, August 19, 2022, https://www.nytimes.com/2022/08/19/opinion/saudi-arabia-women-rights.html.; Neil King, "Saudi Announces New Cultural Vision, including Residency for International Artists," *Gulf Business*, March 28, 2019, https://gulfbusiness.com/saudi-announces-new-cultural-vision-including-residency-international-artists/.

45 Chris Smith, "Saudi Arabia Is Taking Steps That Could Upend the Sports World," *Sports Business Journal*, October 31, 2022, https://www.sportsbusinessjournal.com/Journal/Issues/2022/10/31/Portfolio/Saudi-Arabia.aspx.; Sarah Leah Whitson, "How Not to Artwash Saudi Arabia's Gruesome Human Rights Record," *Hyperallergic*, March 14, 2023, https://hyperallergic.com/808064/how-to-not-artwash-saudi-arabias-gruesome-human-rights-record/.; Rory Jones, "Flush with Oil Profits, Saudi Arabia Pours $7.5 Billion into U.S. Stocks from Amazon to Microsoft," *Wall Street Journal*, August 16, 2022, https://www.wsj.com/articles/saudi-fund-spends-oil-windfalls-on-7-5-billion-in-u-s-stocks-from-amazon-to-microsoft-11660645409.

46 Ben Chapman, "Investors Pull $1bn Out of Saudi Arabia's Stock Market as Fallout from Jamal Khashoggi Death Deepens," *The Independent*, October 22, 2018, https://www.independent.co.uk/news/business/news/saudi-arabia-stock-market-jamal-khashoggi-death-murder-finance-economy-a8595781.html.

revolving-door buyouts of Saudi Arabia and the UAE.[47] Saudi Arabia's sovereign wealth fund has been a particularly useful tool in this regard, with eye-popping payouts to former Trump administration officials, including $2 billion to former Senior Advisor to Trump Jared Kushner, $1 billion to former Treasury Secretary Steven Mnuchin, and unknown millions to Donald Trump himself.[48] The defense industry also cannot match the eye-popping salaries and business deals that Gulf states are paying to over 500 US military officials, including the 15 former US generals and admirals that Saudi Arabia has been paying as consultants since 2016.[49]

It is not hard to understand how such payouts compromise the integrity, independence, and decision-making of US policymakers, who are naturally counting how much money they could garner if they make decisions that would please their future business partners and employers. While President Biden signed a law prohibiting former intelligence officials from working for foreign governments for 30 months after leaving their jobs, no such laws prohibit civilian or military officials from doing the same.[50] Moreover, the promise of future rewards to sitting officials is increasingly coupled with direct efforts to influence and bribe election candidates.[51]

From the perspective of Middle East countries, which are long accustomed to seeing their government officials bought and sold by external actors, there is nothing new here, and the shoe is now merely on the American foot. From a US perspective, not only does the Gulf Arab states' influence in Washington hinder the ability of elected officials to direct

---

47   Craig Whitlock and Nate Jones, "Key Findings from the Post's Series on Veterans' Lucrative Foreign Jobs," *Washington Post*, October 18, 2022, https://www.washingtonpost.com/investigations/interactive/2022/veterans-foreign-jobs-foia-takeaways/.
48   Adam Klasfeld, "Watchdog Sues for Details about Jared Kushner and Steven Mnuchin's Mideast Travels after Saudis Reportedly Poured Billions into Duo's Funds," *Law and Crime*, October 6, 2022, https://lawandcrime.com/high-profile/watchdog-sues-for-details-about-jared-kushner-and-steven-mnuchins-mideast-travels-after-saudis-reportedly-poured-billions-into-duos-funds/.; "US: Investigate New Evidence of President Trump's Business Dealings with MBS," DAWN, January 15, 2023, https://dawnmena.org/u-s-investigate-new-evidence-of-president-trumps-business-dealings-with-mbs/.
49   Craig Whitlock and Nate Jones, "Retired U.S. Generals, Admirals Take Top Jobs with Saudi Crown Prince," *Washington Post*, October 18, 2022, https://www.washingtonpost.com/investigations/interactive/2022/veterans-us-foreign-jobs-saudi-arabia/.
50   "US: Investigate."
51   James Bamford, "The Trump Campaign's Collusion With Israel," *The Nation*, March 23, 2023, https://www.thenation.com/article/world/trump-israel-collusion/.

policies toward the interests of the American people but it constitutes an unprecedented attack on US democracy itself. The United States' Middle East policy under the Biden administration has fallen back in line with the decades-long practice of maintaining support for abusive regimes and contributing to their heinous abuses against the people of the region. The oft-touted US commitment to democracy and human rights is therefore entirely absent from the Middle East.

The US Pivot and Great Cyberpower Competition in the MENA Region

Tamara Kharroub

Over the last few years, the United States' global strategy and national security priorities have shifted significantly from focusing on counterterrorism and Middle East conflicts to dedicating increasing attention to deterring the threat posed by China and Russia. Meanwhile, information and communication technologies (ICT) have emerged as vital tools in the global political order, as technology has become the backbone of political, economic, and military structures across the globe. In this ever-expanding environment of digital omnipresence, cyberspace has become the new battleground for power and influence. Countries around the world are prioritizing cyber strategies and investing in cyber capabilities and technological infrastructures, especially in the realm of cybersecurity, which includes cyber weapons and defense systems. With rapid advancements in technology and the relatively low-cost and high-impact nature of cyber tools compared to conventional weapons systems, cyberspace has become a major arena for global influence, and no less so when it comes to great power competition.

Recent US defense and national security postures have not only renewed America's strategic focus on great power competition with

Russia and China, they have also elevated the importance of cybersecurity. This chapter aims to explore the emergence of global cyber powers, to assess Chinese and Russian influence in the information and technology domains in the Middle East and North Africa (MENA), and to analyze the impacts of US shortcomings in the cyber environment of the Arab world. Although the US may not be completely pivoting away from the Middle East, its policy recalibration in the region reflects a renewed narrow focus on security while it continues to lose influence on other fronts, including cyberspace. Washington's cyber strategy prioritizes cybersecurity and cyberthreats from adversaries like China, Russia, Iran, and North Korea, but in the process loses much-needed leverage over information and technology infrastructures that are poised to determine the future of power and influence, especially in the MENA region.

The Global Battle Over Cyberspace

Cyberspace is becoming increasingly central to all political and geopolitical domains, including governance, diplomacy, economics, and defense; and it is also being used as a weapon of war and aggression, especially in the form of espionage and cyberattacks. While state and nonstate actors alike are leveraging cyber capabilities to advance their political agendas, a comprehensive understanding of cyberpower and information about various states' cyber capabilities remain limited. Cyberpower can be defined as the effective deployment of cyber capabilities and the use of cyberspace by a state or other actor to create both advantage and influence in other environments in order to achieve its (national) objectives.[1]

A few initiatives in recent years have begun assessing the cyberpower of some countries. According to a 2021 report by the International Institute for Strategic Studies (IISS), which analyzed the cyber capabilities of 15 countries, the United States is the world's dominant cyber power, partly because it has been building its cyberpower since the 1990s and has established cyber alliances like the Five Eyes.[2] The report lists Russia and China in the second tier (along with five other countries), but concludes that China

---

1 Julia Voo et al., "National Cyber Power Index 2022," Belfer Center for Science and International Affairs, September 2022, https://www.belfercenter.org/sites/default/files/files/publication/CyberProject_National%20Cyber%20Power%20Index%202022_v3_220922.pdf.

2 "Cyber Capabilities and National Power: A Net Assessment," International Institute for Strategic Studies, June 2021, https://www.iiss.org/globalassets/media-library---content--migration/files/research-papers/cyber-power-report/cyber-capabilities-and-national-power---a-net-assessment___.pdf.

is on track to join the US in the first tier due to its "Made in China 2025" strategy and its focus on developing artificial intelligence (AI) and growing its indigenous technologies to achieve economic independence. However, the seven categories used by IISS to assess cyberpower are primarily security-focused, for example, national strategies, governance and military structures, cyber espionage abilities, defense and resilience against cyberthreats, and offensive cyber operations. Taking a more holistic approach to cyberpower, the 2022 National Cyber Power Index (NCPI), ranked 30 countries across eight categories that conceptualize cyberpower in terms of cyberwar components (similar to those found in the IISS study), in addition to a wide range of non-military capabilities, namely information manipulation and control, domestic surveillance, national commercial cyber competence, defining international cyber norms, and cyber operations to amass wealth.[3] The NCPI found that the United States tops the list, especially when it comes to destructive capabilities and intelligence, followed by China in the second spot and then Russia ranking third. Although the United States ranks first on most categories, China beats the United States when it comes to cyber surveillance, cyber commerce, and cyber defense.

The expanding cyberpower of China and Russia has presented the United States with an additional challenge in its strategic global competition. As cyber technologies are becoming ever more central in the realm of power and influence and as instruments of warfare, China and Russia are racing to develop their cyber capabilities and their malicious operations around the world—and especially against the United States—to achieve geopolitical and strategic goals. Russia has arguably carried out the most damaging cyberattacks against the United States, primarily in the form of information warfare, espionage, and destructive cyber operations.[4] The most prominent examples of Russian cyber aggression include the hacking and release of stolen emails and documents from the Democratic National Committee, disinformation operations to influence US presidential elections, and more recently the 2020 SolarWinds hack that compromised the supply chain and infiltrated US government networks. Other influential Russian operations to aid its political and expansionist geostrategic goals include a broad 2007 attack on the Estonian cyber grid that crippled both public and private organizations, a similar 2008 cyberattack

---

3 Voo et. al, "National Cyber Power Index 2022."
4 Andrew S. Bowen, "Russian Cyber Units," Congressional Research Service, updated February 2, 2022, https://crsreports.congress.gov/product/pdf/IF/IF11718.

against Georgia, a 2015 attack on the power grid in Ukraine, a 2018 hack of a Saudi Petrochemical plant, and the 2017 NotPetya attack aimed at Ukraine, which paralyzed multinational companies and threatened global economic and political systems. Evidently, the Kremlin views the targeting of critical infrastructure and information environments in the United States and around the world as a key part of its cyber strategy for achieving its hegemonic aspirations.

Similarly, China's cyberthreats to the United States have relied on methods of espionage and information control, albeit with a larger focus on economic and industrial goals. Chinese President Xi Jinping has made it very clear that he plans to turn China into a "cyber superpower." The 2023 Annual Threat Assessment of the US Intelligence Community considers China the top cyber espionage threat to the American government and the US private sector, mainly due to its commitments to boost its indigenous commercial and military technologies to become self-sufficient and to continue to dominate global technology supply chains, and because of its growing dedication to information operations to shape public perception in the United States, spread Chinese propaganda, and undermine US leadership.[5] Commercial espionage in particular has become a trademark of Beijing's efforts to control the global economic environment through illegally acquiring technological and trade secrets and intellectual property.[6] Additionally, the Chinese Communist Party, through its Made in China 2025 plan, encourages private companies to develop dual-use technologies that can also be employed for military purposes.[7] Another major concern for the United States is China's attempts to politicize and take control over technical standards and protocols in order to dominate the global tech ecosystem, including by investing in a national standards strategy, pushing for membership and influence in standards development organizations like the International Organization for Standardization, and using its Belt and

---

5 "Annual Threat Assessment of the US Intelligence Community," Office of the Director of National Intelligence, February 6, 2023, https://www.dni.gov/files/ODNI/documents/assessments/ATA-2023-Unclassified-Report.pdf.

6 Yudhijit Bhattacharjee, "The Daring Ruse That Exposed China's Campaign to Steal American Secrets," *New York Times Magazine*, March 7, 2023, https://www.nytimes.com/2023/03/07/magazine/china-spying-intellectual-property.html.

7 Meia Nouwens and Helena Legarda, "China's Pursuit of Advanced Dual-Use Technologies," International Institute for Strategic Studies, December 18, 2018, https://www.iiss.org/research-paper//2018/12/emerging-technology-dominance.

Road Initiative to lock countries into its standards.[8] This is especially the case with the 5G wireless networks that provide the backbone for the next generation of connectivity, where Chinese company Huawei is leading the world in the race for 5G, having signed more 5G contracts than any company (including with European countries)—and this coming after it has already built 70 percent of the African continent's 4G network.[9]

Both Russia and China have recognized the importance of data and cyberspace in each country's competition with the United States and quest for global dominance. The more digitally connected society and governance become, the more susceptible they are to cyberattacks and information operations that can paralyze entire nations, compromise critical national security data and economic infrastructures, and change public opinion and the political landscape. As the opportunities and threats afforded by cyberpower are becoming apparent, states are racing to not only protect their national security but also to amass influence and control in the global digital ecosystem. In response, the United States is emphasizing the importance of cyber capabilities in its national security and defense strategies. For example, the Biden administration's 2022 National Security Strategy highlights the role of emerging technologies in the global political order and in geopolitical competition with major global powers.[10] However, cyberattacks appear to take center stage in the United States' concerns, as evidenced by the administration's Cybersecurity Strategy of 2023, which emphasizes cybersecurity components such as defending critical infrastructure and disrupting threat actors, investing in security and the resilience of data and systems, and forging international partnerships to counter cyberthreats and defend allies against them.[11]

Much of the United States' discussion about cyberpower is focused on the concept of cybersecurity, which involves defensive cyber tools to

---

8   Tim Rühlig, "China, Europe and the New Power Competition over Technical Standards," Swedish Institute of International Affairs, January 2021, https://www.ui.se/globalassets/ui.se-eng/publications/ui-publications/2021/ui-brief-no.-1-2021.pdf.
9   David Sacks, "China's Huawei Is Winning the 5G Race. Here's What the United States Should Do To Respond," Council on Foreign Relations, March 29, 2021, https://www.cfr.org/blog/china-huawei-5g.
10 "National Security Strategy," The White House, October 2022, https://www.whitehouse.gov/wp-content/uploads/2022/10/Biden-Harris-Administrations-National-Security-Strategy-10.2022.pdf.
11 "National Cybersecurity Strategy," The White House, March 2023, https://www.whitehouse.gov/wp-content/uploads/2023/03/National-Cybersecurity-Strategy-2023.pdf.

protect data and systems, cyber breaches to collect intelligence and information, and offensive cyber operations that cause harm and damage to rival governments' infrastructures. Understandably, Washington is especially prioritizing cyber defense and security capabilities with regard to Russian aggression, while at the same time focusing on containing China economically and decoupling it from the technology supply chain. However, this narrow focus on defense and cybersecurity underestimates the long-term impact of Chinese and Russian investments in the worldwide information environment and communications infrastructures. While the US is busy with its tech cold war with China and with Russia's conventional war on Ukraine, a different kind of cyber battle is emerging in the MENA region.

MENA: The Cyber Battleground the United States Is Losing

The tech ecosystem is rapidly evolving and emerging technologies will be the determining factor in strategic power competition, where control over information, access to data, artificial intelligence, and communication networks provide competitive advantages. Cyberspace in the Middle East and North Africa is a crucial battleground that both China and Russia are attempting to dominate. Both nations have been investing in long-term cyber strategies in the MENA region aimed at garnering influence and control and advancing their respective global and geopolitical agendas.

China's cyber strategy is being implemented through its Digital Silk Road (DSR), which is the technological component of its Belt and Road Initiative. By making the DSR one of its foreign policy priorities, Beijing is aiming to expand its digital footprint in the region and become the top technological global power, thereby amassing greater control over communication and data networks. Through the DSR, Chinese companies have built critical digital infrastructure across the MENA region, and Beijing has forged agreements with various countries there. The major components of this cyber architecture include memoranda of understanding (e.g., with Egypt, Saudi Arabia, and the UAE), comprehensive mass surveillance and Huawei's "safe cities" public monitoring projects, ICT training centers and labs, cloud services and quantum computing networks, subsea fiber-optic cables, 4G and 5G communication networks, and the BeiDou Navigation Satellite System, which is now more accurate in Asia than GPS.[12] Chinese

---

12 Thomas Blaubach, "Chinese Technology in the Middle East: A Threat to Sovereignty or an Economic Opportunity?," Middle East Institute, March 2021, https://mei.edu/sites/default/files/2021-03/Chinese-Tech.pdf.

surveillance companies Hikvision and Dahua account for the production of almost 40 percent of surveillance cameras in the world, and comprehensive surveillance systems (including those using AI and big data analytics) have been sold to over 80 countries, including many in the MENA region such as the UAE, Morocco, and Lebanon.[13] When it comes to fiber-optics, HMN Technologies (formerly Huawei Marine Networks) is laying undersea fiber-optic cables to connect the Middle East with Europe and Africa as part of its Pakistan and East Africa Connecting Europe (PEACE) subsea cable. China is the fourth largest provider of international subsea cables, which transmit 95 percent of the world's data.[14] Huawei has also been developing the MENA region's 5G communication networks in eight countries, including the UAE, Saudi Arabia, Qatar, Morocco, and Egypt.[15]

As MENA countries plan to diversify their economies and embark on processes of digital transformation, China is taking advantage of this opportunity to take control over Arab technological infrastructures and the region's digital communications ecosystem. While many of the Chinese companies involved are private firms, their ties to the Chinese Communist Party present a significant concern. To be sure, Chinese companies are not the only ones with this level of control over communication and information systems, as American and other western companies also have large global market shares, but the close relationship between the Chinese private sector and the government, as well as China's laws, give the government greater control and access. These companies' access to massive amounts of data therefore grants Beijing unprecedented power and influence in the region. The Chinese government can use these tech networks to collect intelligence and monitor opponents, obtain intellectual property and trade secrets, and shut down entire communication channels and digital infrastructures to use them as leverage and implement coercive measures for strategic ends. Moreover, some analysts have referred to the affordability arrangements that Chinese companies provide to developing countries in exchange for supplying them with crucial technologies as debt traps, wherein an inability to pay results in the loss

---

13   "Mapping China's Digital Silk Road," Reconnecting Asia, October 19, 2021, https://reconasia.csis.org/mapping-chinas-digital-silk-road/.
14   Ibid.
15   Dale Aluf, "China's Tech Outreach in the Middle East and North Africa," *The Diplomat*, November 17, 2022, https://thediplomat.com/2022/11/chinas-tech-outreach-in-the-middle-east-and-north-africa/.

of critical infrastructure and a broader threat to national autonomy.[16] Such powerful control over the global tech ecosystem enables Beijing to become the global cyber power it envisions and to exert control over the international order to advance its political and economic interests.

While Russia has also invested in surveillance systems and exported them to some countries, including supplying the UAE's Oyoon surveillance system, it has primarily devoted its foreign cyber strategy to the arena of information operations, and especially cross-border political influence disinformation campaigns. Without a commercial tech industry and burdened by a weakened military in the post-Soviet era, Russia employs cyber operations as part of its great-power strategy to recover its global dominance. In the Arab world, Russia began waging a systematic disinformation war and deploying Arabic-language propaganda operations even prior to the Arab Spring uprisings of 2011, efforts that were led by the launch of *RT Arabic* (formerly *Russia Today*) in May 2007.[17] Today, the Kremlin operates a large network of Arabic media outlets and social media campaigns using bot factories and troll farms to spread Russian propaganda and anti-American content in the Arabic-language digital sphere. Narratives on social media platforms and those coming out of Russia's state-funded media outlets, such as the various outlets of *RT Arabic* parent company RT and the news agency *Sputnik*, aim to manipulate public opinion about the United States and the West and control current narratives, especially regarding Russia's war on Ukraine. The Russian playbook frames the war as one that challenges US imperialism and counters both encirclement by NATO and the American-led hegemonic global order. Russian media outlets have even propagated false claims, including a statement that Ukrainian President Volodymyr Zelenskyy had fled the country and conspiracy theories about the existence of secret laboratories for biological weapons in Ukraine. Another critical part of Russian cross-border political influence operations involves orchestrated social media campaigns in support of the Assad regime in Syria and military leaders in Libya and Sudan.[18]

---

16 Blaubach, "Chinese Technology."
17 Elene Janadze, "The Digital Middle East: Another Front in Russia's Information War," Middle East Institute, April 19, 2022, https://www.mei.edu/publications/digital-middle-east-another-front-russias-information-war.
18 "Evidence of Russia-Linked Influence Operations in Africa," Stanford Internet Observatory, October 30, 2019, https://cyber.fsi.stanford.edu/io/news/prigozhin-africa.

Russian government perspectives are pervasive in the Arabic-language media sphere. Some evidence shows that *RT Arabic* ranks among the top three most watched news outlets in several Arab countries, and both *RT Arabic* and *Sputnik* have been found to post significantly more content on social media platforms than other major media outlets, thus flooding the Arabic-language digital sphere with the Kremlin's narrative.[19] Public opinion polling suggests that these information operations may be working. For example, according to the UAE-based Arab Youth Survey, young Arabs believe that the United States and its NATO allies are more to blame for the Ukraine war than Russia.[20] Multiple factors contribute to the success of Russian disinformation campaigns and help its information warfare rank among the world's most effective. First, Russian operations exploit existing sentiments and societal divides and employ them to augment its chosen narrative, often cloaking said narrative in supposedly authentic indigenous voices. For example, Russia builds on extant anti-American views and the history of the United States' failures and war crimes in the MENA region to demonize the United States and present itself as an anti-imperialist power fighting both US and broader western hegemony. Second, the Kremlin's information warfare strategy is premeditated, long-term, and ongoing, as it does not make a distinction between times of peace and times of war. Equally important is the lack of credible information sources in the MENA region's state-controlled media environment and the overreliance of a primarily young population on social media platforms for news and political engagement. Furthermore, social media platforms by design elevate and amplify extreme, unexpected, and inflammatory content and create online echo chambers and ideological silos that continue to perpetuate these disinformation campaigns.[21] Importantly for the United States, there is a severe lack of counternarratives in the Arabic-language digital environment to confront Russia's information campaigns in the MENA region, part of an information vacuum that Moscow has successfully exploited to win the hearts and minds of the Arab people. Control over the information ecosystem allows Russia to shape not only opinions but ultimately events on the ground.

---

19 Janadze, "The Digital Middle East."
20 "14th Annual ASDA'A BCW Arab Youth Survey," BCW Global, September 21, 2022, https://www.bcw-global.com/newsroom/global/14th-annual-asdaa-bcw-arab-youth-survey.
21 Tamara Kharroub, "Identity Politics 2.0: Cyber Geopolitics and the Weaponization of Social Media," Arab Center Washington DC, June 1, 2019, https://arabcenterdc.org/resource/identity-politics-2-0-cyber-geopolitics-and-the-weaponization-of-social-media/.

Data and Connectivity Represent Power

While information and military technology have always been an important part of warfare, the evolution of cyberpower has no doubt significantly enabled China and Russia to rise on the world stage, to reemerge as serious threats to the US, and to expand their global influence. Both Russia and China are flexing their cyber muscles in the MENA region, and Washington should not underestimate the power that technological infrastructure and information hold for determining the future of the Middle East. As the United States moves forward with recalibrating its policies and strategies in the Middle East to prioritize the Abraham Accords, security alliances with oppressive and authoritarian regimes, and cybersecurity collaboration, it is losing the long-term cyber war in the region.[22] While it is true that both Russia and China are signing cyber agreements to support Iran's cyber capabilities and are helping Tehran build its cyber strategy and offensive technologies, a narrow US focus on the MENA region using the lens of an Iran-deterrence security strategy does not match up with the region's rapidly evolving technological ecosystem.

As the US intelligence community continues to prioritize espionage operations and cyberattack threats to American national security, the United States is underestimating the power and long-term impact of China and Russia's expanding investments in information and technology infrastructure around the world, and especially in the MENA region. Such heavy foundational operations undermine US influence and power, as Russia and China aim to set telecoms standards, control the information environment, and secure a monopoly over telecommunications infrastructure and data facilities. Data is a source of power, and increased connectivity brings additional layers of vulnerabilities that can be exploited for espionage, cyberattacks, sanctions, and shutdowns. The United States' overemphasis on security in the region and its miscalculations regarding the power of information and telecoms infrastructure risk it losing not only the cyber war but its ongoing great power competition as well.

To be sure, MENA countries, especially in the Gulf, are forging their own cyber strategies. States like Saudi Arabia and the UAE are emerging as regional (authoritarian) digital powers by leading disinformation

---

22   On cybersecurity alliances under the Abraham Accords, see: Ines Kagubare, "US, Middle Eastern Allies Include Cyber Collaboration in Abraham Accords," *The Hill*, January 31, 2023, https://thehill.com/policy/cybersecurity/3838236-us-middle-eastern-allies-include-cyber-collaboration-in-abraham-accords/.

campaigns and political influence operations, obtaining and implementing large-scale surveillance systems, investing in smart cities and tech capabilities, passing laws that protect their data sovereignty, and harnessing AI, predictive policing, and spyware programs. Non-Arab MENA countries like Israel, Iran, and Turkey remain the largest cyber powers in the region, with extensive cybersecurity and cyberattack capabilities. But China and Russia are far ahead of the competition, representing the most capable cyber powers in the world after the United States. As part of their respective great-power strategies, they will continue to jockey for influence and control over both global and MENA cyberspace and to dominate the region's information and technology infrastructures for decades to come.

2 CURRENT US ENGAGEMENTS AND ENTANGLEMENTS

The US-Israel Nexus and the Question of a Pivot
Yousef Munayyer

The United States and the Arabian Peninsula
Kristian Coates Ulrichsen

Declining American Influence in the Middle East:
Afghanistan, Iraq, and Libya
Nabeel Khoury

The Syrian Conflict: A Turning Point in US Middle East Policy
Lina Khatib

The Mutual Pivot to Asia in US-Egypt Relations
Sahar Aziz

Iran and the Perceived US Pivot Away from the Middle East
Mahsa Rouhi

The US in the Middle East: Staying Put While Simultaneously Pivoting
Imad K. Harb

The US-Israel Nexus and the Question of a Pivot

Yousef Munayyer

How would a pivot in American foreign policy toward Asia impact the US-Israel relationship? I start answering this question by challenging the premise in order to modify it and provide an alternative frame that offers greater analytical leverage than a hypothetical proposition that is not borne out by observable facts. I argue that by understanding the evolution of US foreign policy as one that features a transition between paradigms rather than a geographic repositioning, we are both better able to understand the world and the relationships in question as they exist and to also think about the implications for those relationships as a transition occurs. Then, I will discuss the historical context of the US-Israel relationship across previous foreign policy paradigms and ask what another shift could bring given what we know about the two nations' history.

Pivoting Away Is the Wrong Question
As the United States' wars in Iraq and Afghanistan drew to a close, and as China continued to grow economically and expand its influence, it was expected that many would ask whether the United States was shifting its

focus from the Middle East to East Asia. The question of a so-called pivot to Asia has been often discussed in the last decade or more, as the foreign policy conversation tries to capture what the next focal point of US foreign policy will be. The idea of a pivot following a drawdown suggests not only a refocus but a repositioning of assets. The notion of a pivot suggests moving from a position one occupies to a new position that one does not yet occupy. Is the United States capable of such a maneuver? To answer this, we have to think about where around the globe the United States currently is, and where it is not. There are not many places on the map where the United States is not present through relationships, interests, and military ties and bases. According to a 2021 report by the Quincy Institute for Responsible Statecraft, "The United States continues to maintain around 750 military bases abroad in 80 foreign countries and colonies (territories)."[1] How can the United States pivot from one place to another if it is already everywhere?

Similarly, when one considers economic interests and diplomatic ties, the United States is one of the most integrated and connected countries in the world. According to the World Bank, the United States lags behind only China in gross exports of goods and services.[2] When it comes to trading partners, as of 2020 and according to World Bank data, the United States has 222 trading partners, which puts it ahead of China's 214. Diplomatically, according to the Lowy Institute, which tracks global diplomatic missions across the globe, the United States has 267 global diplomatic posts, second only to China which has 275.[3] While China has managed to integrate itself across the globe economically and diplomatically, the United States is at least just as integrated, and when one brings the military dimension into the equation, the United States stands in its own category of global hegemony.

For these reasons, pivoting is not something the United States is in a position to do, as it is already well entrenched around the globe. However, the end of the Global War on Terror era, which itself was a period

---

1 David Vine, et al., "Drawdown: Improving U.S. and Global Security Through Military Base Closures Abroad," Quincy Institute for Responsible Statecraft, September 20, 2021, https://quincyinst.org/report/drawdown-improving-u-s-and-global-security-through-military-base-closures-abroad/.
2 "Exports of Goods and Services (Current US$)," World Bank, accessed July 18, 2023, https://data.worldbank.org/indicator/NE.EXP.GNFS.CD?most_recent_value_desc=true.
3 "Global Diplomacy Index: 2021 Country Ranking," Lowy Institute, undated, https://globaldiplomacyindex.lowyinstitute.org/country_rank.html.

characterized by destruction, counterproductive policy, and the overreach of a hyperpower in a post-bipolar moment, is an important time to be asking questions about the dominant paradigm shaping US foreign policy. The answers to this question will undoubtedly have significant impacts on the US-Israel relationship. Historically, this relationship has been greatly shaped and affected by the dominant paradigms that set the parameters of geostrategic competition.

The US-Israel Relationship and Paradigms Past

How do we understand the structure and distribution of power in the international system? The United States, as discussed above, is not a small state or even a regional power; instead, it is the top competitor for global hegemony and has been since the Second World War reordered global power. For these reasons, understanding US foreign policy requires a global outlook and an understanding of competition on such a scale. Since the Second World War, two paradigms or interpretive frameworks have dominated the analysis of US foreign policy: the Cold War paradigm, and later and more briefly, the War on Terror paradigm. Below I will discuss each framework, the interregnum between them, and what they meant for the US-Israel relationship at each stage.

"City on a Hill" vs "Evil Empire" - The Cold War Paradigm

The State of Israel was established at the very outset of the Cold War era. The United States and the Soviet Union both recognized the new nation shortly after its declaration of statehood in May 1948.[4] The competition between the United States and the Soviet Union would take place in various spots across the globe, each with their own sets of allies and movements, and each seeking to establish and maintain spheres of influence. The Middle East was a strategically important region in this global competition, and while it was far closer to Moscow and its satellite nations than to Washington, the region's energy sources were vital. Washington's relationship with Israel was heavily shaped by these dynamics. Early on, particularly as evidenced by the US position during the Suez Crisis, Washington was taking a more balanced position toward Israel in the region; but this would all change in the 1960s, and particularly during and after the 1967 War. The Israeli military's performance during the

---

4 "Israel International Relations: International Recognition of Israel," Jewish Virtual Library, undated, https://www.jewishvirtuallibrary.org/international-recognition-of-israel.

1967 War, especially against Soviet-backed allies in Syria and Egypt, elevated the competition in the region between the two global powers, with both sides increasing investment in their respective allies, an increase that impacted the next major war in 1973.

It was during this era that the most important element of the US military relationship was established: consistent military support through financing and arms transfers, which not only ensured that Israel would be well armed but that it would maintain a qualitative military edge. Israel's strategic partnership with the United States, which developed significantly during this era, cemented the foundation of the US-Israel relationship as one that was not only based on geostrategic interests but also around being on the same side of the so-called moral divide that characterized the Cold War paradigm. Much like the US relationship with South Africa, Israel was seen as an outpost supporting US interests and also sharing western values in a region of strategic importance otherwise populated by non-western peoples. So long as this paradigm remained in place, the shared interests and values that were perceived through its lens made it easier to downplay any differences that may have existed between the United States and Israel during this time.

The Interregnum and the War on Terror Paradigm

The fall of the Berlin Wall and the end of the Cold War paradigm brought significant changes and numerous questions around US foreign policy and the US-Israel relationship. How the United States would relate to Israel and its many other allies now that the defining framework had ended was an open question. The end of the conflict was welcomed by Washington as the beginning of a wave of democratization; but what would it mean for populations oppressed by America's Cold War allies? Would democracy and rights come their way as well? For South Africa, the moment coincided with the fall of apartheid after a long battle for freedom that was led against its government both locally and globally. For Palestinians, a window of hope appeared to open as the first Palestinian Intifada (uprising) gave way to an Israeli-Palestinian peace process. An Israeli-Jordanian agreement would follow, suggesting more change was possible in the region after the Cold War.[5]

---

5 "The Oslo Accords and the Arab-Israeli Peace Process," U.S. Department of State, undated, https://history.state.gov/milestones/1993-2000/oslo.

Importantly, outside of the Cold War framework, the plight of the Palestinians could no longer be as easily ignored as it had been previously. The US-Israel relationship was also shaped by other US campaigns in the region, including the Gulf War in 1990-1991, during which Washington sought to maintain the support of Arab friends. But with a new world order being declared, Israel no longer fit as neatly into the role it had once occupied as a strategic American outpost in a region contested by another superpower. In other words, Israel's strategic value decreased. This is not to say that it offered no strategic value to the United States in the region, but that regional conditions had changed in a way that made what it had to offer less valuable than before. The historic cooperation between the United States and Israel during the Cold War did, however, have a legacy effect, and the ties built by national institutions and agencies on both sides of the relationship continued to exist. At the same time, the shared values that form part of the relationship would increasingly come into question as the plight of the Palestinians remained unresolved. These shifts laid the groundwork for a rift to grow in the US-Israel relationship, but the growth of that rift would be delayed for nearly two decades as a new paradigm took shape that would once again bolster the relationship.

The attacks on New York City and the Pentagon on September 11, 2001 left nearly 3,000 Americans dead and shocked the nation and the world. The United States suffered a horrifying blow on its homeland for the first time in modern history. Further, the attacks were orchestrated not by a global superpower, but by a non-state actor operating in war-torn Afghanistan. All the previous rules and strategies of global politics fell short of explaining and addressing the challenges the United States saw itself facing in that moment, and from here the Global War on Terror would be born.[6] Former President George W. Bush declared that other countries would either be "with us or [...] with the terrorists."[7] American defense spending grew significantly (doubling from 2001 to 2008) and the United States launched major land wars in Afghanistan and Iraq and drone wars across much of the Middle East and North Africa.[8]

---

6   "2001-2004: How 9/11 Reshaped Foreign Policy," Council on Foreign Relations, undated, https://www.cfr.org/timeline/how-911-reshaped-foreign-policy.
7   George W. Bush, "Address to a Joint Session of Congress and the American People," The White House, September 20, 2001, https://georgewbush-whitehouse.archives.gov/news/releases/2001/09/20010920-8.html.
8   Stephen Daggett, "Costs of Major U.S. Wars," Congressional Research Service, June 29, 2010, https://sgp.fas.org/crs/natsec/RS22926.pdf.

Underscoring the world-altering impact of this moment, NATO exercised Article 5 of its charter, pertaining to collective defense, for the first time in the alliance's history.[9]

While the Global War on Terror paradigm did not last nearly as long as the Cold War, it nonetheless provided an interpretive framework of world politics that allowed Israel to neatly place itself alongside the United States. This was not lost on Benjamin Netanyahu, who would go on to become the longest serving Israeli prime minister in history. He initially told the *New York Times* on September 11 that the attacks would be "very good" for the US-Israel relationship and would inevitably draw the two countries much closer together.[10] With terrorism becoming the new communism—i.e., the global threat around which Washington would order its foreign policy—Israel once again found itself easily making the argument for being a strategic asset as a counterterrorism partner and a like-minded nation that was part of the western family's shared fight.

After two decades, the United States' land wars in Iraq and Afghanistan drew to a close, leaving behind a profound sense of loss and folly. While the United States continues its numerous counterterrorism operations and the lasting impact of the Global War on Terror is still being felt, the power of the paradigm as an interpretive framework is not what it once was. The question now is what, if anything, will replace this paradigm and how will it impact the US-Israel relationship?

Essential Considerations as Paradigms Shift

Whatever the new prevailing paradigm will be (if a clear one indeed emerges to define US foreign policy), several essential questions arise that deserve attention in the interim. For example, could the US leave Israel behind given the two nations' long-standing relationship? Where does normalization with Arab states, for which both the US and Israel have been pushing, fit into the bigger question of refocusing US foreign policy beyond the region? What role does US domestic politics play in shaping Washington's changing position in the region? I will attempt to address these questions below.

---

9   "Collective Defence and Article 5," North Atlantic Treaty Organization, updated July 4, 2023, https://www.nato.int/cps/en/natohq/topics_110496.htm.
10 James Bennet, "Spilled Blood Is Seen as Bond That Draws 2 Nations Closer," *New York Times*, September 12, 2001, https://www.nytimes.com/2001/09/12/us/day-terror-israelis-spilled-blood-seen-bond-that-draws-2-nations-closer.html.

Would/Could the US Leave Israel Behind?

A complete American detachment from Israel does not seem possible, but as the relationship has evolved over time, the nature of American support has undeniably changed. While the core of the relationship is military financing, there used to be a much greater economic component to the aid relationship. As Israel grew to possess a more financially stable and independent economy, this support was phased out. Similarly, US military financing for Israel has included a unique component of the United States' offshore procurement exemption, which no other recipients of US military financing received, and which permitted Israel to spend roughly a quarter of US military financing in its own domestic military industry.[11] This support, given over years, has contributed to the significant growth and development of the Israeli military industry to the point where Israel is annually among the largest per capita arms exporters in the world. This unique component of US military financing is also being phased out as part of the memorandum of understanding around US military financing currently in place, as negotiated during the Obama administration.[12]

The clear pattern here in US policy around military financing is that as Israel becomes more independent and no longer needs American assistance, some assistance is reduced or modified. Israeli leaders often make the point of thanking the United States for helping Israel "defend itself by itself." In the last two decades, the United States has authorized additional spending to support Israeli missile defense systems to respond to strategic challenges posed by projectile fire from the Gaza Strip and Lebanon.[13] While Israel's domestic military industries excel in technology and surveillance and also have the capacity to produce some small arms and heavier equipment, Israel continues to rely on American weapons for its most significant power projection, specifically for its air force. Despite this, the Israeli economy has grown significantly, and Israel today exports

---

11* Josh Ruebner et al., "Bringing Assistance to Israel in Line With Rights and U.S. Laws," Carnegie Endowment for International Peace, May 12, 2021, https://carnegieendowment.org/2021/05/12/bringing-assistance-to-israel-in-line-with-rights-and-u.s.-laws-pub-84503.
12 Jeremy M. Sharp, "U.S. Foreign Aid to Israel," Congressional Research Service, updated February 18, 2022, https://crsreports.congress.gov/product/pdf/RL/RL33222/44#:~:text=According%20to%20USAID%20Data%20Services,1946%2D2021%20is%20%24247%20billion.
13 Michael Merryman-Lotze, "5 things to know about U.S. funding for Israel's 'Iron Dome,'" American Friends Service Committee, September 29, 2021, https://afsc.org/news/5-things-know-about-us-funding-israels-iron-dome.

in arms some three to four times what it receives in military aid from the United States.[14] And US military aid as a percentage of Israeli GDP is less than one percent. Israel is clearly financially independent enough to pay for the weapons it buys from the United States without military financing, which is itself a product of the Arab-Israeli wars of the Cold War era, and of a time when the Israeli economy was not capable of responding to the strategic military challenge on its own.

Much has changed since then; not only is the Israeli economy in a fundamentally different position, but Israel also now has peace agreements with the neighbors with which it shares most of its borders, namely Egypt and Jordan. The argument for US military financing for Israel is far weaker today that it ever was before. As with economic assistance and offshore procurement, the conditions that once necessitated military financing in the eyes of policymakers have ceased to exist. Could the US reevaluate military financing for Israel while still making its weapons systems available for purchase, as it does with many other Middle Eastern clients? While the phasing out of previous programs like economic assistance and offshore procurement show that change is in fact possible when conditions necessitate a policy shift, military financing is such a staple of the US-Israel relationship that this policy question takes on a bitter political dimension, making change far more difficult.

What about US Domestic Politics?

For more than a century, American support for Zionism has had a domestic political component. From the early days when Americans saw Palestine through the lens of biblical history to the present where well organized interest groups lobby policymakers around US relations with Israel, the US-Israel relationship has always been about more than US geopolitical interests. As paradigms shift, how will this shape the domestic political component of the US-Israel relationship?

To understand how the domestic political component might shift during this period between paradigms, or even without a dominant paradigm, it is important to understand how it operated when other paradigms prevailed. During both the Cold War years and the War on Terror, domestic supporters of the US-Israel relationship made two key arguments that had significant traction within these frameworks. First, they emphasized that Israel is

---

14 Josh Ruebner et al., "Bringing Assistance to Israel in Line With Rights and U.S. Laws."

a strategic partner and an asset, not a liability, to the United States in the region. Second, they stated that the US and Israel share key values around democracy, rights, and pluralism. These were easy arguments to make in the past, especially as Israel was fighting Soviet client states in the region and combatting Islamist militant groups during the Second Intifada. But do they still make sense today? For a growing number of Americans, it seems that they now have much less resonance. The strategic partner argument is undercut by the fact that the Middle East is no longer viewed through the lens of great power competition, and furthermore, Americans have grown weary of endless engagements in the region which never seem to justify the cost expended and only generate more enemies. Further, the values argument is undercut by Israel's treatment of the Palestinians, its policies of apartheid, and the continued rightward and religious-nationalist drift of Israeli politics. This has had a significant impact on the American Jewish community, which mostly belongs to the Reform branch of Judaism, and which increasingly sees itself as having less in common with a more religious Israel.

There is little doubt that the pro-Israel arguments which used to be hegemonic in American public discourse are now regularly challenged, and notable shifts have taken place in American public opinion.[15] There is, however, a significant gap between American opinion and American policy. This is where political institutions, from interest groups to elections, will have the most sway. The pressure to shift US policy away from Israel will continue to grow in this period, but the legacy of past policy, entrenched for decades, will be bitterly held onto by interest groups and policymakers alike. Over time, as a new paradigm takes hold new arguments for Israel's strategic value in the global competition with China will likely be developed, perhaps focusing on technological tools. And a new values-based argument will be needed as well, perhaps centered on neoliberal economics. During the interim period however, the US-Israel relationship will continue to come under stress as domestic politics shift away from where they were in response to the situation on the ground.

How Does Normalization with Arab Countries Fit In?

The primary American interest in the Middle East continues to be the stable flow of natural resources from the region into global markets. This

---

15 Lydia Saad, "Democrats' Sympathies in Middle East Shift to Palestinians," Gallup, March 16, 2023, https://news.gallup.com/poll/472070/democrats-sympathies-middle-east-shift-palestinians.aspx.

has always been the most important determinant in shaping US policy over the decades. Does normalization between Israel and Arab states with which it does not yet have relations contribute to the emergence of a more stable regional political structure?

There is little evidence to suggest that that is the case. Israel continues to be unpopular among Arab publics, and regimes normalizing with the country have resorted to repressive measures to deal with domestic opponents of this policy.[16] Further, normalization seeks to isolate Iran by creating an Arab-Israeli alliance against it. While that might seem attractive to some, Iran is likely to see it as hostile and thus fuel confrontations across the region.

Washington also has domestic political interests in pursuing normalization because of the importance of Israel in American domestic politics. At the same time, expanding cooperation between American client states, like Israel and Saudi Arabia for example, is likely to be viewed positively; but when and how this happens and what the US relationship with Iran is going to be like over time will determine the extent to which this will contribute to regional security. In sum, there are too many open questions around the implications of normalization for it to reliably be considered an effective placeholder allowing a more significant American retreat from the region.

What Comes Next?

Is there a coherent organizing principle or interpretive framework that clearly orders American relationships around the globe today? It is hard to identify one, and none exist that are as defined as the preceding ones. That, however, can and likely will change, though it is not clear when.

If the timeline is not clear then the likely destination is; and that destination is China. Still, global American competition with China is probably in its very early stages. The Biden administration outlined the current American foreign policy in Secretary of State Antony Blinken's "Foreign Policy for the American People" speech in 2021.[17] In his speech, Secretary Blinken identified eight principles of the administration's foreign policy. Last on the list was what Blinken called "the biggest geopolitical test of the twenty-first century: our relationship with China." This was a challenge

---

16 Dana El Kurd, "Peace and Authoritarian Practices: The Impact of Normalization with Israel on the Arab World," Social Science Research Network, July 9, 2022, https://papers.ssrn.com/sol3/papers.cfm?abstract_id=4143656.

17 Antony Blinken, "A Foreign Policy for the American People," U.S. Department of State, March 3, 2021, https://www.state.gov/a-foreign-policy-for-the-american-people/.

of a different order, according to America's top diplomat, because unlike Russia, Iran, and North Korea only China has "the economic, diplomatic, military, and technological power to seriously challenge the stable and open international system – all the rules, values, and relationships that make the world work the way we want it to, because it ultimately serves the interests and reflects the values of the American people."

There is much to dissect in this loaded quotation, but one thing is very clear: this is not analogous to the post-World War II order that was defined by superpower competition, but is instead something quite different. The United States is looking at China and at what it could become over time. Blinken noted that this would be the geopolitical test of the twenty-first century, suggesting a long view of China's rise and America's relationship to it. So what does the coming stage of that relationship look like and how does it order alliances and relationships around itself?

In the short to medium term, this looks like an attempt to manage and limit the proliferation of China's instruments of leverage across the globe, which at this stage is overwhelmingly in the form of economic investment and trade relationships and not weapons transfers (although that component has been growing over time). But absent the zero-sum ideological component and the threat that the "evil empire" and "global terror" presents to the American way of life, it is much harder to create a Manichean order today.

This may change over time, and it sounds as if Blinken expects it to, but it is not the case now. That leaves other American principles to shape relationships, including supporting allies and strengthening democracy while pushing back against authoritarianism. When it comes to the US-Israel relationship, these principles militate against each other, especially as Israel descends further down the path of apartheid with no end in sight.

This spells turbulence on the path forward in the US-Israel relationship. The strength of the relationship will continue to rely on the legacy of the past, but over time it will become increasingly hard to attract new supporters for it in the United States, especially as the situation on the ground (i.e., under occupation) becomes explicitly more undemocratic. Trends for over a decade have shown a growing partisan divide in support for Israel and have demonstrated that younger and diverse demographics sympathize more with Palestinians. Increasingly, the American Jewish community is expressing frustration with the Israeli government and its policies. Absent a Manichean global paradigm that buttresses the US-Israel alliance, these differences are likely to be magnified in the coming years.

The United States and the Arabian Peninsula

Kristian Coates Ulrichsen

This chapter examines whether and how policymakers in the six states of the Gulf Cooperation Council (GCC) perceive the US "pivot" away from the Middle East, and also explores the degree to which there is regional consensus as to the nature and depth of any such disengagement. Beginning in the Obama administration and continuing through both the Trump presidency and the Biden White House, aspects of US-Gulf relations have come under strain at different times over a range of issues. These have included, at various points, US responses to the Arab Spring uprisings, nuclear negotiations with Iran, the 2017–2021 blockade of Qatar, and attacks on maritime and energy targets in Saudi Arabia and the United Arab Emirates. While concerns have varied in intensity and played out in sometimes contradictory ways, their cumulative effect was to inject some uncertainty into regional calculations regarding the United States as a reliable, or even a long-term partner.

There are three sections in this chapter, beginning with an overview of how the perception of US disengagement from the Middle East, and from the Gulf in particular, took root. This leads into a second section that examines the varying reactions across the six GCC capitals and explores the specific issues that animate the concerns raised by Gulf officials at US policy shifts, whether real or perceived. Section three delves into the rise of other extra-regional partners and assesses whether any of them could ever realistically replace the role the United States has played in the Gulf since the 1980s.

Perceptions of Disengagement

No single incident triggered the perception that the United States was losing interest in the Middle East; rather, an accumulation of factors across a yearslong period contributed to the view expressed by some in the Gulf that US engagement was becoming more uncertain and less reliable. Some of these factors were fair reactions to policy decisions in Washington that caused concern in some GCC capitals, while others were indicative of the power that perceptions hold to take root and reinforce patterns of analysis. An additional factor is a broader contextual one, namely that the US military presence in the Gulf and the broader Middle East had increased enormously during America's "war on terror" and its invasions of Afghanistan in 2001 and Iraq in 2003, before subsequently declining. Combat operations in both countries meant that US troop levels in Afghanistan and Iraq rose from 5,200 in fiscal year 2002 to a peak of 187,900 in fiscal year 2008.[1] Most US forces withdrew from Iraq in 2011 and their numbers declined in Afghanistan to 13,000 in 2019, before the Doha Agreement signed by US and Taliban representatives in February 2020 set a timeline for a full withdrawal.[2]

An elevated US military presence in the Arabian Peninsula, with basing arrangements and access to facilities that provided administrative and logistical support to the "forever wars" that followed the September 11 attacks, may have come to resemble a "new normal" in the eyes of ruling circles in GCC states. Moreover, the passage of time and the ascendance of a younger generation of leaders in the Gulf may have occluded the fact that the emergence of the United States as an extra-regional power was

---

1 Amy Belasco, "Troop Levels in the Afghan and Iraq Wars, FY2001-FY2012: Cost and Other Potential Issues," Congressional Research Service, July 2, 2009: 8–9, https://sgp.fas.org/crs/natsec/R40682.pdf.
2 Michael E. O'Hanlon, "5,000 Troops for 5 Years: A No Drama Approach to Afghanistan For the Next US President," Brookings Institution, December 5, 2019, https://www.brookings.edu/policy2020/bigideas/5000-troops-for-5-years-a-no-drama-approach-to-afghanistan-for-the-next-us-president/.

not a foregone conclusion but rather the outcome of a series of largely reactive decisions over a period of more than a decade in the 1980s and 1990s.[3] The United States did not automatically or immediately fill the void left by the British after their withdrawal from longstanding security and defense arrangements with the smaller Gulf States in 1971. It took the internationalization of the Iran-Iraq War (through the "Tanker War" phase in 1984–88) and the Iraqi invasion of Kuwait in August 1990 to establish the United States as a significant military presence in the Gulf. Even then, most US forces left the Arabian Peninsula after the conclusion of the Gulf War in 1991 and only returned on a permanent basis in 1994 after then Iraqi President Saddam Hussein again moved Iraqi troops toward Kuwait.[4]

A return to the long-term "mean" of the US presence in the region was therefore to be expected. However, a perception of relative US "disinterest" gradually took root over the 2010s, beginning with the Obama administration after it took office in 2009. Leaders in the Gulf appeared to interpret the phrase "pivot to Asia" (which began to more frequently pop up in American discourse around this time) to mean a rebalancing away from the Middle East, when it actually signaled a US desire to shift from a Cold War-era focus on Europe to concentrate on the Pacific as a fulcrum of twenty-first century geopolitics.[5] A series of policy responses by consecutive US administrations to developments in the Middle East and North Africa also fed into a narrative of uncertainty about the United States' posture. The perceived "abandonment" (as it was seen in the Gulf) of then Egyptian President Hosni Mubarak in 2011 left some wondering which US partner might be the next to suffer the same fate. And the United States' acceptance of Egypt's post-revolution electoral outcomes and its willingness to work with the Muslim Brotherhood presidency of Mohamed Morsi caused dismay in Riyadh and Abu Dhabi.[6]

---

3 Kristian Coates Ulrichsen, "Rebalancing Regional Security in the Persian Gulf," Baker Institute for Public Policy, February 2020, p. 4, https://www.bakerinstitute.org/research/rebalancing-regional-security-persian-gulf.

4 Anthony Cordesman, *Kuwait: Recovery and Security After the Gulf War* (Boulder: Westview Press, 1997), 127.

5 Kenneth G. Lieberthal, "The American Pivot to Asia," Brookings Institution, December 21, 2011, https://www.brookings.edu/articles/the-american-pivot-to-asia/.

6 Bruce Riedel, "Saudi Arabia Blames America for the Turmoil in Egypt," Brookings Institution, August 19, 2013, https://www.brookings.edu/opinions/saudi-arabia-blames-america-for-the-turmoil-in-egypt/.

Between 2013 and 2015, the fact that US officials negotiated with Iranian counterparts, initially directly and in secret, and subsequently as part of the P5+1 (the United Nations Security Council members and Germany), unnerved GCC (and Israeli) officials, not least because of their exclusion from the process. Shortly after the November 2013 breakthrough that produced an interim agreement on Iran's nuclear program, Prince Turki bin Faisal Al Saud, the former Saudi ambassador to the United States, declared, "How we feel is that we weren't part of the discussions at all, in some cases we were—I would go so far as to say we were lied to, things were hidden from us."[7] During the run-up to the agreement on the Joint Comprehensive Plan of Action (JCPOA) in July 2015, an alignment of skepticism toward the Iran deal drew some of the Gulf States, notably the UAE and Saudi Arabia, closer to Israel, with tacit coordination of talking points and meetings of intelligence officials.[8] By the end of Obama's time in office, relations with Riyadh and Abu Dhabi had cooled to the extent that officials in both capitals reacted with fury to a "free riders" comment Obama made in a lengthy interview with *The Atlantic*, as they felt (erroneously) that it was directed at them.[9]

Reactions and Responses

There was no single or consensual response across the six GCC states to US policy moves or presumed shifts in approach. Leaders in three of the Gulf States—Oman, Kuwait, and Qatar—did not react especially strongly to the vicissitudes of the Obama administration, with Oman in particular engaging closely with Obama's secretary of state, John Kerry, during the Iran nuclear negotiations.[10] Kuwait and Qatar also sent their respective

---

[7] "Iran and P5+1 Sign Breakthrough Nuclear Deal," *Gulf States Newsletter* 37, no. 959 (November 28, 2013): 3, https://www.gsn-online.com/news-centre/article/iran-and-p5-plus-1-sign-breakthrough-nuclear-deal.

[8] Hagar Shezaf and Rori Donaghy, "Israel Eyes Improved Ties with Gulf States after 'Foothold' Gained in UAE," *Middle East Eye*, January 19, 2016, https://www.middleeasteye.net/news/israel-eyes-improved-ties-gulf-states-after-foothold-gained-uae.

[9] Turki al-Faisal Al Saud, "Mr. Obama, We Are Not 'Free Riders,'" *Arab News*, March 24, 2016, https://www.arabnews.com/columns/news/894826. A careful reading of Obama's interview with Jeffrey Goldberg suggests that he made the comment "free riders aggravate me" about the United Kingdom. See: Jeffrey Goldberg, "The Obama Doctrine," *The Atlantic*, April 2016, https://www.theatlantic.com/magazine/archive/2016/04/the-obama-doctrine/471525/.

[10] William Burns, *The Back Channel: American Diplomacy in a Disordered World* (London: Hurst & Co., 2019), 357–59.

heads of state, Sabah al-Ahmad al-Sabah and Tamim bin Hamad Al Thani, to the US-GCC summit at Camp David in May 2015 amid rumors that Saudi and Bahraini leaders had stayed away as displays of frustration at the Obama administration's regional policy approach.[11] Saudi Arabia and the UAE separately intervened militarily in Yemen in March 2015, in a move that suggested that, for them, pushing back assertively against (perceived) Iranian-backed regionally-destabilizing groups such as the Houthi movement took priority over the limited negotiations in Vienna on Iran's nuclear program.[12]

By the time of the transition from the Obama administration to the Trump presidency in 2016–17, the Saudis and the Emiratis were seen by some in the outgoing White House as having taken sides in domestic US politics. Speaking after Obama left office, Ben Rhodes, the former president's deputy national security advisor, suggested that Saudi and Emirati lobbying was "more responsible for the image of Obama being soft in the Middle East than anyone else. They trashed us all around town."[13] During the transition period, a visit by Abu Dhabi's then crown prince (but de facto leader), Mohammed bin Zayed Al Nahyan (MBZ), to Trump Tower in New York caused controversy among US officials who had not been notified of his arrival in the US, in apparent contravention of diplomatic protocol.[14] Both MBZ and Saudi Arabian Crown Prince Mohammed bin Salman Al Saud (MBS) grew close to the Trump administration in early 2017 and Trump himself made his first overseas visit as president to Saudi Arabia in May 2017, where he was lavishly hosted by King Salman bin Abdulaziz.[15]

---

11 Nahal Toosi and Michael Crowley, "A Saudi Snub?," *Politico*, May 10, 2015, https://www.politico.com/story/2015/05/saudi-king-salman-to-skip-obamas-camp-david-summit-117801.
12 Peter Salisbury, "Risk Perception and Appetite in UAE Foreign and National Security Policy," Chatham House, July 2020, pp.32–33, https://www.chathamhouse.org/sites/default/files/2020-07-01-risk-in-uae-salisbury.pdf.
13 Dexter Filkins, "A Saudi Prince's Quest to Remake the Middle East," *The New Yorker*, April 2, 2018, https://www.newyorker.com/magazine/2018/04/09/a-saudi-princes-quest-to-remake-the-middle-east.
14 Manu Raju, "Exclusive: Rice Told House Investigators Why She Unmasked Senior Trump Officials," *CNN*, September 18, 2017, https://www.cnn.com/2017/09/13/politics/susan-rice-house-investigators-unmasked-trump-officials/index.html.
15 David D. Kirkpatrick and Mark Mazzetti, "How 2 Gulf Monarchies Sought to Influence the White House," *New York Times*, March 21, 2018, https://www.nytimes.com/2018/03/21/us/politics/george-nader-elliott-broidy-uae-saudi-arabia-white-house-influence.html.

This visit to Riyadh for the Arab Islamic American Summit was a break with the precedent of US presidents traditionally choosing to first visit Canada or Mexico, and Trump's time in Riyadh became controversial as it was followed two weeks later by the blockade of Qatar. In a series of three explosive tweets in June 2017, Trump referred back to his time in Riyadh and indicated that his support for the Saudi-Emirati-Bahraini-Egyptian move against Qatar had roots in meetings he had held in Saudi Arabia, as he asserted, "So good to see the Saudi Arabia visit with the King [sic] and 50 countries already paying off. They said they would take a hard line on funding extremism and all reference was pointing to Qatar."[16] Trump's comments caused shockwaves, not only in Doha, where Qatari officials wondered if Trump was greenlighting possible military action against their country, but also within his administration, as the secretaries of state and defense, Rex Tillerson and James Mattis, respectively, hurriedly sought to repair the damage caused by his remarks.[17]

Any potential Saudi or Emirati escalation against Qatar, which was deemed by many observers as a realistic possibility in June 2017, was forestalled not by Trump but by the actions of the Turkish government, which pledged military support to Qatar and indicated that Doha would neither be alone nor isolated.[18] This was significant given that in the post-1990 context of regional security it had been supposed that it would be the United States that would come to the assistance of Gulf partners should such intervention ever be necessary. Instead, it was Turkey that did so, amid unprecedented uncertainty in other Gulf capitals, such as Muscat and Kuwait City, as well as Doha, as to whether US security partnerships still held meaning in the Trump era. Thus, just as Saudi, Emirati, and Bahraini officials had expressed their concerns about aspects of Obama's

---

16 Patrick Wintour, "Donald Trump Tweets Support for Blockade Imposed on Qatar," *The Guardian*, June 6, 2017, https://www.theguardian.com/world/2017/jun/06/qatar-panic-buying-as-shoppers-stockpile-food-due-to-saudi-blockade.
17 Mark Perry, "Tillerson and Mattis Cleaning Up Kushner's Middle East Mess," *The American Conservative*, June 27, 2017, https://www.theamericanconservative.com/tillerson-and-mattis-cleaning-up-kushners-middle-east-mess/.
18 "How Turkey Stood by Qatar Amid the Gulf Crisis," *Al Jazeera*, November 14, 2017, https://www.aljazeera.com/news/2017/11/14/how-turkey-stood-by-qatar-amid-the-gulf-crisis.

approach to regional affairs, in the Trump administration it was the turn of the Qataris, the Kuwaitis, and the Omanis to do so.[19]

Ironically, in light of their proximity to the Trump White House and to officials such as Jared Kushner, in 2019 it was the Saudis and the Emiratis' turn to feel the shock of US (in)action in time of crisis. This came as the US withdrew from the JCPOA in May 2018 and adopted a policy of "maximum pressure," which included new punitive economic sanctions on Iran and terror designations for Iranian entities.[20] One response to the US pressure was a series of acts of "maximum resistance," which revolved around attacks against maritime and energy targets in Saudi Arabia and the UAE between May and September 2019. The incidents, never formally attributed to Iran, included hits on shipping and pipeline infrastructure, and culminated in missile and drone strikes on Saudi oil infrastructure that temporarily knocked out half the kingdom's oil production.[21] A declaration by Trump two days after the Abqaiq attack, which drew a distinction between US and Saudi interests and emphasized that the US had not been a target, caused shockwaves in Riyadh, and in Abu Dhabi.[22] Beginning in 2019, both Saudi Arabia and the UAE began to separately engage with Iran in attempts to de-escalate regional tensions, as leaders in each capital felt they could no longer be assured of US backing.

---

19 Speaking alongside former President Trump at the White House in September 2017, Emir Sabah al-Ahmad of Kuwait referred to the prospect of military escalation against Qatar, though without going into detail, saying, "What is important is that we have stopped any military action." See: "Remarks by President Trump and Emir Sabah al-Ahmed al-Jaber al-Sabah of Kuwait in Joint Press Conference," The White House, September 7, 2017, https://trumpwhitehouse.archives.gov/briefings-statements/remarks-president-trump-emir-sabah-al-ahmed-al-jaber-al-sabah-kuwait-joint-press-conference/.

20 Colum Lynch, "Iran: Maximum Pressure, Minimum Gain," *Foreign Policy*, December 23, 2020, https://foreignpolicy.com/2020/12/23/iran-maximum-pressure-trump-policy/.

21 Natasha Turak, "How Saudi Arabia Failed to Protect Itself from Drone and Missile Attacks Despite Billions Spent on Defense Systems," *CNBC*, September 19, 2019, https://www.cnbc.com/2019/09/19/how-saudi-arabia-failed-to-protect-itself-from-drones-missile-attacks.html.

22 Steve Holland and Rania El Gamal, "Trump Says He Does Not Want War After Attack on Saudi Oil Facilities," *Reuters*, September 16, 2019, https://www.reuters.com/article/us-saudi-aramco-trump-says-he-does-not-want-war-after-attack-on-saudi-oil-facilities-idUSKBN1W10X8.

Internationalizing the Gulf

In August 2021, the chaotic nature of the final American withdrawal from Afghanistan offered an additional signal for those doubting the United States' commitment to its partners and allies around the world, indicating that this uncertainty would continue into a third consecutive presidency, that of Joe Biden. Barely six months later, the sight of the Biden administration engaging intensively with international partners over Russia's military buildup and its subsequent full-scale invasion of Ukraine ought to have countered any such perceptions of US disengagement; but instead, the course of the war underscored how the Gulf States, like many parts of the Global South, were loath to formally pick sides in a great power rivalry.[23] Both MBZ and MBS reportedly rebuffed US and other western entreaties to raise oil production to bring down prices, and the Saudi crown prince even replied, "Simply, I do not care," when he was asked what he thought of Biden's opinion of him.[24] For his part, Biden had, during a campaign debate of Democratic presidential candidates in 2019, claimed that if elected he would make Saudi Arabia "the pariah that they are" and force them to "pay the price" for the killing of Jamal Khashoggi in 2018.[25]

Relations between the Biden administration and the Gulf States have been colored by the fact that the Russia-Ukraine war has caused the White House to be focused elsewhere, and the administration has struggled to articulate a clear approach to the Middle East. In 2022, Qatar joined Kuwait and Bahrain as the third GCC state to be named a Major Non-NATO Ally of the United States, in recognition of the wide-ranging assistance Doha provided during the US withdrawal from Afghanistan and its aftermath.[26] Saudi Arabia and the UAE remain outside the major non-NATO ally process and have instead deepened ties with Russia and

---

23 Kristian Coates Ulrichsen, "The Russia-Ukraine War and the Impact on the Persian Gulf States," *Asia Policy* 18, no. 2 (April 2023): 43–44, https://muse.jhu.edu/article/893919.
24 Emile Hokayem, "Fraught Relations: Saudi Ambitions and American Anger," *Survival: Global Politics and Strategy* 64, no. 6 (December 5, 2022): 9, https://www.tandfonline.com/doi/full/10.1080/00396338.2022.2150422.
25 Alex Emmons et al., "Joe Biden, In Departure from Obama Policy, Says He Would Make Saudi Arabia a 'Pariah,'" *The Intercept*, November 21, 2019, https://theintercept.com/2019/11/21/democratic-debate-joe-biden-saudi-arabia/.
26 R. Clarke Cooper, "As Qatar Becomes a Non-NATO Ally, Greater Responsibility Comes with the Status," Atlantic Council, March 3, 2022, https://www.atlanticcouncil.org/blogs/menasource/as-qatar-becomes-a-non-nato-ally-greater-responsibility-coveys-with-the-status/. Bahrain and Kuwait were accorded major non-NATO ally status by the George W. Bush administration, in 2002 and 2004, respectively.

China, primarily in economic and energy issues, but also with some security cooperation. Such moves may be understood as exercises in hedging, as policymakers in GCC states engage pragmatically in a changing global order with a multipolarity of centers of power and influence, including in the Gulf itself.

A complete US disengagement, and still less a withdrawal, from the Gulf remains a highly unlikely prospect, but GCC states are participating proactively in shaping a new regional landscape, one in which China looms large as a long-term partner in economic, energy, and, increasingly, political affairs. The trilateral Iran-Saudi-China statement that was issued in Beijing on March 10, 2023, and that set a roadmap for the restoration of diplomatic ties between Tehran and Riyadh, may be a harbinger of a more polycentric approach to regional affairs, one in which the United States remains an important security and defense partner for GCC states, but not the only one, and where the Gulf States increasingly function in a non-aligned manner that projects their own interests in picking a path between the strategic rivalries and great power competition around them.[27]

---

27 Natasha Turak, "The China-Brokered Saudi-Iran Deal Has Big Repercussions for the Middle East—And the U.S," *CNBC*, March 15, 2023, https://www.cnbc.com/2023/03/15/does-chinas-role-in-saudi-iran-rapprochement-represent-a-new-order-.html.

Declining American Influence in the Middle East: Afghanistan, Iraq, and Libya

Nabeel Khoury

American influence in the Middle East is declining due to a shifting global balance of power and an ambivalent US foreign policy toward key issues in the region. From Syria to Yemen, North Africa, and elsewhere, the United States has struggled to find a clear strategy, even while the government's much-touted pivot to East Asia has yet to take shape, let alone yield tangible diplomatic results. US withdrawals from Afghanistan and Iraq have not yet been replaced with robust diplomacy in an increasingly complicated region that has been crowded and clouded by multiple foreign interventions. Just as problematic is the American role in Libya after its uprising in 2011, which saw the United States take a largely hands-off approach that continues to this day.

The collapse of the Soviet Union in 1991, and with it the Warsaw Pact, is one of those historic shifts that take a decade or so to fully unfold. During the Cold War, two global powers competed for influence; the lines were clearly drawn and there was a stable balance of power. Only once, and very briefly, was there a danger of another world war, during the fitful 13 days of the Cuban Missile Crisis, when the United States and the Soviet Union got their signals crossed and almost stumbled into nuclear war.[1]

The world witnessed a moment of American ascendency in the 1990s, which some confused as evidence of the balance of power shifting to a unipolar system. China, however, had been preparing itself to step from economic growth to military build-up, and finally to become a global power in every sense of the word. This recently became fully apparent with China having brokered a rapprochement between Iran and Saudi Arabia, thereby taking a clear diplomatic step in the Middle East while also moving closer to Russian President Vladimir Putin in his hour of need during the war in Ukraine.[2] This rise in Chinese power and influence coincided with a reduced US footprint under the Obama administration, which talked up its proposed pivot to the Pacific, but did very little to move resources or diplomatic energy from one region to the other. At a recent G-7 summit in Tokyo, US Secretary of State Antony Blinken signaled an affinity of views among these allies vis-à-vis China, but announced no new action, diplomatic or economic, to try to influence Chinese policy.[3]

The changing balance of power and the consequent decline in American influence was nowhere more clearly demonstrated than in the Middle East. Under the Obama administration, the fate of Syria was decided by Russia, Turkey, Iran, and Israel. More recently, the United Arab Emirates and Saudi Arabia, after staying away for almost a decade, have reentered the Syrian fray and, in the process of rehabilitating Bashar al-Assad's regime, are now players and influencers in that game of nations.[4] The United States, on the other hand, has remained at best a marginal player. Nevertheless, President Obama's desire to avoid another Iraq debacle led

---

1   "The Cuban Missile Crisis, October 1962," U.S. State Department Office of the Historian, https://history.state.gov/milestones/1961-1968/cuban-missile-crisis.

2   Yasmine Farouk, "Riyadh's Motivations Behind the Saudi-Iran Deal," Carnegie Endowment for International Peace, March 30, 2023, https://carnegieendowment.org/2023/03/30/riyadh-s-motivations-behind-saudi-iran-deal-pub-89421.; Karl Ritter and David Keyton, "China and Russia Are Increasing Their Military Collaboration, Japan's Foreign Minister Warns," *Associated Press*, May 13, 2023, https://apnews.com/article/japan-china-ukraine-war-russia-taiwan-c11b5c5ad28f438574643d9dcb28ccc2.

3   Edward Wong, "Blinken and Top Diplomats Stress Unity on Russia and China," *New York Times*, April 18, 2023, https://www.nytimes.com/2023/04/18/world/asia/blinken-g7-russia-china.html?smid=url-share.

4   Kali Robinson, "Syria Is Normalizing Relations With Arab Countries. Who Will Benefit?," Council on Foreign Relations, May 11, 2023, https://www.cfr.org/in-brief/syria-normalizing-relations-arab-countries-who-will-benefit.

to a declining role in Syria and lay the groundwork for the pull-out from Afghanistan, fully implemented by the Biden administration—sometimes labeled as "Obama part two."

The Carter Doctrine, as laid out in former President Jimmy Carter's 1980 State of the Union Address, emphasized that, "An attempt by any outside force to gain control of the Persian Gulf region will be regarded as an assault on the vital interests of the United States of America, and such an assault will be repelled by any means necessary, including military force." That message was a response to the 1979 Islamic Revolution in Iran and the Soviet invasion of Afghanistan that took place in the same momentous year. However, after a decade of struggle, the Soviets withdrew from Afghanistan and the USSR collapsed, thus ending the Cold War. Bolstered by the Soviet defeat and prompted into action by the September 11, 2001 terrorist attacks on the United States, the George W. Bush administration invaded Afghanistan, launching a two-decade occupation that ended without much to show for the international effort that it led in the country.

The US intervention in Afghanistan became much more problematic one year on, when it turned into a full-fledged occupation. The twenty-year occupation was often described as an experiment in nation-building and the establishment of US dominance in the region—an experiment that failed on both counts. When it ended, the chaos of a sudden total pull-out while the Taliban were closing in on Kabul left the American public and the world stunned by the futility of it all.[5] Turned upside-down, Bush's "shock and awe" phrase exposed a superpower clearly ill-disposed to steer the region toward a more democratic path. Middle East media outlets have since reflected a prevailing conclusion in the region that the US withdrawal from Afghanistan was first and foremost a defeat and a manifestation of declining US commitment to its friends and allies.[6] For the Kingdom of Saudi Arabia and the UAE, the Afghan withdrawal enhanced planning that was already underway in the waning years of the US occupation, and that was focused on balancing these two Gulf powerhouses' dependence on the United States with stronger relations with Russia and China.

---

5   Karoun Demirjian, "G.O.P. Inquiry on Afghan Withdrawal Opens With Searing Witness Accounts," *New York Times*, March 8, 2023, https://www.nytimes.com/2023/03/08/us/politics/afghanistan-withdrawal-house-hearing.html.

6   Omar al-Sharif, "The US Withdrawal from Afghanistan," *Arab News*, April 20, 2021, https://www.arabnews.com/node/1846041.

US Power after Afghanistan

When the end to the United States' involvement in Afghanistan came, it came quickly. The Ashraf Ghani government folded without a fight, mercifully choosing to avoid further bloodshed in the capital, in what would have been in any case a losing battle.[7] After twenty years of occupation, thousands of American deaths, tens of thousands of Afghan deaths, and over a trillion dollars spent by the Department of Defense alone, the US failed to secure its friends in power and left them at the mercy (or lack thereof) of the Taliban, with whom US diplomats had negotiated for more than a decade regarding the transition.[8] Worse still, when the US embassy closed and all the troops pulled out, over 100,000 Afghan allies and former employees were left with incomplete special immigrant visas (SIV) and could not be evacuated in time.[9]

To be fair, US/NATO military intervention dealt a serious blow to al-Qaeda's terror capabilities in the first year of the invasion. However, the 19 years that followed were mostly dedicated to nation-building, an attempt to shore-up anti-Qaeda and Taliban forces in the country and to support the building of political and academic institutions that would, if properly supported, defend against the return of extremism to the country.[10] Well before the actual withdrawal of troops from Afghanistan, however, both the United States and its NATO allies concluded that their goal was unachievable, though the speed with which the pro-West government fell was a surprise to most.[11] The haste and chaos of the withdrawal took a toll on Afghans who had for years loyally served with US and NATO forces.[12]

---

7 "Afghan President Ghani Relinquishes Power, Taliban Form Interim Gov't," *Daily Sabah*, August 15, 2021, https://www.dailysabah.com/world/asia-pacific/afghan-president-ghani-relinquishes-power-taliban-form-interim-govt.

8 "Human and Budgetary Costs of the U.S. War in Afghanistan, 2001-2022," Watson Institute for International and Public Affairs, August 2021, https://watson.brown.edu/costsofwar/figures/2021/human-and-budgetary-costs-date-us-war-afghanistan-2001-2022.

9 Loren Voss, "How to Save Thousands of Afghan Allies," *Lawfare*, January 30, 2023, https://www.lawfareblog.com/how-save-thousands-afghan-allies.

10 Jessica T. Mathews, "American Power After Afghanistan: How to Rightsize the Country's Global Role," *Foreign Affairs*, September 17, 2021, https://www.foreignaffairs.com/articles/united-states/2021-09-17/american-power-after-afghanistan.

11 "NATO and Afghanistan," North Atlantic Treaty Organization, August 31, 2022, https://www.nato.int/cps/en/natohq/topics_8189.htm.

12 Franco Ordoñez, "For Biden, the Chaotic Withdrawal from Kabul Was a Turning Point in His Presidency," *National Public Radio*, August 15, 2022, https://www.npr.org/2022/08/15/1117037318/for-biden-the-chaotic-withdrawal-from-kabul-was-a-turning-point-in-his-presidenc.

More fundamentally, the delay in realizing that the occupation itself was flawed is inexcusable. Simply put, the enterprise of recreating the country in the image of its occupiers was too costly, especially when compared to the meagre results it produced.

Despite twenty years of occupation and ambitious (perhaps overly ambitious) development goals, western powers and international institutions consistently failed to implement their grandiose designs for economic and political development. This was partly due to short-term budgeting processes and complacency toward their lack of success; but it was mostly due to the corrupt warlords and drug lords who remained empowered, either directly by the occupying powers or indirectly via the lackluster leadership installed in Kabul.[13]

The story on the military side of things is even worse, and was riddled with failures in achieving stability in most of Afghanistan's provinces. The US military could not be everywhere at once in such a geographically large and difficult terrain and the local armed forces were never able to hold cities and villages for long after international forces cleared them of the Taliban. Kunduz is one example of a large city liberated from the Taliban on more than one occasion, only to be lost again once NATO forces left it in the hands of the Afghan military.[14] Smaller cities and villages suffered the same fate, especially in the southern Helmand Province. In short, once the al-Qaeda fighters left and the battle turned into an undeclared war with the Taliban, US/NATO forces had at best a tenuous hold on most provinces in the country. No one was more aware of this fact early on than then Secretary of Defense Donald Rumsfeld, whose harsh words to US generals (mostly conveyed in secret documents) clearly expressed his frustrations.[15]

The twin invasions of Iraq and Afghanistan were supposed to transform the Middle East, making it a safer environment for all democracy-loving people and for American interests in the region. Former US Secretary

---

13   Dipali Mukhopadhyay, "Warlords As Bureaucrats: The Afghan Experience," *Carnegie Endowment for International Peace Middle East Program*, no. 101 (August 2009), https://carnegieendowment.org/files/warlords_as_bureaucrats.pdf.

14   Craig Whitlock, "The Grand Illusion: Hiding the Truth about the Afghanistan War's 'Conclusion,'" *Washington Post*, August 12, 2021, https://www.washingtonpost.com/investigations/2021/08/12/obama-afghan-war-ending-afghanistan-papers-book-excerpt/.

15   Craig Whitlock, "At War with the Truth," *Washington Post*, December 9, 2019, https://www.washingtonpost.com/graphics/2019/investigations/afghanistan-papers/afghanistan-war-confidential-documents/.

of State Condoleezza Rice, confounding Israel's war against Hezbollah in 2006 with the American war against al-Qaeda in Afghanistan and conflating the forces fighting against the US occupation in Iraq with terrorists everywhere, labeled the whole US endeavor a struggle for "a new Middle East."[16] Misunderstanding the origins of conflict in Iraq, Afghanistan, and Lebanon is, to a large degree, responsible for the results: Israel ended its Lebanon war with Hezbollah's power still intact and the US left Afghanistan and Iraq with its influence in both countries significantly diminished.

Invading Iraq

The 2003 US invasion of Iraq, perhaps more than any other American adventure in the Middle East, demonstrated the hubris and the ignorance that drive such interventions. State Department reports warned of resistance to invasion and the potential human rights abuses that might ensue.[17] Regardless of the antipathy to former Iraqi President Saddam Hussein that existed in many corners of the Arab world, the fall of a city like Baghdad to foreign forces had a deep and disturbing impact. The popular reaction in the Arab street during and after the invasion manifested itself in demonstrations, newspaper articles, and live coverage on major media outlets throughout the region.[18] The ascendency of satellite TV and the prominence that year of the *Al Jazeera* network in particular, splashed a blow-by-blow description of the violence and chaos unleashed by the Iraq War across screens and newspapers in the region, which prompted many in the Bush administration to question not their own motives and methods but rather those of the media organizations that they saw as attacking them. This author, present in Baghdad as a State Department spokesperson in 2003, included *Al Jazeera* reporters in press conferences and briefings and was once told by a nonplussed administration official that, "The *Al Jazeera* cameras might as well be guns pointed at us."

The bureaucratic reality in Baghdad, especially during the early years of the occupation, reflected the ascendancy of the Department of Defense over career foreign service diplomats, sending a clear message that the

---

16 Jeremy Bransten, "Middle East: Rice Calls For A 'New Middle East,'" Radio Free Europe/Radio Liberty, July 25, 2006, https://www.rferl.org/a/1070088.html.
17 "State Department Experts Warned CENTCOM Before Iraq War about Lack of Plans For Post-war Iraq Security," National Security Archive Electronic Briefing Book No. 163, August 17, 2005, https://nsarchive2.gwu.edu/NSAEBB/NSAEBB163/index.htm.
18 "Arab Reactions to War on Iraq," Amnesty International Norway, July 4, 2003, https://amnesty.no/arab-reactions-war-iraq.

military was the driving force behind the occupation. Nation-building, both in the political and economic sense, was driven by what political appointees conceived as the needs of the US national interest and not those of the people of Iraq. From the early trust placed in corrupt and sectarian Iraqi politicians like Ahmad Chalabi to twice supporting Nouri al-Maliki for prime minister, the US demonstrated short-sighted self interest in its decisions and policies in Iraq.[19]

The United States' mistaken support for al-Maliki as prime minister in 2006 was, incredibly, repeated after the 2010 parliamentary elections (which his coalition lost by a small margin), despite his obvious sectarian tendencies and his engagement in corruption. It was exactly those characteristics that were responsible for his vindictiveness against Iraq's Sunni communities and the artificially inflated ranks of the Iraqi Army under his leadership. It was only in 2014, and after the Iraqi military's disastrous failures against the Islamic State in Iraq and Syria (ISIS)—now the Islamic State (IS)—that the Obama administration finally lost faith in its ally, and this only after he had decided to reject the continued presence of US military trainers and advisors in the country.[20]

The brutality of occupation, any occupation, can in principle be ameliorated by a genuine concern for its impact on the occupied population at large and by taking responsibility for a full reconstruction and development effort afterward. And indeed, the State Department's Future of Iraq Project warned that neglect of this responsibility could have serious consequences.[21] *New York Times* columnist Thomas Friedman (as well as others in the US media) also emphasized this important matter (however crudely), once telling a crowd at a speaking event, "If you break Iraq, you

---

19 Sewell Chan, "Ahmad Chalabi, Iraqi Politician Who Pushed for U.S. Invasion, Dies at 71," *New York Times*, November 3, 2015, https://www.nytimes.com/2015/11/04/world/middleeast/ahmad-chalabi-iraq-dead.html.; David Rohde et al., Our Man in Baghdad: How America Empowered Nouri al-Maliki—and Then Failed to Keep That Power in Check," *The Atlantic*, July 1, 2014, https://www.theatlantic.com/international/archive/2014/07/nouri-maliki-united-states-iraq/373799/.
20 Martin Chulov and Spencer Ackerman, "How Nouri al-Maliki Fell Out of Favour with the US," *The Guardian*, June 19, 2014, https://www.theguardian.com/world/2014/jun/19/how-nouri-al-maliki-fell-out-favour-with-us-iraq.
21 "New State Department Releases on the 'Future of Iraq' Project," National Security Archive Electronic Briefing Book No. 198, September 1, 2006, https://nsarchive2.gwu.edu/NSAEBB/NSAEBB198/index.htm.

own Iraq."[22] In spite of such warnings, however, mistakes accumulated, from the early dismissal of the Iraqi military to the empowerment of opposition leaders who had long detached themselves from conditions on the ground, and, perhaps most importantly, to the lack of attention paid to the broken infrastructure that frustrated the lives of average Iraqis. Fixing the electric grid is but one example of trying to do reconstruction on the cheap, leading Iraqi journalists and citizens to question whether chaos in the streets and darkness at home was quite the democracy that the US had promised. The frustrations felt on the street certainly contributed to the building of resentment and the strengthening of opposition to the United States—opposition that, in turn, helped build up the ranks of al-Qaeda in Iraq and fueled the rise of IS.

The US invasion certainly removed the despot at the top, thereby opening the possibility for Iraqis to rebuild their own state once the occupation ended in 2011. Twenty years after the invasion of Iraq, however, the population remains rebellious against what they perceive as an inept and corrupt state that has failed to lay the foundations of a modern nation that can provide its citizens with the basic services they need.[23] Nor has the United States' involvement in Iraq brought long-term benefits to the US, as evidenced by the controversial status of the 2,500 American soldiers who remain as trainers and advisors in the country.[24] Although current Iraqi Prime Minister Mohammed Shia' al-Sudani is much more positively disposed toward the US than al-Maliki ever was, he supports this limited number of US troops mainly to balance Iran's military presence and influence. Culturally and politically, Iraq's majority Shia population is much closer to Iran than it is to the United States, which is evident in the prevalent pro-Iran sentiment found among the country's numerous armed militias.

In the end, the cost of the war in Iraq has to be calculated not only in the billions spent on fighting, the thousands of American deaths, and the hundreds of thousands of Iraqi deaths but also in the spread of the

---

22 Jim Romenesko, "Friedman: Break Iraq, You Own Iraq—Like at Pottery Barn," Poynter, February 24, 2003, https://www.poynter.org/reporting-editing/2003/friedman-break-iraq-you-own-iraq-like-at-pottery-barn/.
23 Anthony H. Cordesman, "Iraq as a Failed State," Center for Strategic and International Studies, November 12, 2019, https://www.csis.org/analysis/iraq-failed-state.
24 Jack Detsch, "'They Have to Balance': New Iraqi Leader Tilts the Scales Toward U.S.," *Foreign Policy*, January 24, 2023, https://foreignpolicy.com/2023/01/24/iraq-new-prime-minister-sudani-us-troops/.

resentment toward the United States and the rise of Jihadism throughout the region.[25] It is this cost, more than any rational decision to pivot eastward that precipitated the withdrawal of US forces in 2011 and the limited scope of military operations afterward in what has often been described as the global war on terror.

Libya and the Aftermath of Qaddafi's Fall

For President Obama, 2011 was a tough year in the Middle East. The so-called Arab Spring produced popular uprisings against authoritarian rule, and Arab civil society responded warmly to Obama's speeches on democracy and the US pledge to be on "the right side of history." However, other strings were pulling at Obama, emanating from his pledge not to enter another quagmire like Iraq. That same year, the president announced that the Iraq War was over and that all US troops stationed there would come home.[26] The US pullout would be temporary, however, as US Special Forces returned to Iraq in 2015 to help liberate its cities from an IS surge.

As the war in Libya heated up, the US was pressed by its NATO partners to intervene, and an impending attack by former Libyan dictator Muammar Qaddafi's forces on Benghazi lent urgency to that call. NATO action in Libya was predicated on an international mandate to protect civilians, and Qaddafi's repeated threats to "cleanse Benghazi" of the opposition forces there certainly put tens of thousands of the city's inhabitants in harm's way.[27] However, NATO's military action also had the goal of tipping the balance in favor of the opposition—a goal that succeeded in ending the Qaddafi regime. President Obama, reluctant to get involved in Libya, was convinced nevertheless that the United States was obliged to not only support the NATO action but also to lead it. Consequently, Obama authorized military action, provided that no troops

---

25 Neta C. Crawford, "The Iraq War Has Cost the US Nearly $2 Trillion," *Military Times*, February 6, 2020, https://www.militarytimes.com/opinion/commentary/2020/02/06/the-iraq-war-has-cost-the-us-nearly-2-trillion/.

26 "Barack Obama Announces Total Withdrawal of US Troops from Iraq," *The Guardian*, October 21, 2011, https://www.theguardian.com/world/2011/oct/21/obama-us-troops-withdrawal-iraq.

27 Matthew Green, "To What Extent Was the NATO Intervention in Libya a Humanitarian Intervention?," E-International Relations, February 6, 2019, https://www.e-ir.info/2019/02/06/to-what-extent-was-the-nato-intervention-in-libya-a-humanitarian-intervention/.

would be deployed on the ground—instead supplying only naval vessels offshore and intelligence officers on the ground, which resulted in the media-popularized phrase "leading from behind."[28]

The fall of Qaddafi was followed by fierce competition for power inside the country and a host of competing foreign interventions from Russia, Turkey, Egypt, and the UAE, in addition to the continued involvement of Europe.[29] The United Nations has been trying valiantly to help establish stability, but the political scene remains chaotic more than a decade after the Libyan uprising, as Turkish economic interests in Libya clash with those of Russia, Greece, and Israel, and compete politically and ideologically with the UAE and Egypt.[30] After briefly championing General Khalifa Haftar, the leader of the so-called Libyan National Army, the US role in the attempt to shape the future of Libya has been, at best, minimal. Sadly, this restraint did not protect the United States from the terrorist attack that took the life of US Ambassador Chris Stevens and three other embassy staff members in September 2012.[31]

Qaddafi, the longest serving Arab authoritarian leader, had governed the country with a minimum of modern state infrastructure, leaving the majority of Libyans directly dependent on him and his Green Book-inspired popular committees for salaries and services, without the mediation of political parties or civil society organizations. In the aftermath of the fall of the regime, the task of reconstruction was even more challenging than in the cases of Iraq and Afghanistan, where an occupying power could take action and succeed or fail accordingly. A plethora of military groups and militias thrived and competed in Libya instead, and claimed the right to speak for the Libyan people in national and international circles.[32] The lack of national consensus was further exacerbated

---

28 Charles Krauthammer, "The Obama Doctrine: Leading from Behind," *Washington Post*, April 28, 2011, https://www.washingtonpost.com/opinions/the-obama-doctrine-leading-from-behind/2011/04/28/AFBCy18E_story.html.

29 Patricia Karam, "Can Libya's Stalemate Be Overcome?," Arab Center Washington DC, April 4, 2023, https://arabcenterdc.org/resource/can-libyas-stalemate-be-overcome/.

30 Ezel Sahinkaya, "Why Is Turkey Involved in Libyan Conflict?," *Voice of America*, June 4, 2020, https://www.voanews.com/a/extremism-watch_why-turkey-involved-libyan-conflict/6190551.html.

31 Luke Harding, Chris Stephen et al., "Chris Stevens, US Ambassador to Libya, Killed in Benghazi Attack," *The Guardian*, September 12, 2012, https://www.theguardian.com/world/2012/sep/12/chris-stevens-us-ambassador-libya-killed.

32 Stephanie T. Williams, "Libya's Hybrid Armed Groups Dilemma," Brookings Institution, January 27, 2023, https://www.brookings.edu/articles/libyas-hybrid-armed-groups-dilemma/.

by the multiple regional and international powers pushing for their own interests in the country.

The chaos that is Libya today, and the lingering trauma over Stevens' murder, have much to do with why the United States has conducted a barebones diplomacy in the country since 2014.[33] Security concerns, however consequential, do not fully explain the minimal US role, which is based on Obama's reluctance after the 2011 Arab uprisings to fully invest in supporting democratic development in the Middle East. Simply put, both Obama and current President Joe Biden have failed to find a credible strategy that straddles both security concerns and a value-based foreign policy. Saudi Arabia is a case in point, where security and economic ties pull the US right back to its long-standing regional partner every time harsh words or actions over human rights abuses drive the two apart. In Libya, the US seems to be similarly pulled in opposing directions, struggling to balance between the abuses of General Haftar, who is supported by traditional US friends like Egypt and the United Arab Emirates, and the lack of both alternative forces to champion and a direct role to play using American diplomats on the ground. As a result, US influence has fallen behind that of Russia, which has adopted Haftar; behind Turkey, which supports its own friendly forces on the ground; and behind European countries intent on trying to stymie illegal immigration to their shores, coordinated by Libyan traffickers.

Toward a US Strategy

Biden has prioritized diplomacy and the withdrawal of forces from "forever wars"; but in an article published in 2020 in *Foreign Affairs* that very much resembled a mission statement for his presidency, he still insisted that America must lead.[34] And to the extent that he referred to building partnerships, he highlighted the need for a coalition of democracies aligned against fascism, something that he has since launched at democracy summits in 2021 and 2023. This obsession with leadership belies a lack of awareness that the challenge for the United States in the twenty-first century is to work well with a concert of powers, turning hostility and

---

33 Frederic Wehrey, "Why Isn't the U.S. in Libya?," *Foreign Policy*, April 6, 2023, https://foreignpolicy.com/2023/04/06/libya-us-embassy-state-department-diplomacy-wagner-group/.
34 Joseph R. Biden, Jr., "Why America Must Lead Again: Rescuing U.S. Foreign Policy After Trump," *Foreign Affairs*, January 23, 2020, https://www.foreignaffairs.com/articles/united-states/2020-01-23/why-america-must-lead-again.

competitiveness with other global powers into a better understanding of common interests and a collaborative approach to common threats.

In early 2023, US Special Presidential Envoy Brett McGurk laid out "the Biden Doctrine," with several references to "threats from Iran" and to deterrence of an alleged preparation by Iran to attack Saudi Arabia.[35] In the midst of the US girding itself for hostilities rather than putting diplomacy first, Beijing made a diplomatic splash by brokering an Iran-Saudi Arabia agreement on March 10, 2023.[36] The Biden administration responded professionally and publicly welcomed the rapprochement. However, administration officials expressed some resentment and belittled the Chinese achievement through other channels.[37] The agreement, whether it holds and leads to concrete results or not, left an atypical image of China moving to center stage in a region that has for decades been dominated by the United States.

The United States' nation-building and its nurturing of democracy via a foreign military force and occupation have clearly failed in the Middle East, in part because the occupying power was motivated by its own national interest and allied itself with corrupt and authoritarian figures. Reluctance to intervene and increased caution in the use of force by the United States, though fully understandable in this context, have not been replaced with a dramatic increase in creative diplomacy or in Marshall Plan-like planning that relies on development assistance rather than force to induce a desired change. The United States could have used the three cases discussed here—Afghanistan, Iraq, and Libya—to showcase that it can achieve more during peace than it can during war. Thus far, this has not been the case. Meanwhile, Tunisia, once regarded as the Arab country most likely to succeed post-2011 in building a democracy without violence, has managed to avoid foreign military intervention but has descended into a harsh autocracy against the background of relative US neglect. Clearly, the search for a new and more creative American foreign policy in the Middle East continues.

---

35   "Brett McGurk Sets Out the 'Biden Doctrine' for the Middle East," Atlantic Council, February 15, 2023, https://www.atlanticcouncil.org/commentary/transcript/brett-mcgurk-sets-out-the-biden-doctrine-for-the-middle-east/.

36   Maria Fantappie and Vali Nasr, "A New Order in the Middle East?: Iran and Saudi Arabia's Rapprochement Could Transform the Region," *Foreign Affairs*, March 22, 2023, https://www.foreignaffairs.com/china/iran-saudi-arabia-middle-east-relations.

37   Peter Baker, "Chinese-Brokered Deal Upends Mideast Diplomacy and Challenges U.S.," *New York Times*, March 11, 2023, https://www.nytimes.com/2023/03/11/us/politics/saudi-arabia-iran-china-biden.html.

The Syrian Conflict: A Turning Point in US Middle East Policy

Lina Khatib

The Syrian conflict represents a significant turning point in American policy toward the Middle East. The past decade has seen the United States downgrade the region on its list of priorities, and Syria has in many ways been a bellwether of US engagement in the Middle East. Arab states have recently normalized with the Syrian regime of President Bashar al-Assad.[1] They are accepting—pragmatically—that he has managed to remain in power despite the war. This acceptance is driven in no small part by US foreign policy toward Syria since 2011.

Linked to this is what many Arab countries see as a problematic American take on Iran's interventions in the Middle East. Despite the different priorities of successive US administrations since 2008, the Iran focus since former President Barack Obama's first term has been on the Islamic Republic's nuclear program rather than its regional role. Some Arab countries now going down the path of normalization with Assad are

---

1 Mohamed Wagdy and Kareem Chehayeb, "Pariah No More? Arab League Reinstates Bashar Assad's Syria," *Associated Press*, May 7, 2023, https://apnews.com/article/syria-arab-egypt-saudi-qatar-jordan-f0298c40488470eb28274b2ffb859396.

driven by the desire to de-escalate tensions in the region after waiting for years for US support vis-à-vis Iran's interventions in the Middle East—support that never came.

Assad is enjoying the legitimacy that normalization with Arab countries brings. Full normalization in the Arab world would signal the beginning of the end of international isolation for the regime, even if the end goal is still a way off. Understanding how Syria got here merits looking back at how the United States has approached the main milestones in the Syrian conflict since its beginning. This chapter lays out the key policy decisions taken by the United States at each of those milestones to argue that America has been the main driver behind the dynamics leading Arab countries to normalize with Assad.

Iran and US Nonintervention in Syria

With signing a nuclear deal with Iran having been the main Middle East priority for the US administration during Obama's first term, the American position toward the Syrian conflict in its first two years was noninterventionist.[2] When the Syrian uprising began in March 2011, Syrians had seen the Obama administration express support for the revolutions that had begun earlier in Tunisia, Egypt, and Libya. The Libyan context, with the violent crackdown by the Muammar Qaddafi regime on peaceful demonstrations leading to UN Security Council Resolution 1973 authorizing a NATO-led military campaign to help remove Qaddafi from power, stood out as an illustration of the international community's solidarity with movements for political change in the Arab world.[3] Pro-reform activists across the region saw the US as a leading player in this context. Though the Syrian uprising started as a peaceful one, the implicit expectation in the Arab world was that the United States would not hesitate to use all available tools to aid the Syrians demanding freedom and dignity.

It took little time for the Syrian uprising to turn into a conflict due to the violent crackdown on protesters by the Assad regime. The US made statements condemning the violence and imposed some sanctions on the

---

2   Barbara Plett Usher, "Obama's Syria Legacy: Measured Diplomacy, Strategic Explosion," *BBC News*, January 13, 2017, https://www.bbc.com/news/world-us-canada-38297343.
3   United Nations Security Council Resolution 1973 (2011), March 17, 2011, https://www.un.org/securitycouncil/s/res/1973-%282011%29.

regime, and by August 2011 had called on Assad to resign.[4] But Washington did not invest in serious diplomatic efforts to resolve the conflict. Running parallel to this was Iran's intervention in the Syrian scenario, which began early on as both Iran and its Lebanese ally Hezbollah played an active role in advising the Assad regime on quelling protests.[5] US policymakers knew of Hezbollah and Iran's role but did not initiate stepped-up diplomatic action on Syria.[6]

The main factor behind the United States' reluctance to engage further in this regard was Iran's nuclear file. While campaigning for his first term, Obama made sealing a nuclear deal with Iran his priority for the Middle East, and he pursued this goal during both of his presidential terms. In 2011, the goal was still a long way from being achieved. The Obama administration did not want to further complicate its relationship with the Islamic Republic by adding another variable, namely Iran's regional interventions, to the negotiating table as part of a "grand bargain."[7] Instead, it decided to focus only on the nuclear deal. This left Iran and Hezbollah with a wide-open space to increase their activities inside Syria to aid the Assad regime.

Obama's Red Line

"Assad must go"; no other words better summarize the Obama administration's rhetoric on the Arab Spring. When President Obama uttered these words during a press conference on March 20, 2013—adding that Assad and his regime "will be held accountable for the use of chemical weapons or their transfer to terrorists"—he implied that after two years of the Syrian crisis, the US was finally ready to act to effect regime change in

---

4   Scott Wilson and Joby Warrick, "Assad Must Go, Obama Says," *Washington Post*, August 18, 2011, https://www.washingtonpost.com/politics/assad-must-go-obama-says/2011/08/18/gIQAelheOJ_story.html.
5   Ian Black and Dan Roberts, "Hezbollah Is Helping Assad Fight Syria Uprising, Says Hassan Nasrallah," *The Guardian*, April 30, 2013, https://www.theguardian.com/world/2013/apr/30/hezbollah-syria-uprising-nasrallah.
6   Mark Hosenball, "Iran Helping Assad to Put Down Protests: Officials," *Reuters*, March 23, 2012, https://www.reuters.com/article/us-iran-syria-crackdown-idUSBRE82M18220120323.
7   Michael R. Gordon, "John Kerry, in Saudi Arabia, Reassures Gulf States on Iran Nuclear Talks," *New York Times* March 5, 2015, https://www.nytimes.com/2015/03/06/world/middleeast/john-kerry-in-saudi-arabia-reassures-gulf-states-on-iran-nuclear-talks.html.

Syria.[8] This was especially poignant, as the press conference during which Obama made the remarks was a joint one with Israeli Prime Minister Benjamin Netanyahu while the US president was in Israel on an official visit. The reality is that the US position on Syria at the time remained hostage to the Iran nuclear file. The Obama administration's rhetoric on the Arab Spring in general, and on Syria in particular, was mainly one of false hope.

Obama's words in March 2013 came the day after the Syrian regime launched two chemical weapon attacks in Aleppo and Damascus.[9] In his remarks, Obama said that the use of chemical weapons was a "game changer" and a "red line."[10] When the Assad regime continued to use chemical weapons later that summer, Assad's allies and opponents alike, as well as those within the regime itself, expected that the US was going to engage in military action in Syria. But such action never took place, partly due to continued concerns in Washington that addressing Iran's regional interventions would risk progress toward signing a nuclear deal, in addition to hesitation regarding both who would replace Assad and the challenge of stabilizing Syria.

Obama's red line in the sand was a pivotal moment for US foreign policy. Assad understood it as an illustration that the United States was not serious about removing him from power. Iran and Hezbollah joined Assad in seeing the last-minute change of mind in Washington as further proof of US weakness. But above all else, the United States' inaction frustrated its allies in the Arab world, particularly in the Gulf. Qatar and Saudi Arabia had thrown their weight behind various elements of Syria's opposition and its rebel factions and saw in the backtracking a significant blow to their efforts.[11] US credibility—in the eyes of America's friends and enemies alike—was damaged. Saudi Arabia and Israel were both unhappy with Obama's pursuit of the Iran nuclear deal at the expense of their own

---

8 "Remarks by President Obama and Prime Minister Netanyahu of Israel in Joint Press Conference," The White House Office of the Press Secretary, March 20, 2013, https://obamawhitehouse.archives.gov/the-press-office/2013/03/20/remarks-president-obama-and-prime-minister-netanyahu-israel-joint-press-.

9 "Timeline of Syrian Chemical Weapons Activity, 2012-2022," Arms Control Association, May 2021, https://www.armscontrol.org/factsheets/Timeline-of-Syrian-Chemical-Weapons-Activity.

10 "Remarks by President Obama and Prime Minister Netanyahu of Israel."

11 "Qatar's Emir, a U.S. Ally, Assails Obama's Syria Policy," Reuters, September 20, 2016, https://www.reuters.com/article/us-mideast-crisis-syria-qatar-idUSKCN11Q2RX.

national political and security interests. Obama's much coveted nuclear deal, the Joint Comprehensive Plan of Action (JCPOA), was eventually adopted in October 2015 and implemented in January 2016.[12]

The Rise of IS and the Empowerment of Iran-Backed Groups

If US foreign policy toward the Middle East during the first three years of the Syrian conflict was dominated by the objective of securing a nuclear deal with Iran, the next three years were dominated by the fight against the so-called Islamic State in Iraq and Syria (ISIS), now known as the Islamic State (IS). The US focus on countering IS had fundamental long-term consequences for actors in the Syrian conflict. It not only resulted in the empowerment of Kurdish factions in northeast Syria but also in the consolidation of power for Iran-backed armed groups that were also fighting IS in Syria and Iraq. This, in turn, further strengthened Iran's influence in the two countries and beyond.

In Syria and Lebanon, Hezbollah used the fight against IS to paint its intervention in support of the Assad regime as being about countering what it labeled "takfiri jihadists," saying that its actions were protecting Lebanon and the rest of the Arab world from the spread of IS and other Sunni extremist groups.[13] In Iraq, the Iran-backed Popular Mobilization Forces (PMF) presented itself as the national liberation force needed to defeat IS, especially as the Iraqi Army had failed to stand up to it on its own when it took over Mosul in 2014 and declared the establishment of its so-called caliphate.[14]

Both Hezbollah and the PMF eventually cashed in their military gains in the form of political advantages, consolidating their positions as the dominant political actors in their respective countries.[15] Both continue to promote an

---

12 Jennifer R. Williams, "A Comprehensive Timeline of the Iran Nuclear Deal," Brookings Institution, July 21, 2015, https://www.brookings.edu/blog/markaz/2015/07/21/a-comprehensive-timeline-of-the-iran-nuclear-deal/.
13 Nour Samaha, "Hezbollah Chief Urges Middle East to Unite against ISIL," *Al Jazeera*, February 16, 2015, https://www.aljazeera.com/news/2015/2/16/hezbollah-chief-urges-middle-east-to-unite-against-isil.
14 Ned Parker et al., "Special Report: How Mosul Fell - An Iraqi General Disputes Baghdad's Story," *Reuters*, October 14, 2014, https://www.reuters.com/article/us-mideast-crisis-gharawi-special-report/special-report-how-mosul-fell-an-iraqi-general-disputes-baghdads-story-idUSKCN0I30Z820141014.
15 Farah Najjar, "Iraq's Second Army: Who Are They, What Do They Want?," *Al Jazeera*, October 31, 2017, https://www.aljazeera.com/news/2017/10/31/iraqs-second-army-who-are-they-what-do-they-want.

anti-US agenda and have used their political clout to either block opponents from reaching positions of power or to limit their influence if they do reach such positions. In both countries, these Iran-backed groups have played a major role in stalling processes of cabinet formation following parliamentary elections.[16] Meanwhile, Iran consolidated its presence in Syria through the expansion of Shia shrines under its supervision, the buying of property, and demographic engineering in key areas near the Lebanese border through population transfers.[17] The latter practice served to give Hezbollah and its Syrian allies de facto control over the Lebanon-Syria border, which in turn has facilitated their movement of goods and people between the two countries in both directions, including the illicit trade in drugs.[18] Working in partnership with the Fourth Armored Division of the Syrian Army, which is led by Bashar al-Assad's brother, Maher al-Assad, Hezbollah is playing a major role in making Syria an international hub for the Captagon drug trade.[19]

The Instrumentalization of Syrian Kurdish Factions

As the United States gathered and led a global coalition to fight IS, Kurdish factions were the coalition's chosen local forces on the ground in northeast Syria, though their name, the Syrian Democratic Forces, was meant to convey that they were not exclusively Kurdish but also had Arabs in their ranks. One military member of the global coalition said in 2017 that the coalition preferred to work with Kurdish groups because, "Arab Sunni groups are too divided, whereas the Kurds are more ideologically coherent and therefore easier to command."[20]

---

16 Philip Loft, "Iraq in 2022: Forming a Government," UK Parliament House of Commons Library, November 2, 2022, https://commonslibrary.parliament.uk/research-briefings/cbp-9605/.
17 Martin Chulov, "Iran Repopulates Syria with Shia Muslims to Help Tighten Regime's Control," *The Guardian*, January 13, 2017, https://www.theguardian.com/world/2017/jan/13/irans-syria-project-pushing-population-shifts-to-increase-influence.
18 Mazen Ezzi, "Lebanese Hezbollah's Experience in Syria," *Middle East Directions*, March 13, 2020, https://cadmus.eui.eu/bitstream/handle/1814/66546/MED_WPCS_2020_4.pdf.
19 Rouba El Husseini and Jean Marc Mojon, "Captagon Connection: How Syria Became a Narco State," *Al-Monitor*, November 2, 2022, https://www.al-monitor.com/originals/2022/11/captagon-connection-how-syria-became-narco-state.
20 Interview with the author, June 2017.

Kurdish factions saw a double gain in joining the fight against IS; it was a way to both liberate their areas from the organization's control and obtain political favors from the United States. The latter goal was important because Kurdish groups, especially the People's Protection Units (YPG) and Women's Protection Units (YPJ), saw an alliance with the US as helping their objective of gaining autonomy. Turkey had entered the Syrian conflict to support groups from the Syrian opposition against Assad, but used this support as a pretext for trying to prevent Kurdish groups in Syria from establishing a Kurdish-governed region near its border, citing the YPG's relationship with the Kurdistan Workers' Party (PKK)—which Turkey lists as a terrorist group—as proof that the former are terrorists. Ironically, the United States also recognizes the PKK as a terrorist group.

The presence of oil fields in Syrian areas where Kurdish factions prevail is a motivation for the United States to continue to have a presence in those areas because Washington will not want Assad to regain control over those resources. The United States can also instrumentalize Kurdish factions in standoffs with Turkey. But it would be a stretch to see the US partnership with the Kurds in Syria as a long-term political alliance. It is more of a relationship of convenience. Kurdish factions have periodically signaled their willingness to strike a deal with Assad whenever they saw that the direction of the conflict was heading toward his remaining in power. This trend is reinforced by the gradual restoration of bilateral ties between Syria and other Arab countries.[21]

The Rise of Russia

The overall approach of the United States to the Syrian conflict during its first four years paved the way for Russia to enter militarily in September 2015 in support of the Assad regime. As the above overview shows, with the US mainly throwing its weight behind the fight against IS rather than supporting the opposition against Assad, Russia saw in the United States' disengagement from the Syrian conflict an opportunity to assert its geopolitical weight—namely against the United States—at a relatively low cost. Although Russia provided airpower, it deployed limited troops on the ground, relying on Iran-backed groups to perform that role. Russia also used its support for Assad to consolidate its presence on the Mediterranean

---

21 Amberin Zaman, "Syria's Kurds Make Their Own Pitch as Arab States Court Assad," *Al-Monitor*, April 20, 2023, https://www.al-monitor.com/originals/2023/04/syrias-kurds-make-their-own-pitch-arab-states-court-assad.

Sea through its naval base in Tartus, in addition to controlling an air base in Humaymim.[22]

Russia's intervention in the Syrian conflict came at a time when, despite Iran's backing, the Assad regime was under significant pressure from Syrian rebel groups. The Russian intervention can therefore be seen as having provided Assad with a crucial lifeline. The Obama administration hoped that the nuclear deal with Iran would serve to build some trust that could later be harnessed to address other issues like Iran's ballistic missile program and its regional interventions, but the nuclear deal had no bearing on Iran's behavior on either front.[23]

Russia later used its military might to present itself as a power broker, launching the Astana Process with Iran and Turkey in 2017 under the pretext of seeking a peace settlement.[24] The Astana Process came after years of the political process led by the United Nations, which aimed to achieve political transition in Syria according to UN Security Council Resolution 2254, having failed to yield major results, mainly because Assad and Russia deliberately sought to render UN efforts ineffective.[25]

Although the United States continued to paint Iran and Russia as destabilizing actors in the Middle East, successive administrations in Washington chose not to engage Russia bilaterally to try to reach a deal on Syria; nor did the US change course regarding Iran's regional interventions. Under the Trump administration, the US announced a "maximum pressure" policy on Iran, but said policy was limited to increasing sanctions on Iran (and Russia) in 2017, withdrawing from the JCPOA in 2018, and assassinating Islamic Revolutionary Guard Corps leader Qassem Soleimani in Iraq in 2020.[26]

Russia and Iran, meanwhile, continued their military alliance in Syria, using it to project power vis-à-vis the West in general and the United States in particular. They helped one another in evading sanctions, with

---

22 Yuliya Talmazan, "Russia Establishing Permanent Presence at Its Syrian Bases: Minister of Defence," *NBC News*, December 26, 2017, https://www.nbcnews.com/news/world/russia-establishing-permanent-presence-its-syrian-bases-minister-defense-n832596.
23 Based on interviews conducted by the author with US State Department personnel, April 2021.
24 "Syria: The Astana Peace Process," *France 24*, May 9, 2018, https://www.france24.com/en/20180905-syria-astana-peace-process.
25 United Nations Security Council Resolution 2254 (2015), adopted December 18, 2015, https://www.securitycouncilreport.org/atf/cf/%7B65BFCF9B-6D27-4E9C-8CD3-CF6E4FF96FF9%7D/s_res_2254.pdf.
26 Colum Lynch, "Iran: Maximum Pressure, Minimum Gain," *Foreign Policy*, December 23, 2020, https://foreignpolicy.com/2020/12/23/iran-maximum-pressure-trump-policy/.

Iran facilitating Russia's access to the global economy through trade routes across the Middle East, especially for the trade of oil.[27] They both maintained economic relations with various Middle Eastern countries, including countries with which each had political disagreements, such as US allies and partners Turkey and the United Arab Emirates.

Accountability Replaces Diplomacy

The Joe Biden administration has continued on a path of US disengagement in Syria that is similar to those of the administrations of Obama and Trump. When Biden took office, the Middle East in general did not feature highly on the list of US foreign policy priorities, being overshadowed by concerns about China and Russia.[28] The exception was the JCPOA, which Biden wanted the US to rejoin. On Syria, Biden appeared to largely follow in the footsteps of Obama, but without the former president's rhetoric. He even appointed some former Obama administration officials to serve in the National Security Council and other government bodies.

Iran came to indirectly benefit from this increased US disengagement. Among other issues, Biden's criticism of Saudi Arabia while on the campaign trail, as well as his desire to resurrect the nuclear deal with Iran, contributed to frosty relations with the kingdom. This also encouraged other US partners in the Arab world to pursue their own diplomatic deals to try to de-escalate regional tensions—such as the China-brokered rapprochement between Saudi Arabia and Iran in March 2023—in order to protect their national security.[29] Such moves served to signal to the United States that its own Arab partners are willing to keep all options open if America is not going to increase the extent of its engagement in the region to support their national interests.[30]

---

27 Matthew Karnitschnig, "Iran Teaches Russia Its Tricks on Beating Oil Sanctions," *Politico*, November 9, 2022, https://www.politico.eu/article/iran-russia-cooperation-dodging-oil-sanctions/.
28 Joseph Stepansky, "US Foreign Policy in 2021: Key Moments in Biden's First Term," *Al Jazeera*, December 24, 2021, https://www.aljazeera.com/news/2021/12/24/us-foreign-policy-in-2021-key-moments-in-bidens-first-term.
29 Peter Baker, "Chinese-Brokered Deal Upends Mideast Diplomacy and Challenges U.S.," *New York Times*, March 11, 2023, https://www.nytimes.com/2023/03/11/us/politics/saudi-arabia-iran-china-biden.html.
30 Lina Khatib, "Saudi Arabia, Iran and China Offer the U.S. a Lesson in Pragmatism," *World Politics Review*, March 14, 2023, https://www.worldpoliticsreview.com/saudi-arabia-iran-relations-yemen-war-china-us/.

Syria began to fade into the background as a foreign policy agenda item. The United States and the European Union kept insisting that reconstruction funds would only flow into Syria in accordance with UN Security Council Resolution 2254 and that they remain committed to a Syrian-led political transition in the country.[31] They both maintained the sanctions on the Syrian regime that they had implemented and added to throughout the duration of the conflict. The Biden administration continues to uphold the Caesar Act—legislation sanctioning the Assad regime for war crimes—which the 116th Congress passed in December 2019, and which the Trump administration began implementing in 2020.[32]

While measures of accountability are important in the Syrian context, they are not a replacement for diplomacy. Sanctions alone are not a sufficient tool for exerting political pressure. Although the Assad regime's financial and diplomatic status was damaged as a result of western sanctions, the regime, with Iran and Russia's help, continues to survive, and has found an important lifeline in illicit trade. As Assad has now regained control of most of Syria, and as Syrian rebel groups have found themselves with less foreign support than before, it is safe to conclude that Russia, China, Iran, and Arab countries all regard the US role in Syria as diminished. One of the starkest contradictions in US policy is that Washington's concern about Russia did not seem to extend to the country's activities in Syria, where it continued to act with impunity. This contributed in a meaningful way to emboldening Russia in its subsequent invasion of Ukraine in 2022.

The Route to Peace in Syria Passes Through Washington

Russia, Iran, Turkey, and other Middle Eastern actors have all been pursuing geopolitical interests based on pragmatism and the compartmentalization of economic, military, and political relationships instead of adhering to clear political camps. US disengagement in Syria has contributed to this ongoing dynamic. It is therefore not surprising that many Arab countries are heading in the direction of normalization with Assad. It is unlikely

---

31 "No Normalization for Syria without 'Permanent Political Change': Washington," *The Cradle*, April 27, 2023, https://thecradle.co/article-view/24102/no-normalization-for-syria-without-permanent-political-change-washington.

32 U.S. Congress, House, *Caesar Syria Civilian Protection Act of 2019*, H.R.31, 116th Congress, 1st sess., introduced in House January 3, 2019, https://www.congress.gov/bill/116th-congress/house-bill/31.

that re-engaging Assad means that any Arab country is going to fund reconstruction in Syria in a major way or trust the Assad regime. Serious contentious issues remain unresolved, mainly the matter of the thousands of detainees held by the regime, Syria's heavy involvement in the international drug trade, the status of millions of Syrian refugees and internally displaced persons, and the presence of Iran-backed militias in Syria.

The Assad regime wanted to return to the Arab League without conditions, and appears to have succeeded in doing so, having been reinstated on May 7, 2023, despite objections from Qatar and other member states.[33] But with US elections looming in 2024, some Arab countries like Saudi Arabia remain keen to see a new US administration that is more engaged in the region in ways that serve their political and security interests. Meanwhile, the UN Syria peace process is stalled indefinitely. What is clear is that the route to peace in Syria still passes through Washington, at least in part. US inaction and disengagement are just as consequential as engagement, and as the Russian intervention in Ukraine shows, the consequences of inaction in the Middle East can stretch far beyond the region itself.

---

33 Aidan Lewis and Sarah El Safety, "Arab League Readmits Syria as Relations with Assad Normalise," *Reuters*, May 7, 2023, https://www.reuters.com/world/middle-east/arab-league-set-readmit-syria-relations-with-assad-normalise-2023-05-07/.

The Mutual Pivot to Asia in US-Egypt Relations

Sahar Aziz

The current geopolitical inflection point in international relations puts into question the significance of the Middle East in US foreign policy over the next few decades. Egypt, the most populous nation in the Middle East and strategically located at the northeast tip of Africa, is betting its significance to the United States can withstand this shift to a multipolar order. While many of the factors binding Egypt-US relations today also shaped the Anwar al-Sadat and Hosni Mubarak regimes' reliance on American backing, the Obama administration's support for the people in the 2011 Egyptian Revolution set off alarms for prospective Middle East autocrats. Exclusive reliance on US patronage for political survival is no longer a secure bet.

Since coming to power in 2014, Egyptian President Abdel Fattah el-Sisi's top foreign policy priority has been to diversify Egypt's foreign relations and military purchases. After strengthening ties with and securing foreign aid from Saudi Arabia and the United Arab Emirates, Sisi expanded Egypt's military purchases to France and Russia, while also welcoming China's investments in his ambitious infrastructure plans.

Simultaneously, the US government's "pivot to Asia," announced under the Obama administration but begun in earnest under President Joe Biden, further incentivized Sisi to diversify Egypt's economic and military relations.[1] Hence a mutual pivot East, for different reasons.

Four factors are most likely to impact the contours of Egypt-US relations during this new era of global competition. First, Egypt's substantial and decades-long dependence on US military aid is likely to remain steady so long as Israel retains its special favored-nation status in US foreign policy. Second, Egypt's control of the Suez Canal secures its geopolitical significance since maritime shipping remains a substantial means of global trade. Third, rapidly worsening economic conditions for the most populous nation in the Middle East could trigger mass uprisings, increased undocumented migration to Europe, and political conflict in a volatile region. Finally, China's increased interest in trade and infrastructure investments in Egypt as part of its expanding interests in Africa is likely to erode America's ability to influence the Egyptian government's policies.

Notably peripheral in the bilateral relations calculus are human rights and the promotion of democracy. The dual failures of the Arab Spring and America's military interventions in Afghanistan and Iraq leave little appetite among Americans for exporting democracy to the Middle East. Whatever pledges Biden has made to put human rights at the heart of his foreign policy, they are likely intended to condemn communist China, which is eclipsing the Middle East's significance in Washington.[2] The Middle East is now a secondary or tertiary foreign policy priority.

America's Pivot Away from the Middle East

The Biden administration's 2022 National Security Strategy unequivocally identifies China as the top global priority. Having declared victory in the Global War on Terror, Biden announced "a consequential new period of American foreign policy that will demand more of the United States in the Indo-Pacific than has been asked of us since the Second World War. No region will be of more significance to the world and to everyday

---

1 Hillary Clinton, "America's Pacific Century," *Foreign Policy*, October 11, 2011, https://foreignpolicy.com/2011/10/11/americas-pacific-century/.; Elise Labott, "Can Biden Finally Put the Middle East in Check and Pivot Already?," *Foreign Policy*, March 2, 2021, https://foreignpolicy.com/2021/03/02/biden-middle-east-china-pivot-clinton-obama/.
2 Simon Lewis and Humeyra Pamuk, "Biden Put Rights at Heart of US Foreign Policy. Then He Pulled Punches," *Reuters*, Sept. 13, 2021, https://www.reuters.com/world/asia-pacific/biden-put-rights-heart-us-foreign-policy-then-he-pulled-punches-2021-09-13/.

Americans than the Indo-Pacific."[3] As a result, the US is seeking to contain the rise of China through military alliances in Southeast Asia, South Asia, and the Pacific. The US "will seek greater strategic stability through measures that reduce the risk of unintended military escalation, enhance crisis communications, build mutual transparency, and ultimately engage Beijing on more formal arms control efforts."[4]

Not until the final pages of the National Security Strategy is the importance of the Middle East acknowledged, and only in connection with America's "ironclad commitment" to Israel's security. In a turnabout from the past two decades, Biden states that the US "will not use our military to change regimes or remake societies, but instead limit the use of force to circumstances where it is necessary to protect our national security interests and consistent with international law, while enabling our partners to defend their territory from external and terrorist threats."[5] The strategy's emphasis on building integrated air and maritime defense structures signals that only countries that further those goals will remain relevant. That the promotion of human rights and the values enshrined in the United Nations charter is the final point in the strategy is further evidence of America's shift away from democracy promotion after the Arab Spring.

Although there is no specific mention of Egypt in the National Security Strategy, control of the Suez Canal, a shared border with Israel, and having the largest population in the region all make Egypt too important for the United States to ignore. Moreover, the Egyptian military is the most powerful institution in the country and maintains strong strategic relations with the United States.[6] These factors keep Egypt relevant, though not a priority, in US foreign policy.

Egypt's Strategic Location and Military Dependence on the US

When Egypt signed a peace treaty in 1979 with Israel—America's strongest ally outside of Europe—its relevance was secured in US foreign policy for decades to come. Since then, Egypt has received military aid from the

---

3 "National Security Strategy 2022," The White House, October 2022, p. 38, https://www.whitehouse.gov/wp-content/uploads/2022/11/8-November-Combined-PDF-for-Upload.pdf.
4 Ibid., 25.
5 Ibid., 43.
6 "Strengthening the US-Egyptian Relationship, Council on Foreign Relations, May 30, 2002, https://www.cfr.org/report/strengthening-us-egyptian-relationship.

United States that surpasses $1 billion per year.[7] The latest aid package of $1.4 billion in 2023 ($1.3 billion in military assistance) brought total US aid to Egypt since 1946 to $87 billion.[8] Military aid thus constitutes a significant portion of the Egyptian military's annual budget. Pursuant to US law, the aid can only be spent on purchases of US military equipment, arms, and training, thereby maintaining relations between the Egyptian and American militaries.[9]

While the Israel-Egypt peace deal was the impetus for establishing the large annual military aid package, the United States' significant economic interests in the global arms market also incentivize large foreign military aid packages. According to a 2020 survey, 42 of the world's 100 largest defense firms are based in the United States, including seven of the top ten.[10] Successive administrations have thus understood that foreign aid packages boost American arms sales, which are essential for keeping the nation's defense industry competitive and innovative.

The Middle East has long been a key driver of the global weapons trade, to a disproportionate degree relative to its population. Some states in this heavily militarized region are major arms purchasers, empowered by partnerships with foreign allies and wealth derived from vast energy reserves. For example, from 2015 to 2019, the Middle East accounted for an estimated 35 percent of global arms imports.[11] Notably, the United States has been the single largest arms supplier to the Middle East by volume and value for decades.[12] Between 1950 and 2017, the Middle East accounted for over $379 billion in US foreign military sales agreements.[13] Russia and France were the second and third largest arms suppliers, at 19.3

---

7   Jeremy M. Sharp, "Egypt: Background and U.S. Relations," Congressional Research Service, updated May 2, 2023, https://crsreports.congress.gov/product/pdf/RL/RL33003/122.
8   "Fact Sheet – U.S. Military Assistance to Egypt: Separating Fact from Fiction," Project on Middle East Democracy, July 30, 2020, https://pomed.org/publication/fact-sheet-u-s-military-assistance-to-egypt-separating-fact-from-fiction/.; Edward Wong and Vivian Yee, "U.S. to Move Forward on Military Aid to Egypt Despite Lawmakers' Concerns," *New York Times*, September 14, 2022, https://www.nytimes.com/2022/09/14/us/politics/egypt-military-aid-biden.html.
9   Sharp, "Egypt: Background and U.S. Relations."
10 Clayton Thomas et al., "Arms Sales in the Middle East: Trends and Analytical Perspectives for U.S. Policy," Congressional Research Service, updated November 23, 2020, https://crsreports.congress.gov/product/pdf/R/R44984/7.
11 Ibid., 1–2.
12 Ibid., 2.
13 Ibid.

percent and 11.4 percent respectively, of all Middle East arms imports between 2015 and 2019.[14] Meanwhile, China accounted for a mere 2.5 percent of arms imported into the region between 2000 and 2019.[15] Thus, China's regional impact is primarily in the economic sphere.

The Egyptian Army is the second largest in the Middle East, making it a critical regional ally and global arms importer. Most of Egypt's arms purchases are paid with US foreign military financing (FMF) grants offered in the annual military aid package. FMF grants must be spent on US defense equipment, services, and training, which explains why 47 percent of Egyptian arms acquisitions came from the United States between 2010 and 2014.[16]

However, the Obama administration's policies toward Egypt angered its military generals. The United States' failure to stand by former General Hosni Mubarak during the 2011 Revolution, its acceptance of Muslim Brotherhood candidate Mohamed Morsi's presidential victory, and its freeze on a substantial portion of aircraft, tank, and missile sales to Egypt for two years after the military deposed Morsi in 2013 rang alarm bells within the military. Sisi responded by diversifying Egypt's military suppliers for the stated purpose of decreasing reliance on the United States.[17] Egypt's arms purchases from the US dropped to 15 percent of its total purchases from 2015 to 2019, while they simultaneously increased from France and Russia to 35 percent and 34 percent, respectively.[18] The tens of billions of dollars in aid to Egypt from the Gulf countries since 2013 increased the percentage of the military budget that could be spent on non-US military equipment.[19] As a result, between 2018 and 2022, Egypt

---

14 Ibid.
15 Ibid., 7.
16 Ibid., 15.
17 Bradley Bowman et al., "Egypt's Transition Away from American Weapons Is a National Security Issue," *Defense News*, May 25, 2021, https://www.defensenews.com/opinion/commentary/2021/05/25/egypts-transition-away-from-american-weapons-is-a-national-security-issue/.; "Policy of 'Diversification' Allows Egypt Not to Be Hostage to US Pressures," *The Arab Weekly*, February 22, 2022, https://thearabweekly.com/policy-diversification-allows-egypt-not-be-hostage-us-pressures.
18 Thomas et al., "Arms Sales in the Middle East," 15.
19 Nadeen Ebrahim, "Gulf States Have Given Billions in Aid to Egypt. Now They Want to See Returns," *CNN*, March 1, 2023, https://www.cnn.com/2023/03/01/business/egypt-gulf-states-aid-mime-intl/index.html.; Khalil al-Anani, "Gulf Countries' Aid to Egypt: It Is Politics, Not the Economy, Stupid!," Arab Center Washington DC, May 5, 2022, https://arabcenterdc.org/resource/gulf-countries-aid-to-egypt-it-is-politics-not-the-economy-stupid/.

was the sixth largest arms importer globally, with Russia, Italy, and France being its principal suppliers.[20]

Despite this diversification of arms purchases, the decades-long pipeline of US ammunition, spare parts, and maintenance makes Egypt's military dependent on the United States for sustained military operations. A grave economic crisis, combined with record levels of external debt, may give Sisi no choice but to rely primarily on US aid for future military supplies. But as Egypt increasingly relies on China and the Gulf states for foreign investments, US influence is waning in the economic sphere.

Egypt's Economic Crisis Attracts Chinese Investment and Influence

Twelve years after the historic January 25, 2011 Revolution, the most pervasive grievance among Egyptians arises from the country's deteriorating economic conditions.[21] Skyrocketing inflation, the devaluation of the Egyptian pound, and stagnant wages have sliced the average Egyptian household's purchasing power in half.[22] As a result, the World Bank classifies 60 percent of Egyptians as poor or vulnerable.[23] All the while, Egypt's hundreds of thousands of college graduates each year struggle to find gainful employment in the formal sector that matches their skills. To be sure, political instability arising from the Arab Spring initially triggered an economic decline. But government mismanagement and Sisi's ambitious infrastructure projects have caused the national debt to reach an unprecedented $165 billion.[24]

Since the military forcibly removed President Mohamed Morsi in 2013, the Egyptian economy has been propped up by over $100 billion in grants from the Gulf countries. This aid includes Central Bank deposits, fuel assistance, and other forms of aid, most of which are provided with

---

20 Jeremy M. Sharp, "Egypt: Background and U.S. Relations."
21 Michel Martin and Aya Batrawy, "Egypt Faces a Deepening Economic Crisis. Is the Government Taking Steps to Fix It?," *National Public Radio*, March 28, 2023, https://www.npr.org/2023/03/28/1166422786/egypt-the-middle-easts-biggest-country-is-facing-a-deepening-economic-crisis.; Samy Magdy, "In Egypt, Government and Poor Struggle with Troubled Economy," *Associated Press*, March 1, 2023, https://apnews.com/article/egypt-economic-crisis-inflation-russia-ukraine-war-0bf22bb11d5b7fe2060eac52279b9df3.
22 Cathrin Schaer, "Economic Crisis: Is Egypt the 'New Lebanon?,'" *Deutsche Welle*, January 20, 2023, https://www.dw.com/en/economic-crisis-is-egypt-the-new-lebanon/a-64469810.
23 Sharp, "Egypt: Background and U.S. Relations," 5.
24 Yezid Sayigh, "Egypt Is Missing Its IMF Loan Program Targets," Carnegie Endowment for International Peace, July 6, 2023, https://carnegie-mec.org/diwan/90134.

few conditions.[25] Additionally, Egypt has received over $13 billion from International Monetary Fund (IMF) grants conditioned on macroeconomic reforms.[26] But rather than using these and other funds to strengthen the economy, President Sisi went on a spending spree, expanding the Suez Canal, building a new administrative capital on the outskirts of Cairo, and purchasing billions of dollars' worth of military equipment.

By 2022, Egypt had a debt service provision of $28 billion, which exceeded the total value of exports and amounted to four times the annual revenues from the Suez Canal.[27] As a result, the country's annual debt service consumes nearly half of the state budget, among the highest ratios in the world, which led Moody's to downgrade Egypt's sovereign credit rating from B2 to B3 in 2023.[28] Egypt is also the second largest IMF debtor after Argentina, which, combined with other external debt, has produced a budget financing gap of $17 billion over the next four years.[29] Sisi is presumably relying on his Gulf allies and China to assist in covering this shortfall. The assistance is sure to increase China's influence in Egypt's domestic and foreign policy over time.

---

25 Jonathan Fenton-Harvey, "Why Unconditional Gulf Financing for Egypt is Dwindling," *The New Arab*, February 15, 2023, https://www.newarab.com/analysis/why-unconditional-gulf-financing-egypt-dwindling.

26 "Egypt: History of Lending Commitments as of February 28, 2021," International Monetary Fund, February 28, 2021, https://www.imf.org/external/np/fin/tad/extarr2.aspx?memberKey1=275&date1key=2021-02-28.; "IMF Executive Board Approves 46-month US $3 Billion Extended Arrangement for Egypt," International Monetary Fund, December 16, 2022, https://www.imf.org/en/News/Articles/2022/12/16/pr22441-egypt-imf-executive-board-approves-46-month-usd3b-extended-arrangement.; Richard Thompson, "GCC States Pledge to Invest $12bn in Egyptian Economy," *Middle East Business Intelligence*, March, 14, 2015, https://www.meed.com/gcc-states-pledge-to-invest-12bn-in-egyptian-economy/.

27 Mahmoud Hassan, "Creditors Are Standing on Egypt's Doorstep," *Middle East Monitor*, April 3, 2023, https://www.middleeastmonitor.com/20230403-creditors-are-standing-on-egypts-doorstep/.; "Egypt's Suez Canal Revenue Hits $7 Billion Record Peak," *Reuters*, July 5, 2022, https://www.reuters.com/business/egypts-suez-canal-revenue-hits-7-bln-record-peak-2022-07-04/.

28 Vansh Agarwal, "Moody's Cuts Egypt Rating to B3, Changes Outlook to Stable," *Reuters*, https://www.reuters.com/world/africa/moodys-cuts-egypt-rating-b3-changes-outlook-stable-2023-02-07/.

29 Lee Ying Shan, "Egypt's Pound Is Among the Worst Performing Currencies in 2023. And It's Expected to Plummet Further," *CNBC*, April 4, 2023, https://www.cnbc.com/2023/04/05/the-egyptian-pound-is-amongst-the-worst-performing-currencies-in-2023.html.

Meanwhile, Egypt's foreign exchange reserve stands at just $34.35 billion, of which $28 billion are deposits made by Saudi Arabia, Kuwait, Qatar, and the United Arab Emirates.[30] The Gulf states' outsized influence in Egypt is driven by their own domestic politics. The monarchies' largesse was initially driven by their desire to prevent the Arab Spring from spreading to their countries and stop the Muslim Brotherhood's electoral success in Egypt from expanding regionally. Having accomplished these goals, the Gulf nations are not as motivated to give Egypt unconditional loans. Indeed, recent influxes of Gulf funds have been limited to purchases of Egyptian state-owned assets or private companies.[31]

China has also leveraged the precarity of Egypt's economy to expand its sphere of influence in Africa. For example, in 2014 Egypt signed a strategic partnership agreement with China that pledged cooperation on defense, technology, and the economy.[32] Two years later, 20 more bilateral agreements were signed that increased China's investments in Egypt by more than 300 percent.[33] Most recently, in 2023 China committed to investing $2 billion in iron and steel plants in the Suez Canal Economic Zone.[34] Another entry point into Egypt's economy is China's Belt and Road Initiative (BRI), which aims to develop new trade linkages, cultivate export markets, boost Chinese incomes, and export China's excess productive capacity.[35] Almost 139 countries—accounting for nearly two-thirds of

---

30 "Egypt's Foreign Reserves Surge to over $34Bn in February," *Arab News*, March 6, 2023, https://www.arabnews.com/node/2263416/business-economy.
31 "Gulf States Play Hardball over Sending Billions to Rescue Egypt," *Middle East Monitor*, February 25, 2023, https://www.middleeastmonitor.com/20230225-gulf-states-play-hardball-over-sending-billions-to-rescue-egypt/.; "Cash-Strapped Egypt Prompts Unprecedented Gulf Acquisition of Stakes in Major State-Companies," *Middle East Monitor*, February 16, 2023, https://www.middleeastmonitor.com/20230216-cash-strapped-egypt-prompts-unprecedented-gulf-acquisition-of-stakes-in-major-state-companies/.
32 "China, Egypt Sign Strategic Partnership Agreement," *The Economic Times*, December 24, 2014, https://economictimes.indiatimes.com/news/international/business/china-egypt-sign-strategic-partnership-agreement/articleshow/45629765.cms?from=mdr.
33 Mohamed Maher and Mohamed Farid, "The Growth of Chinese Influence in Egypt: Signs and Consequences, Fikra Forum, April 27, 2023, https://www.washingtoninstitute.org/policy-analysis/growth-chinese-influence-egypt-signs-and-consequences.
34 "China's Xinxing to Invest $2 Bln in Suez Canal Economic Zone—Egyptian Cabinet," *Reuters*, March 23, 2023, https://www.reuters.com/markets/commodities/chinas-xinxing-invest-2-bln-suez-canal-economic-zone-egyptian-cabinet-2023-03-23/.
35 Jacob J. Lew et al., "China's Belt and Road: Implications for the United States," Council on Foreign Relations, updated March 2021, https://www.cfr.org/task-force-report/chinas-belt-and-road-implications-for-the-united-states/.

the world's population and 40 percent of global GDP—have signed on to BRI projects.[36] Seventeen of those countries are in the Middle East and North Africa, including Egypt.

Consequently, China was Egypt's largest trading partner for eight consecutive years after 2013. In the first 11 months in 2022, China exported over $13 billion worth of goods to Egypt, and Egypt exported $1.7 billion to China.[37] Egyptian industry is heavily reliant on Chinese imports for machinery, electrical appliances, boilers, and mechanical tools. Meanwhile, Egypt ranked as merely the 54th largest US trading partner in 2022 at $9.4 billion, even though it is the largest export market for US goods in Africa.[38]

China is also investing in major infrastructure and construction projects in Sisi's New Administrative Capital and the coastal city of al-Alamein. The China Fortune Land Development Company, for example, invested $20 billion in 2016 toward construction of the new capital.[39] In 2015, China State Construction Engineering Corporation signed a $15 billion deal to build the Iconic Tower building in the new capital.[40] In comparison, US foreign direct investment in Egypt has been approximately $11 billion a year since 2016, largely limited to the oil and natural gas sectors.[41] As Egypt's fourth largest creditor and largest trading partner, China has effectively purchased influence in Egypt's economic future alongside the Gulf nations. The impact on US-Egypt relations is twofold: a confinement of US influence to military and security policy as they relate to Israel and the Suez Canal, and a loss of leverage for improving Egypt's human rights record.

---

36 David Sacks, "Countries in China's Belt and Road Initiative: Who's In and Who's Out," Council on Foreign Relations, March 24, 2021, https://www.cfr.org/blog/countries-chinas-belt-and-road-initiative-whos-and-whos-out.
37 "Egypt's Exports to China Rises by Nearly 21% in 2022," *Arab News*, updated March 12, 2023, https://www.arabnews.com/node/2267171/business-economy.
38 Sharp, "Egypt: Background and U.S. Relations."
39 Kieron Monks, "Egypt Is Getting a New Capital – Courtesy of China," *CNN*, October 10, 2016, https://www.cnn.com/style/article/egypt-new-capital/index.html.
40 Grady McGregor, "China Emerges as Lead Funder for Egypt's New Administrative City," *Al-Monitor*, December 20, 2022, https://www.al-monitor.com/originals/2022/12/china-emerges-lead-funder-egypts-new-administrative-city.
41 "Egypt - International Trade and Investment Country Facts," Bureau of Economic Analysis, undated, https://apps.bea.gov/international/factsheet/factsheet.html#410.

A Pivot Away from Human Rights

Mainstream narratives on US human rights policy in the Middle East posit security and human rights as competing, rather than complementary, foreign policy interests. Put another way, "Confronting partner governments over their political shortcomings risks triggering hostility that would jeopardize the security benefits that such governments provide to Washington. Yet giving them a free pass on democracy and rights issues undercuts the credibility of US appeals to values, bolstering the damaging perception that America only pushes for democracy against its adversaries or in strategically irrelevant countries."[42] The record of successive US administrations clearly demonstrates that purported security benefits always supersede stated commitments to human rights.

Former President George W. Bush, for example, declared a goal of democracy promotion, but its implementation translated into a military occupation of Afghanistan and Iraq and superficial electoral reforms in Egypt.[43] The resulting civil wars and political violence caused the Obama administration to prioritize stability over political and human rights. Despite initially supporting the 2011 Egyptian Revolution, President Obama refused to label the military's forced removal of Egypt's democratically elected president in 2013 a coup to avoid triggering US legal prohibitions on military aid.[44] Congress, in contrast, enforced its human rights agenda through appropriations measures that withheld certain portions of Egypt's foreign military funds unless the executive branch could certify Egypt's progress on various metrics related to human rights.[45] However, these laws grant the executive branch the authority to waive such restrictions on national security grounds, which successive secretaries of state have routinely done. By the time Donald Trump became US

---

42 Thomas Carothers and Benjamin Press, "Navigating the Democracy Security Dilemma in US Foreign Policy: Lessons from Egypt, India, and Turkey," Carnegie Endowment for International Peace, November 04, 2021, https://carnegieendowment.org/2021/11/04/navigating-democracy-security-dilemma-in-US-foreign-policy-lessons-from-egypt-india-and-turkey-pub-85701.

43 Sahar F. Aziz, "Revolution Without Reform? A Critique of Egypt's Election Laws," *George Washington International Law Review* 45 (2012): 101–180, https://dx.doi.org/10.2139/ssrn.2026475.

44 Christopher M. Blanchard, "Congress and the Middle East, 2011-2020: Selected Case Studies," Congressional Research Service, May 21, 2021, https://crsreports.congress.gov/product/pdf/R/R46796/6.

45 Ibid., 28.

president, the changes in human rights policy were more in rhetoric than policy. While Trump made no secret of his disregard for human rights when executing multibillion-dollar arms deals with Saudi Arabia and the United Arab Emirates, Biden is continuing business as usual with Middle East nations whose human rights records remain abysmal.[46]

In attempting to fulfill his pledge to put human rights at the heart of his foreign policy, Biden withheld $130 million in security aid from Egypt in 2021 and 2022 over its human rights record.[47] A separate tranche of $75 million was released in 2022 after the State Department made the contested conclusion that Egypt had met the congressional requirement of exhibiting "clear and consistent progress in releasing political prisoners and providing detainees with due process of law."[48] Human rights groups criticized this decision on the grounds that Sisi's prisoner releases were offset by new arrests of political prisoners. The split decision on military aid to Egypt continues the standard US practice of applying pressure on Egypt over its poor human rights record while rewarding incremental steps by this Middle East ally.

Meanwhile, the growing influence of China and the Gulf nations is likely to make US policy irrelevant in this realm. Not only do all these countries possess poor human rights records but they also intentionally exclude individual rights or political freedom from their foreign policy calculus. Thus, whatever pressure the Biden administration is willing to place on Egypt to comply with human rights laws is likely to fall on deaf ears in Cairo, unless the national security waivers for military aid are not granted.

---

46 Wajahat Ali, "Why Is Trump Still Ignoring Saudi Arabia's Brutal Human Rights Abuses?" *NBC News*, April 2, 2019, https://www.nbcnews.com/think/opinion/why-trump-still-ignoring-saudi-arabia-s-brutal-human-rights-ncna989806.; "Trump's First International Tour Raises Red Flags for Human Rights in Middle East," Amnesty International, May 19, 2017, https://www.amnesty.org/en/latest/news/2017/05/trumps-first-international-tour-raises-red-flags-for-human-rights-in-middle-east/.; Nick Shifrin, "Biden faces criticism for not doing more on human rights during Middle East trip," *PBS Newshour*, July 19, 2022, https://www.pbs.org/newshour/show/biden-faces-criticism-for-not-doing-more-on-human-rights-during-middle-east-trip#audio.; Sahar Aziz, "Sure, the US Cares about Human Rights — When It Benefits Us," *The Hill*, June 28, 2023, https://thehill.com/opinion/international/4070170-sure-the-us-cares-about-human-rights-when-it-benefits-us/.
47 Missy Ryan, "U.S. Blocks $130 Million in Aid to Egypt over Human Rights," *Washington Post*, September 14, 2022, https://www.washingtonpost.com/national-security/2022/09/14/us-blocks-130-million-aid-egypt-over-human-rights/.
48 Wong and Yee, "U.S. to Move Forward."

Despite minor variations across US administrations, human rights have never truly been a top priority in US Middle East policy. Absent domestic pressure on American elected officials, the pivot to Asia risks making human rights even less relevant in global politics. That China and the Gulf states do not care about the human rights records of their allies—much less their own—further emboldens the Egyptian government to ignore its human rights obligations.

Conclusion

Evolving global political realities are sure to change US-Egypt relations.[49] As President Biden deprioritizes the Middle East in his focus on great power competition with China and Russia, President Sisi is deprioritizing the US in his domestic and foreign policy.[50] In turn, the US will streamline its engagement with Egypt to securing the Israeli border, retaining Egypt's dependence on US military equipment through foreign aid, and preventing the collapse of the Egyptian economy through IMF and World Bank loans conditioned on neoliberal economic reforms. Democracy and human rights will remain marginal, except as a strategic tool for shunning President Sisi for any actions that threaten Israel's security or US military dominance in the Middle East.

Looking ahead, domestic developments that threaten Egypt's political stability, and consequently its economy, are likely to be more influenced by China and the Gulf nations than the United States. While this may prove inconsequential for the US pivot to Asia in the short term, Egypt may become firmly set within China's expanding sphere of influence in a multipolar world order gradually replacing American global hegemony. And if past is prologue, merely replacing one great power for another does little to empower the people of the Middle East to establish an indigenous democratic system that values their lives and dignity.

---

49   Brian Katulis and Peter Juul, "Strategic Reengagement in the Middle East," Center for American Progress, December 16, 2021, https://www.americanprogress.org/article/strategic-reengagement-in-the-middle-east/.
50   Natasha Bertrand and Lara Seligman, "Biden Deprioritizes the Middle East," *Politico*, February 22, 2021, https://www.politico.com/news/2021/02/22/biden-middle-east-foreign-policy-470589.

Iran and the Perceived US Pivot Away from the Middle East

Mahsa Rouhi[1]

There is a growing perception in the Middle East that the United States' role in the region is undergoing a significant shift. In the early 2000s, this role was primarily shaped by the post-September 11 environment, as the Bush administration pursued its global war on terror, invading Afghanistan in 2001 and Iraq in 2003. In his first post-9/11 State of the Union address, former President George W. Bush named Iran as a principal threat to international peace and security, one of three countries constituting an "axis of evil."[2] Even though the Bush administration called for the promotion of democracy throughout the Middle East as a strategy to win the war on terror, Iranian leaders believed that their country could be the next target for a US invasion.[3] The scale of the US presence, coupled with the

---

1 Dr. Mahsa Rouhi is a Research Fellow at the Center for Strategic Research at National Defense University's Institute for National Strategic Studies (INSS). The views expressed are her own and do not reflect the official policy or position of the National Defense University, the Department of Defense, or the US government.
2 George W. Bush, "State of the Union Address," The White House, January 29, 2002. https://georgewbush-whitehouse.archives.gov/news/releases/2002/01/20020129-11.html.

Bush administration's rhetoric, led Iran to believe that the US would play and maintain a dominant role in the region. Tehran's perceptions regarding the threat the United States poses have significantly changed over the past decade due to a variety of factors and geopolitical developments.

The introduction of the "pivot to Asia" under the Obama administration in 2011, which sought deeper relations with Asian and Pacific partners (increasingly viewed as the world's "political and economic center of gravity"), along with former President Donald Trump's decision to reduce the number of US troops in Iraq and Afghanistan, current President Joe Biden's withdrawal from Afghanistan, and US efforts to reduce support for the war in Yemen are but a few factors that have contributed to the perception that the United States is and has been pivoting away from the region.[4] US-Iran relations and the occasional conflict in security priorities between the United States and its regional partners regarding Iran, Yemen, and Syria have reinforced emerging perceptions among both regional and global actors of America's waning presence and influence in the Middle East.[5]

Regardless of whether the US pivot is a reality or a myth, these growing perceptions are driving policy decisions in the region, which could create

---

3 "Fact Sheet: President Bush Calls for a 'Forward Strategy of Freedom' to Promote Democracy in the Middle East," The White House, November 6, 2003, https://georgewbush-whitehouse.archives.gov/news/releases/2003/11/20031106-11.html.; Suzanne Maloney, "U.S. Policy Toward Iran: Missed Opportunities and Paths Forward," *The Fletcher Forum of World Affairs* 32, no. 2 (Summer 2008): 25–44, https://www.brookings.edu/wp-content/uploads/2016/06/summer_iran_maloney.pdf.

4 The "pivot to Asia" or "rebalancing" strategy has continued through President Trump and President Biden Administrations, as indicated in national security documents. There is an argument that while this concept was officially introduced or labeled during the Obama administration, "the United States pursued a strategy of reorientation toward Asia from the mid-2000s onward," in: Nina Silove, "The Pivot before the Pivot: U.S. Strategy to Preserve the Power Balance in Asia." *Quarterly Journal: International Security* 40, no. 4. (Spring 2016): 45–88. See also: "Fact Sheet: Advancing the Rebalance to Asia and the Pacific," The White House, November 16, 2015, https://obamawhitehouse.archives.gov/the-press-office/2015/11/16/fact-sheet-advancing-rebalance-asia-and-pacific. On US forces and commitments, see: Jim Garamone, "U.S. Will Draw Down Forces in Afghanistan, Iraq, Acting Secretary Says," *U.S. Department of Defense News*, November 17, 2020, https://www.defense.gov/News/News-Stories/Article/Article/2418416/us-will-draw-down-forces-in-afghanistan-iraq-acting-secretary-says/. And see: "Around the Halls: Brookings Experts on Biden's Performance in the Middle East," Brookings Institution, February 3, 2023, https://www.brookings.edu/blog/order-from-chaos/2023/02/03/around-the-halls-brookings-experts-on-bidens-performance-in-the-middle-east/.

a new reality in the long run. One of the key issues impacting the security strategy for Middle Eastern countries has been tensions surrounding Iran's nuclear program. In the lead-up to the implementation of the 2015 Joint Comprehensive Plan of Action (JCPOA), US allies and partners in the region expressed concerns that the JCPOA would only embolden the Iranian regime since the deal failed to address their principal security concerns, namely the Islamic Republic's ballistic missile program and its network of non-state actors.[6] Since the US withdrawal from the agreement in 2018 and former President Trump's subsequent "maximum pressure" approach, US-Iran relations have been increasingly strained, resulting in a cycle of escalatory exchanges.[7] Iran views US partners in the region as an extension of American interests, and has thus targeted regional rivals as a means of imposing costs on America. Attacks on Saudi Arabian oil facilities, strikes on American military bases in Iraq, and confrontations and attacks in the Strait of Hormuz have all signaled the cost of US-Iran escalation for Gulf Arab states.[8]

Throughout the escalating tensions, there were still efforts to revive the JCPOA, though none meaningfully materialized. After an initial stalemate, negotiations to revive the agreement began in Spring 2021. Returning to the deal, however, proved to be more complicated. The main points of contention included guarantees on US compliance, the limitations of effective sanctions relief, and Iran's nuclear advancements, which rendered the original terms of the deal less effective due to the stockpile

---

5   Max Boot, "As a Post-American Middle East Dawns, Iran and China Rush to Fill the Void," *Washington Post*, May 8, 2023, https://www.washingtonpost.com/opinions/2023/05/08/united-states-influence-middle-east-iran-china.; Gerald M. Feierstein et al., "US-Gulf Relations at the Crossroads: Time for a Recalibration," Middle East Institute, April 2022, https://www.mei.edu/sites/default/files/2022-04/US-Gulf%20Relations%20at%20a%20Crossroads%20-%20Time%20for%20a%20Recalibration.pdf.
6   "The Middle East After the Iran Nuclear Deal," Council on Foreign Relations, September 3, 2015, https://www.cfr.org/expert-roundup/middle-east-after-iran-nuclear-deal.
7   "Fact Sheet: President Donald J. Trump is Ending United States Participation in an Unacceptable Iran Deal," The White House, May 8, 2018, https://trumpwhitehouse.archives.gov/briefings-statements/president-donald-j-trump-ending-united-states-participation-unacceptable-iran-deal/.; "Confrontation with Iran," Council on Foreign Relations, January 6, 2023, https://www.cfr.org/global-conflict-tracker/conflict/confrontation-between-united-states-and-iran.
8   Mahsa Rouhi, "Whatever Iran's Role in the Saudi Attack, the Regional Status Quo Is Unsustainable," *The Guardian*, September 18, 2019, https://www.theguardian.com/commentisfree/2019/sep/18/iran-saudi-attack-nuclear-deal-us.

Iran had acquired, its higher levels of enrichment, and the irreversible nature of research and development knowledge.[9] More recently, both Iran's brutal crackdown on protests in the wake of Kurdish Iranian woman Mahsa Amini's death at the hands of the country's "morality police" and its support for Russia's war in Ukraine effectively dealt the final blows to the chance of reviving the nuclear deal.

The structural challenges, coupled with the political challenges, have left few alternatives to contain Iran's nuclear program in a sustainable manner and little possibility of rapprochement between the United States and Iran, at least in the short run. With no comprehensive agreement on Iran's nuclear program, there exist both a high level of uncertainty and elevated threat perceptions for countries in the region, which fear that the likely outcome of this situation is either a nuclear-armed Iran or a regional conflict between the Islamic Republic and the United States and Israel, with major consequences and costs for regional states, particularly those of the Gulf Cooperation Council (GCC).[10]

This has led to US partners and allies diversifying and revising their security strategies and partnerships in the region and globally, particularly regarding Iran, Russia, and China, thereby positioning themselves to be able to adjust to this unpredictable geopolitical context. Intensifying strategic competition between great powers has been viewed by revisionists such as Iran as an opportunity to capitalize on waning US influence and to challenge the US-led liberal international order. Ultimately, perceptions about a US pivot will have major implications for future Middle East security, and could reshape alliances, partnerships, and eventually the geopolitical landscape itself.

Shifting Strategic Partnerships

After former President Trump withdrew the US from the JCPOA, the remaining parties to the deal—Europe, Russia, China, and Iran—began efforts to salvage it, seeking pathways to circumvent US sanctions and provide Iran the economic relief that was to be exchanged for its continued

---

9   Esfandyar Batmanghelidj and Mahsa Rouhi, "The Iran Nuclear Deal and Sanctions Relief: Implications for US Policy." *Survival* 63, no. 4 (2021): 183–98, https://doi.org/10.1080/00396338.2021.1956192.

10 "Significance of the Iran-Saudi Arabia Agreement Brokered by China," Belfer Center, March 14, 2023, https://www.belfercenter.org/publication/significance-iran-saudi-arabia-agreement-brokered-china.

compliance. However, as these efforts failed to bring any substantial benefits, Tehran began gradually reducing its commitment to the deal, choosing reversible advances to keep its options open.[11] An opening to restore the deal seemed to come with the 2020 US presidential election, as Biden signaled his commitment to return to the agreement.[12] After Biden's election, negotiations to restore the deal began in Vienna. However, any potential progress was cut short by an initial stalling of talks, and more importantly, by the election of hardliner Ebrahim Raisi to the Iranian presidency in summer 2021.

Under the Raisi administration, negotiations to revive the nuclear deal have stalled. From Tehran's perspective, there is a great deal of skepticism on whether there are enough gains to justify reengaging with the United States, especially in the context of the nuclear deal. This skepticism stems from a variety of factors, including the asymmetry between imposing sanctions and providing sanctions relief, where the process is not as clear-cut and implementation is not as effective.[13] Second, part of the limitations in sanctions relief in the case of the JCPOA came from uncertainty over the US position. Just one year after the JCPOA was signed, Donald Trump, who had openly criticized the deal as a presidential candidate, was elected to office, and he signaled early on that the United States would ultimately seek to change the terms of the agreement or withdraw from it altogether. In negotiations to revive the JCPOA, Tehran sought guarantees that a future administration would not simply withdraw again, something that would be impossible for Washington to deliver.[14] Finally, Iranian hardliners in general do not believe in any sustainable rapprochement with the West due to a strong belief that such an entente would be used to weaken the Islamic Republic in preparation for a forced regime change.

Absent an agreement, Iran has continued to ramp up its nuclear program as a means of building leverage and of enhancing its capabilities should it decide to weaponize. Recent reports from the International Atomic Energy

---

11   Mahsa Rouhi, "Iranians Will Tolerate Hardship but Not Capitulation," *Foreign Policy*, May 13, 2019, https://foreignpolicy.com/2019/05/13/iranians-will-tolerate-hardship-but-not-capitulation-rouhani-trump-bolton-sanctions-eu-instex/.
12   Joby Warrick and Anne Gearan, "Biden Has Vowed to Quickly Restore the Iran Nuclear Deal, but That May Be Easier Said than Done," *Washington Post*, December 9, 2020, https://www.washingtonpost.com/politics/2020/12/09/biden-foreign-policy-iran/.
13   Batmanghelidj and Rouhi, "The Iran Nuclear Deal."
14   Suzanne Maloney, "After the Iran Deal: A Plan B to Contain the Islamic Republic," *Foreign Affairs*, February 28, 2023, https://www.foreignaffairs.com/middle-east/iran-nuclear-deal-plan-b-contain-islamic-republic.

Agency indicate alarming results of uranium having been enriched to nearly 84 percent purity, the highest level in the history of Iran's nuclear program, and one that is approaching the 90 percent threshold for weapons-grade uranium.[15] While it is unclear whether Iran will decide to weaponize its enriched uranium, there are dangerous escalatory measures at play, heightening threat perceptions and setting the stage for miscalculations.[16]

The nuclear issue has grown more complicated by recent developments, specifically Iran's brutal repression of protests in the wake of Mahsa Amini's death in September 2022, its support for Russia in its war in Ukraine, and its own emerging relationship with China. For the United States and Europe, however, Iran's repression of protests and its support for Russia's war present a challenge to further engagement, while the burgeoning Iran-China relationship provides Tehran with an alternative economic and strategic partner.[17]

Iran's crackdown on protests in the wake of Amini's death in the custody of the country's morality police put the longevity of the regime in question. The Iranian political elite considered these uprisings to be the product of a western scheme to trigger regime change, and characterized them as the most serious threat to the regime since the 1979 Revolution.[18] And while it was not possible to predict the outcome and timeline of these protests, they could have represented a new framework for political change.[19] There were also domestic political risks for the United States and Europe if they had offered any concessions to the Iranian regime, stemming from fears of

---

15 Stephanie Liechtenstein, "International Atomic Energy Agency Reports Seen by AP Say Iran Resolves 2 Inquiries by Inspectors," *Associated Press*, May 31, 2023, https://apnews.com/article/iran-nuclear-program-iaea-uranium-enrichment-dded37dd0509ff0f469478b5db771027.
16 Mahsa Rouhi et al., "Nuclear Proliferation in the Middle East Beyond Iran," panel discussion, Stimson Center, March 14, 2023, https://www.stimson.org/event/nuclear-proliferation-in-the-middle-east-beyond-iran/.
17 Barak Ravid, "U.S. 'Not Going to Waste Time' on Iran Deal Right Now, Official Says," *Axios*, October 31, 2022, https://www.axios.com/2022/10/31/iran-nuclear-deal-talks-biden.
18 Mohammad Ali Kadivar, "Are Iran's Hijab Protests Different from Past Protest Waves?," *Washington Post*, September 23, 2022, https://www.washingtonpost.com/politics/2022/09/23/amini-hijab-morality-police-iran/.; David Gritten, "Iran Protests: Ex-president Khatami Says Rulers Must Heed Protesters' Demands," *BBC News*, December 6, 2022, https://www.bbc.com/news/world-middle-east-63871863.; "President Raisi Says Iran Thwarted U.S. Destabilisation," *Reuters*, November 5, 2022, https://www.reuters.com/world/middle-east/president-raisi-says-iran-thwarted-us-destabilisation-2022-11-05/.

empowering it and, in turn, suppressing or delegitimizing the protests.[20] In previous political climates, the gravity of nuclear nonproliferation surpassed other concerns, but today there is less latitude for unproductive conversations at the expense of human rights violations.

In a House Armed Services Committee hearing, Under Secretary of Defense for Policy Colin Kahl said that the JCPOA was "on ice" due to changes in Iran's behavior, particularly noting the issue of the war in Ukraine.[21] Since Russia's February 2022 invasion of Ukraine, Tehran and Moscow have cultivated deeper ties, forging a strategic alliance with cooperation in the political, economic, and military spheres. Though Russia is not Iran's largest trading partner, bilateral trade between Moscow and Tehran increased by 20 percent in 2022, and both sides have signaled an interest in further economic cooperation.[22] In the war effort, Tehran has provided Russia with hundreds of drones, and Russia is reportedly seeking more.[23] Tehran's decision to support the war in Ukraine both rhetorically and with provisions is grounded primarily in its desire to challenge US hegemony. The tangible benefits of limited economic relief and access to Russian weapons and technology are important as well, but are secondary.

Iran's strategic relationship with China, which is fostered by a common skepticism of US hegemony, has been a priority for Tehran since the introduction of its "look East" policy in 2005.[24] Economic ties between Tehran and Beijing are extensive, though China's significant role in the world economy and its US trade relationship limit its willingness to invest

---

19 Mahsa Rouhi, "Woman, Life, Freedom in Iran," *Survival Online*, November 29, 2022, https://www.iiss.org/blogs/survival-blog/2022/11/woman-life-freedom-in-iran.
20 Nahal Toosi, "'Everyone Thinks We Have Magic Powers': Biden Seeks a Balance on Iran," *Politico*, October 25, 2022, https://www.politico.com/news/2022/10/25/biden-iran-regime-change-protests-nuclear-weapons-00063312.
21 Jennifer Hansler, "Top US Defense Official Says Iran Could Produce 'One Bomb's Worth of Fissile Material' in 'About 12 Days,'" *CNN*, February 28, 2023, https://www.cnn.com/2023/02/28/politics/kahl-iran-nuclear-deal/index.html.
22 Alex Vatanka, "Russia and Iran Have High Hopes for Each Other," *Foreign Policy*, May 2, 2023, https://foreignpolicy.com/2023/05/02/russia-iran-grain-trade-china-investment-bri/.
23 Aamer Madhani et al., "Russia Is Seeking More Attack Drones from Iran after Depleting Stockpile, White House Says," *PBS News Hour*, May 15, 2023, https://www.pbs.org/newshour/world/russia-is-seeking-more-attack-drones-from-iran-after-depleting-stockpile-white-house-says.
24 Mahsa Rouhi and Clement Therme, "Could Iran's Eastern Ambitions Pave the Way for Future Prosperity?," International Institute for Strategic Studies, March 28, 2019, https://www.iiss.org/online-analysis/online-analysis//2019/03/iran-look-east.

in Iran.[25] Leaders in Iran have also pursued membership in the Shanghai Cooperation Organization (SCO), which they view as a means of boosting legitimacy, as it is both an "anti-western" organization and an opportunity to challenge US hegemony.[26] After 15 years of observer status, Iran is expected to become a full member of the SCO in 2023, after having signed its memorandum of obligations in September 2022.[27]

Because of the potential role that deepening strategic partnerships among Russia, China, and Iran could play in challenging US hegemony, Iran will remain vested in its partnerships with Moscow and Beijing. But this may present some significant challenges in dealing with the nuclear issue. Much of the success of the JCPOA was due to unity among the P5+1 group of nations on the issue of nuclear nonproliferation. However, Iranian leaders now believe that Moscow and Beijing have greater tolerance of a nuclear-armed Iran given Russia's isolation and China's perception of shifting power structures, a fact that will shape Tehran's cost-benefit calculations as it moves forward. Military cooperation between Russia and Iran, including access to Russian technology and weapons, also undermines security in an already fraught situation.

Navigating the Post-JCPOA Environment and Emerging Scenarios

The window for a diplomatic resolution to the nuclear issue has narrowed. In an October 2022 statement, US Special Envoy for Iran Robert Malley declared that the US would not "waste our time" on the stalled talks with an Iran that was unwilling to meaningfully participate, and cited the protests and the Ukraine war as the primary focus of the administration, comments that were later echoed by a White House National Security Council spokesperson.[28] With a now defunct JCPOA, the region and the

---

25 Vatanka, "Russia and Iran Have High Hopes."
26 Nicole Grajewski, "Iranian Membership in the Shanghai Cooperation Organization: Motivations and Implications," Washington Institute for Near East Policy, September 15, 2021, https://www.washingtoninstitute.org/policy-analysis/iranian-membership-shanghai-cooperation-organization-motivations-and-implications.
27 Parisa Hafezi, "Iran to Join Asian Security Body Led by Russia, China," Reuters, September 15, 2022, https://www.reuters.com/world/middle-east/iran-signs-memorandum-joining-shanghai-cooperation-organisation-tass-2022-09-15/.
28 Barak Ravid, "U.S. 'Not Going to Waste Time' on Iran Deal Right Now."; Barak Ravid and Hans Nichols, "Biden in Newly Surfaced Video: Iran Nuclear Deal Is 'Dead,'" Axios, December 20, 2022, https://www.axios.com/2022/12/20/biden-iran-nuclear-deal-dead-video.

world are faced with navigating an environment that provides little clarity on how to contain Iran's nuclear program.

Some officials in Iran dangerously underestimate the possibility of US military action given that the US has no desire to engage in another war in the Middle East. While there are elements of truth to this assessment, options to curb Iran's nuclear program are increasingly limited, giving more credence to military options. Moreover, from Tehran's perspective, an attack would further underscore its need to pursue a nuclear weapon as the only solution for long-term security.[29] Overconfident in its assumptions of Russian and Chinese support and in the United States' lack of willingness to go to war, Iran is likely to continue advancing its nuclear program and taking more risks. As negotiations to restore the deal have failed to materialize, Iran has continued to ramp up its nuclear program as a means of building leverage and has also threatened to withdraw from the Nuclear Non-Proliferation Treaty if snapback sanctions are triggered.[30]

One of the core underlying issues in this post-JCPOA environment is misperceptions regarding "red lines." US officials have declared that America will not allow Iran to obtain a nuclear weapon.[31] The threshold of this red line, however, is unclear. There is no universal definition for the threshold of weaponization; nor is there consensus on how long that process takes, which indicates that determining when Iran has "weaponized" will not be easily predictable for planning.

The Future of the Region: Strategies for Engagement

Despite the serious risk of conflict and strategic competition in the region, there are also important opportunities to manage the possibility of escalation. The US has sought to reassure partners of its commitment to the region, but there is also a need for a redefinition of the partnership, commitment, and expectations between the GCC states and the United States. Some of these relationships have been under strain due to diverging

---

29 Julien Barnes-Dacey and Ellie Geranmayeh, "The West Must Do More to Prevent Conflict with Iran," *Foreign Policy*, March 3, 2023, https://foreignpolicy.com/2023/03/03/biden-eu-iran-nuclear-prevent-war/.
30 Henry Rome and Louis Dugit-Gros, "Snapback Sanctions on Iran: More Bark than Bite?," Washington Institute for Near East Policy, October 25, 2022, https://www.washingtoninstitute.org/policy-analysis/snapback-sanctions-iran-more-bark-bite.
31 Jim Garamone, "Milley Tells House Panel Joint Force is at 'Inflection Point,'" *U.S. Department of Defense News*, March 23, 2023, https://www.defense.gov/News/News-Stories/Article/Article/3339444/milley-tells-house-panel-joint-force-is-at-inflection-point/.

strategic interests.[32] The wars in Yemen and Syria, the attack on Saudi oil facilities, and a long list of other issues over the past decade or so indicate that there is a growing view among GCC states that the US must reassess the balance between its commitments and its expectations. Saudi Arabia and other GCC states believe that the US will not compromise its own interests for the sake of those of its partners in the region, even while it expects its partners to put America's concerns above their own when asked.

Changing perceptions in a highly uncertain security environment produce a significant impact on policies, partnerships, and alliances in the region. This unpredictable environment is ripe for miscalculations and misperceptions that could potentially increase the risk of conflict. US-Iran relations are being closely watched by actors in the region because escalating tensions over the nuclear program could lead to highly consequential scenarios of change in the region, such as living with a nuclear-armed Iran and accompanying proliferation risks or widespread military conflict between the US and Israel, and Iran.[33]

The confluence of the pivot toward Asia and differences in security and economic priorities have increased pressure on Saudi Arabia and other GCC states to move toward strategic diversification. These principles and pressures have resulted in opportunities for a rise in regionalism and parallel great-power relationships that could more substantially address long-term security concerns. Regional actors have sought to hedge their bets and expand partnerships with Iran, Russia, and China. For GCC states, China is a particularly important partner on the economic front, but there is also an attempt to maintain ties with Russia. The GCC states believe that more diverse strategic partnerships, especially with Russia and China, will provide a means of mitigating the security risks of the current situation.

The so-called Abraham Accords of 2020 and the recent Saudi-Iran détente represent regional breakthroughs. The US was the primary broker of the accords, and this normalization of relations was particularly important because of these countries' shared threat perceptions regarding Iran.[34]

---

32 "Fact Sheet: The United States Strengthens Cooperation with Middle East Partners to Address 21st Century Challenges," The White House, July 16, 2022, https://www.whitehouse.gov/briefing-room/statements-releases/2022/07/16/fact-sheet-the-united-states-strengthens-cooperation-with-middle-east-partners-to-address-21st-century-challenges/.
33 Rouhi et al., "Nuclear Proliferation."
34 Gerald M. Feierstein and Yoel Guzansky, "Two Years On, What Is the State of the Abraham Accords?," Middle East Institute, September 14, 2022, https://www.mei.edu/publications/two-years-what-state-abraham-accords.

In a January 2023 meeting in Israel, US National Security Advisor Jake Sullivan and Israeli Prime Minister Benjamin Netanyahu discussed the potential expansion of the Abraham Accords to include the normalization of relations between Saudi Arabia and Israel.[35] While such an effort faces serious obstacles, the Biden administration is negotiating to identify possible opportunities, which it believes would support allies in countering Iran's influence and behavior in the region.[36]

Similarly, Iran also has interests in regional rapprochement with a changing world afoot. The absence of sanctions relief and the growing risk of conflict with the United States and Israel give Iran greater incentive to rely on regional bilateral and multilateral efforts.[37] A deal with Saudi Arabia provides limited economic relief and reduces both brewing regional tensions and the risk of conflict as a result. Iran has also engaged with the UAE and Iraq for similar reasons.[38] Since Iran benefits from these regional partnerships, it is less likely to jeopardize the economic gains it reaps, particularly in the face of US sanctions.[39]

This rise in regionalism provides another means of de-escalating tensions and lowering the temperature. The recent Saudi-Iran rapprochement brokered by China indicates that both Tehran and Riyadh have a vested interest in alleviating escalatory pressures with the US and its regional allies. The attacks on Saudi oil facilities demonstrated Iran's ability to inflict significant damage despite limited conventional military capabilities. And the risk of conflict and the need for economic relief have motivated Tehran to build relations with its rivals in the region. In the long run, these developments could facilitate efforts to address security concerns and provide a foundation for future engagement.

---

35 Rina Bassist, "Iran, Expanding Abraham Accords Top Netanyahu's Meeting with Jake Sullivan," *Al-Monitor*, January 19, 2023, https://www.al-monitor.com/originals/2023/01/iran-expanding-abraham-accords-top-netanyahus-meeting-jake-sullivan.
36 Michael Crowley et al., "Saudi Arabia Offers Its Price to Normalize Relations with Israel," *New York Times*, March 9, 2023, https://www.nytimes.com/2023/03/09/us/politics/saudi-arabia-israel-united-states.html.
37 Mahsa Rouhi, "China's Saudi-Iran Deal Clouded by Uncertainty on Protests, Nuclear Talks," *Al-Monitor*, April 15, 2023, https://www.al-monitor.com/originals/2023/04/chinas-saudi-iran-deal-clouded-uncertainty-protests-nuclear-talks.
38 "Inside Story: After Deal with Saudi Arabia, Top Iranian Security Official 'Due in UAE,'" *Amwaj Media*, March 15, 2023, https://amwaj.media/article/inside-story-after-deal-with-saudi-arabia-top-iranian-security-official-due-in-ua.
39 Rouhi et al., "Nuclear Proliferation."

The US in the Middle East: Staying Put While Simultaneously Pivoting

Imad K. Harb

This volume has endeavored to shed much-needed light on the concept of a US pivot away from the Middle East and America's foreign policy approach to the region. Its publication was necessary as US policy circles across several administrations, as well as Congress, the media, and think tanks have debated and continue to debate the efficacy, value, and fruitfulness of the American presence in the Middle East. The debate is getting even more heated as China flexes its economic—and some fear also its military—muscle in East Asia, one of the geopolitical theaters in which the United States has operated and dominated since the end of the Second World War. To be sure, the dichotomy born out of the continued American presence in the Middle East, which remains a hotspot for conflict, and the necessity to face up to the Chinese challenge is forcing US policymakers to choose between remaining involved in the region, disengaging and devoting all resources to East Asia, or finding a formula for combining both options.

Indeed, policymakers, analysts, and observers know that the United States' involvement in the Middle East has always been rewarding, especially politically and economically, and it would be folly to just pack up and leave the region for would-be hegemons that never before thought that they could replace the United States. But experts also know that stasis would be a disaster for America's long-term strategic interests, especially considering the array of challenges China represents, with its insatiable need for energy, raw materials, and markets. China's challenge in East Asia, the reasoning goes, will not be limited to that strategic theater since Chinese inroads have already been made into other parts of the world, including the Middle East, South Asia, and Africa.

In debating the general idea of a potential US pivot away from the Middle East and a strategic move to East Asia, multiple authors in this volume have drawn the following general conclusions:

1. The United States has chosen to combine a strategy of remaining in the Middle East with a shift in its resources and attention to East Asia. Strategically important factors such as military presence and troop deployment, a reluctance to cede influence to other challengers, a commitment to Israel's security, and uncertainty about future relations with Iran and its nuclear program are decisive in US foreign policy toward the Middle East.
2. Despite appreciating the Middle East's importance to its national security interests, the United States is failing to make democracy and human rights its primary concern in the region, and has in fact emboldened authoritarian leaders there. US policy has even allowed these actors to acquire US-made advanced weapons to ensure the financial well-being of American defense contractors.
3. While sustaining its role in the Middle East, over the last decade the United States has taken steps to prioritize the Indo-Pacific region in its foreign policy. America sees that it must face up to the challenge presented by China but is wary of appearing militarily threatening.
4. Following its strategy since the Obama administration to "end all wars," the United States appears reluctant to interfere in the domestic affairs of its partners and allies in the Middle East. This has given them room to exercise freedom of action and to act independently in choosing to broaden their strategic relations with China, Russia, and others.

These conclusions were derived from the authors' analyses of two sets of factors: those inherent to US policy and influencing the idea of a pivot away from the Middle East, and those emanating from specific conditions in the region and making such a pivot hard to achieve.

Dynamics Influencing the US Pivot from the Middle East

In the initial chapter of this volume, **Charles Dunne** articulates the general agreement among the various authors contributing to this volume that an American disengagement from the Middle East is not possible in the foreseeable future, and most likely never will be. The United States is involved diplomatically, politically, economically, and militarily in the region, an involvement that has not only required decades to take root but has become entangled with US institutions, personnel, policy details, and ideological trends at work in the American body politic. To Dunne, this engagement binds the United States and the Middle East "in ways that resist pragmatic cost-benefit considerations." It is also possible to expand Dunne's judgment in dialectical fashion by looking at US engagement in the Middle East as an instrument of its role elsewhere. Indeed, this engagement is not limited to the benefits geographically accrued to the United States or to interested interlocutors in the region—leaders, elites, institutions, and groups—but transcends them to represent an instrument to reach far beyond the region. Thus, ending the engagement would not only cause "a crisis of confidence" between the United States and the region's leaders, as Dunne argues, but it would immeasurably and negatively impact American policy and practice in surrounding and distant locales as well.

Focusing on American military entanglement in the Middle East—as evident in the tens of thousands of US troops deployed, military bases, weapons sales and training, and other manifestations of raw power—**Waleed Hazbun** argues that decoupling from the region would only lead to the erosion of US influence. Not only does the US global military posture impact the country's relationship with the region, but the contractors and logistics firms that have benefited from decades of military relationships and arms sales present a formidable obstacle to any effort to depart the lucrative Middle Eastern market. Besides, American security commitments to the region's states over the years are very firm arrangements that cannot be easily severed. Hazbun also cogently weaves into his analysis considerations of American domestic politics that strike at the heart of the US relationship with the Middle East: militarized "institutions of strategic development and policy formation" that have had outsized influence over foreign policy, at least since the end of the Second World War. But should the United States decide to take a different approach to the region, it would do well to negotiate regional security arrangements and help promote economic development and climate change policies, as well as other worthy endeavors to de-escalate matters in the region.

Analyzing the economic aspects of a potential pivot from the Middle East, **Mark Finley** focuses on the hydrocarbons sector that has heavily impacted American foreign policy toward the region over the years. He states that becoming a net exporter of oil and gas presents the United States with a dilemma: it is now an economic competitor of the Gulf states while also being a major security supplier to them. If the United States is to pivot away from the Middle East, it risks jeopardizing the continued reliability of Gulf energy exports, not only to the United States but also to the international market. Indeed, the absence of a US security umbrella in the Gulf would threaten oil flows in the region. The 2019 attacks on Saudi oil facilities and on those in the United Arab Emirates can be seen as examples of undesirable outcomes regarding the safe production of energy. To Finley, this begs the question of whether Gulf countries are indeed capable of securing their energy production if or when the United States decides to disengage economically and militarily from the Middle East.

Providing a slightly different analysis on the US pivot to Asia, **Yun Sun** argues that the pivot is indeed taking place and the focus on East Asia and China "is a reality, rather than a myth." Sun considers the continuation of the emphasis in Washington on the Chinese challenge to US hegemony from the Obama to the Biden administration as proof of this reality. To be sure, she asserts, there is a prioritization of the Indo-Pacific region in US foreign policy, which has become a main theme of daily dealings by American policymakers. This prioritization is not temporary or passing, but is a steady and consequential undertaking for the purpose of facing up to "the growing economic, political, security, and ideological challenge" that China presents to US hegemony. But Sun tempers her evaluation of the pivot by stating that while US policymakers see challenging China as a priority, they still believe that abandoning the Middle East is a strategic mistake. She posits that the Middle East is central to the global system that the United States dominates, and its abandonment would constitute "traditional and nontraditional security threats." Besides, Sun concludes, the United States cannot abandon a strategic region that is a focus of US-China competition, a reality that will bind the region as a whole to the outcome of this long-term contest.

Analyzing the context of great power competition surrounding a US pivot from the Middle East, **Patricia Karam** writes that China and other countries' pursuit of influence in the region comes specifically at the expense of the US role there. To Karam, this is a direct result "of what is and what is not working in current US policy"; i.e., it represents the application and choices of US policy that are driving not only the tempo of this influence but also the character of those trying to secure it. Agreeing with Sun that the United States will not leave the Middle East as it faces the Chinese challenge in East Asia, Karam says that the United States must "address and contain socioeconomic challenges within the region." Continuing to fail in that task, she argues, will only open the door wider for its undemocratic competitors, some of whom are already making deals with the region's states.

Rami G. Khouri sees that there may be no love lost between the United States and many state leaders and inhabitants in the region, considering the ill will born out of the hubris that has governed American behavior there over the last few decades and that has resulted in the deaths of millions. If it were not for the nagging security guarantees that American hegemony and weapons provide for many autocrats, the pivot would potentially be the most welcome step Washington could take as far as said autocrats are concerned. After all, many other would-be hegemons would love to indulge the authoritarian nature and structure of the region's regimes without the pretense that the United States has taken pains to show in its relations. Khouri argues that the on-again, off-again relationship between the United States and Middle East countries (with the obvious exception of Israel) is unsustainable, necessitating an apparent drive among Arab states for "self-interest, autonomy, and options to diversify relations." However, the problem remains that the Arab world has "limited leverage and bargaining chips" (except, of course, oil largesse in service of Gulf countries) to be able to make this necessity achievable. In the meantime, the Arab world at large is limping toward more uncertainty and less regional and global influence as it tries to join other regions navigating the new dynamics of the twenty-first century.

Sarah Leah Whitson considers talk of a US pivot away from the Middle East as "greatly exaggerated," not only because of US interests in the region—which do not include promoting democracy and human rights—but also because of regional states' machinations to keep the United States involved. Successive administrations' avoidance of pushing regional actors on democracy and human rights has helped allow the regimes to neglect political and economic development and to secure American corporations' connections and profits. Whitson sees that the Gulf states have great influence in Washington because they have succeeded not only in enticing American corporations but also in hiring many lobbyists, former officials, and retired military officers. She cites the examples of former President Trump's senior advisor Jared Kushner and former Treasury Secretary Steve Mnuchin, who both received substantial funds from Saudi Arabia as former officials who carried water for Saudi interests in Washington. Whitson argues that this harms "the integrity, independence, and decision-making of US policymakers" as they deal with strategic decisions affecting US relations with the Gulf. Ultimately, Whitson writes, this compromises the overall interests of the United States and constitutes a direct assault on American democracy.

Agreeing with the general notion of this volume that the United States is not completely pivoting away from the Middle East, **Tamara Kharroub** exposes US shortcomings in impacting the Arab world's cyber environment. These shortcomings have allowed other actors to develop the infrastructures necessary for information and technology, which are helping them "to determine the future of power and influence" in the MENA region. Not only are actors like China and Russia exploiting this US vulnerability, but Saudi Arabia and the UAE are working on ensuring their dominance of cyberspace in the region, controlling the flow of information, developing surveillance systems, and harnessing artificial intelligence capabilities in order to maintain authoritarian political control. Kharroub argues that the US focus on defense and cybersecurity is shortsighted since it neglects the information and communications environments in which China and Russia have made long-term investments. With the United States failing to develop long-term goals in this regard, Gulf states are using Chinese companies' technology as they embark on efforts to diversify their economies, in the process becoming wedded to China instead of relying on the United States.

Regional Issues Hindering a Pivot

Yousef Munayyer puts the US relationship with Israel in the context of two paradigms that have governed world politics and the US position in them since the Second World War: the Cold War and the Global War on Terror. In the first, Israel was a natural ally and partner of the United

States because it was seen as an extension of the so-called democratic West. In the second, Israel played a role as an active participant alongside the United States. But after the end of US involvements in Iraq and Afghanistan, a new paradigm arose that will govern important issues in the Middle East regarding Israel and its status as the occupying power of Palestinian land. The first issue is that it does not seem possible for the United States to disengage from its traditional support of Israel, even though the latter does not need it for its economic (and arguably military) security. The second is that it is no longer easy to make the argument that Israel is a democratic state that defends human rights since it is an occupying power and practices the crime of apartheid against Palestinians. After seeing Israel's treatment of the Palestinians, domestic public opinion in the United States is beginning to shift away from blind support for the Zionist state. The third issue is that normalizing relations between Israel and Arab states has not necessarily brought stability to the MENA region, not only because it does not have popular support among Arab citizens but also because it does not serve as a resolution to the Question of Palestine.

Kristian Coates Ulrichsen avers that it is quite unlikely that the United States will withdraw, pivot away, or otherwise disengage from the Middle East. But looking at America's policy direction from the perspective of Gulf Cooperation Council states, he argues that they have not been appreciative of the policies of the United States since the original idea of pivoting away was first proposed. To deal with the current state of affairs, Coates Ulrichsen argues, Gulf Arab states are indeed hedging their bets, lest they be left out in the cold if circumstances do lead to a pivot. That is why Gulf states have taken pains to shape "a new regional order" that gives China a role "in economic, energy, and, increasingly, political affairs." The Saudis, for example, are fashioning what he calls a "polycentric approach to regional affairs," where the United States remains an essential security partner, but not the only one. He cites the Saudi-Iran agreement of March 2023, mediated and hosted by China, as an example of a conscious effort to shed the old order of alignment in favor of a multiparty arrangement that serves the interests of the kingdom (and, by extension, other GCC states) in economic prosperity and regional peace. While this hoped-for arrangement is probably far off and arriving at it is a work in progress, it is not hard to see that Saudi Arabia and other GCC states may have finally tired of the expectation that the United States will be their security guarantor as they navigate less certain geopolitical conditions around them.

In his chapter on the declining influence of the United States in the Middle East, **Nabeel Khoury** criticizes what he calls the United States' "obsession with leadership," not only in the MENA region but also globally. He says that the United States appears to lack an awareness of the necessity to work with other powers to have "a better understanding of common interests and a collaborative approach to common threats." Khoury derides Biden administration officials' constant warnings about the supposed threat Iran poses to Saudi Arabia and others in the Gulf, an insistence that made it possible for China to use diplomacy to enter the Middle East and actually strike bargains and reach compromises between local actors, such as occurred last March between Saudi Arabia and Iran. In a sense, Khoury criticizes successive US administrations for not emphasizing a diplomatic approach to the Middle East and for preferring instead to use military force to help nation-building and democracy. This has transformed the United States into an occupying power concerned about its own national interests and allied with corrupt and authoritarian regimes. Instead, Khoury argues, Washington should have introduced a Marshall Plan-like approach that would have assisted in the development of the region—something that could have been implemented in Afghanistan, Iraq, and Libya to show how an enduring peace could be established. Although unlikely, a potential complete US pivot away from the Middle East would indeed bring the region a respite from an adventurous foreign policy that so far has not served American or regional interests.

Lina Khatib analyzes one of the United States' most cumbersome engagements in the Middle East. US policy toward Syria around the start of the latter's civil war in 2011 provided a clear example that Washington was indeed diminishing its attention to the region. Khatib argues that former President Barack Obama's retreat from punishing the Syrian regime in 2013 when it used chemical weapons against civilians—the "red lines" debacle—meant that the United States was not going to use its military power in pursuit of any serious policy objective, in this case accountability for war crimes. This retreat came while major Arab states—Saudi Arabia and Qatar, for example—were supporting rebel groups aiming to topple the Bashar al-Assad regime, a geopolitical and geostrategic partner to Iran. Today, Khatib states, the Arab world sees itself normalizing relations with the same Assad regime that it wanted to depose in the first years of the civil war. To Khatib this is a result of US disengagement from what happens in Syria. However, while asserting that the United States has at best a confused policy toward Syria, she believes that Assad's rehabilitation will not be followed by massive reconstruction funds. The Arab world may accommodate itself to Assad, but there remain serious obstacles and contentious issues such as the thousands of detainees held by the regime, the latter's involvement in the drug trade, the millions of Syrian refugees and internally displaced persons, and the presence of Iranian militias on Syrian soil.

Sahar Aziz sees that Egypt is hedging its bets and is itself pivoting to China while hanging on dearly to US military assistance. Perhaps the only difference between Saudi Arabia and Egypt in courting China is one related to capabilities. While China sees Saudi Arabia as an indispensable oil producer for its economic development and expansion, Egypt appears as a pauper seeking rent and investments from China to address its seriously anemic economic situation. If, for the sake of argument, Saudi Arabia decides to distance itself militarily from the United States, it at least has the financial wherewithal to secure its security needs from China or any other party. Egypt, on the other hand, relies heavily on US military assistance and will not be capable of doing the same in the foreseeable future. Aziz thus proposes that Egypt is seeking to pivot to China to secure its economic needs, while the United States may be partially pivoting to East Asia in order to be able to face up to the Chinese challenge. To Aziz, the United States will not object to Egypt's maneuver so long as the latter keeps its commitment to Israel's security and remains a loyal consumer of American weapons. As for democracy and human rights, Aziz does not believe that they are part of US policy toward Egypt or constitute a pressure point on US foreign relations in the Middle East.

Discussing where Iran fits in the context of the American presence in the Middle East and the possibility of pivoting away from the region, **Mahsa Rouhi** focuses on US-Iran negotiations over the Islamic Republic's nuclear program. She argues that the absence of sanctions relief for Iran and the seeming US adoption of Israel's threat perceptions make the talks more difficult today than they were when the Joint Comprehensive Plan of Action was signed in 2015. From its side, Iran is trying to de-escalate regional tensions and has signed an agreement with Saudi Arabia and engaged with Iraq and the UAE, policies that it believes beneficial at a time of uncertainty with the United States. As for the United States, it cannot think of a pivot away from the Middle East as long as the nuclear situation is unresolved. At the same time, it sees that its Gulf partners are willing and ready to stay on good terms with Iran and is thus trying to accommodate their wishes. In other words, Rouhi argues, the US position in the Middle East and whether the United States disengages from the region or not does not solely depend on what happens with the nuclear issue.

Conclusion

This volume's chapters analyzing the notion of a US pivot away from the Middle East rely in their analyses on past and current conditions in US foreign policy, as well as on regional dynamics that hinder a strategic shift in said policy. Other important issues that this collection was unable to cover are also influencing events and policy developments, and include cultural considerations, the role and opinion of civil society groups in the region, the push and pull of ongoing conflicts, strategic capabilities of US rivals, and many other influential factors. These and other matters may perhaps form the pillars of an additional analysis of the same import in the future. But suffice it to say, the chapters herein have charted a good course for analyzing the realities of US policy in the Middle East at present, as well as those of regional states, with the knowledge that both international and regional conditions are in a state of flux that makes predictions of future trajectories quite difficult. We hope that this volume has increased the sum of knowledge of US policy in the Middle East and beyond, and has offered insight into where MENA countries may be heading as they plan their paths of development and strategic alignment for the future.

Biographies of Contributors

Sahar Aziz is Distinguished Professor of Law, Middle East Legal Studies Scholar, and Chancellor's Social Justice Scholar at Rutgers University Law School. Professor Aziz's scholarship examines the intersection of national security, race, religion, and civil rights with a focus on the adverse impact of national security laws and policies on racial, religious, and ethnic minorities. Professor Aziz is also an expert on rule of law, democracy, and human rights in the Middle East, with a focus on Egypt. She is the author of the book *The Racial Muslim: When Racism Quashes Religious Freedom* and the founding director of the Center for Security, Race and Rights.

Kristian Coates Ulrichsen is a Non-resident Senior Fellow at Arab Center Washington DC and a Baker Institute Fellow for the Middle East at Rice University. His research focuses on political economy and international relations in Middle Eastern and Gulf Arab states, issues of internal security and regional stability, and contemporary and early twentieth century Middle Eastern history. Coates Ulrichsen was previously a research group member at the Middle East Center, London School of Economics and Political Science, and an associate fellow at the Royal Institute of International Affairs (Chatham House). He holds a PhD in History from the University of Cambridge. Select publications include *Insecure Gulf: The End of Certainty and the Transition to the Post-Oil Era* (2011), *The United Arab Emirates: Power, Politics, and Policymaking* (2016), and *Qatar and the Gulf Crisis* (2020), as well as *Centers of Power in the Arab Gulf States* (forthcoming in 2024).

Charles W. Dunne is a former US diplomat who served in the Middle East, South Asia, and Washington. He is currently a Non-resident Fellow at Arab Center Washington DC and a Scholar with the Middle East Institute. Since 2019, he has taught on US foreign policy and political change in the Middle East at the Elliott School of International Affairs at the George Washington University. During his 24 years in the US Foreign Service, Dunne served overseas in Cairo, Jerusalem, and Madras (Chennai), India. He also served as foreign policy advisor to the Pentagon and director for Iraq at the National Security Council. He was also a member of Secretary of State Colin Powell's Policy Planning Staff working on advancing political reform and democracy in the Broader Middle East and North Africa. After leaving government, Dunne was Freedom House's director of Middle East and North Africa programs from 2011 to 2015 and focused on implementing human rights and democracy projects with civil society partners in the region.

Mark Finley is a Fellow in Energy and Global Oil at Rice University's Baker Institute. He has nearly 40 years of experience at the intersections of energy, economics, and public policy. Previously, Finley was a senior economist at BP, where he led analysis of the global oil market and transportation sector for the company's long-term Energy Outlook. He also managed the Statistical Review of World Energy. Prior to joining BP, Finley was an analyst and manager at the Central Intelligence Agency, where he assessed the implications for US strategic interests of global oil and energy market developments and analyzed the energy policies of key producer and consumer countries. He is also a member of the Council on Foreign Relations. Finley holds an undergraduate degree from the University of Michigan and graduate degrees from Northwestern University and the George Washington University.

Imad K. Harb is the Director of Research and Analysis at Arab Center Washington DC. Previously, he worked as an adjunct professor of Middle East Studies at the Center for Contemporary Arab Studies, Georgetown University. He also served as senior analyst at the Abu Dhabi, UAE-based Emirates Center for Strategic Studies and Research and taught political science and international relations at the University of Utah and San Francisco State University. In addition, he worked as senior program officer at the United States Institute of Peace. Harb writes and publishes on a number of topics, including civil-military relations, regional politics, and US policy in the MENA region. He is the co-editor, with Zeina Azzam, of *Biden and the Middle East: A Challenging Road Ahead* (ACW, 2021), and *The Arab World Beyond Conflict* (ACW, 2019), among other volumes. Harb earned a PhD in political science from the University of Utah.

Waleed Hazbun is Richard L. Chambers Professor of Middle Eastern Studies in the Department of Political Science at the University of Alabama, where he teaches international relations and US foreign policy in the Middle East. He holds a PhD in political science from MIT and previously taught at Johns Hopkins University and the American University of Beirut. He is the author of *Beaches, Ruins, Resorts: The Politics of Tourism in the Arab World* (Minnesota, 2008). He also co-edited and contributed to *New Conflict Dynamics: Between Regional Autonomy and Intervention in the Middle East and North Africa* (Danish Institute for International Studies, 2017) and "Exit Empire – Imagining New Paths for US Policy" *Middle East Report* No. 294 (Spring 2020).

Khalil E. Jahshan is a Palestinian American political analyst and media commentator. He serves as Executive Director of Arab Center Washington DC. Between 2004 and 2013, he was a lecturer in International Studies and Languages at Pepperdine University and executive director of Pepperdine's Seaver College Washington DC Internship Program. Previously, Jahshan served as executive vice president of the American-Arab Anti-Discrimination Committee (ADC) and director of its government affairs affiliate, National Association of Arab Americans (NAAA-ADC). Throughout his career, he has held numerous leadership positions in Arab American organizations, including vice president of the American Committee on Jerusalem, president of the National Association of Arab Americans, national director of the Association of Arab-American University Graduates, assistant director of the Palestine Research and Educational Center, and lecturer in Arabic at the University of Chicago Extension and at Northwestern University in Evanston, Illinois. Jahshan has also served on boards of directors and advisory boards of several Middle East-oriented organizations, including ANERA, MIFTAH, and Search for Common Ground. He appears regularly as a political commentator on Arab and American media outlets.

Patricia Karam is a Non-resident Fellow at Arab Center Washington DC. She held multiple senior managerial positions in nongovernmental organizations over the past 20 years, working at the nexus of problem analysis, policy formulation, and impactful program implementation aimed at social and policy change in a range of complex, conflict-ridden settings across the globe. Most recently, Karam was Middle East North Africa (MENA) regional director at the International Republican Institute, where she was responsible for the strategic oversight and leadership of a multimillion-dollar portfolio of programs focused on citizen-responsive governance, political party development, legislative strengthening, and civil society capacity-building. Prior to that, as MENA director at the Natural Resource Governance Institute, Karam was responsible for research, advocacy, grant-making, and technical assistance projects aimed at improving natural resource governance managed through country offices she established in Lebanon, Iraq, Tunisia, and Libya. As a deputy director at the International Center for Transitional Justice, she oversaw educational transitional justice programs and spearheaded the expansion of a Documentation Affinity Group, a global network of action-oriented and grassroots documentation-focused human rights groups. She also held a combination of senior management, fundraising, and grant-making roles at the US Institute of Peace, Iraq Foundation, the Iraqi Embassy, and New York University's Trauma Studies Program.

Tamara Kharroub is Deputy Executive Director and a Senior Fellow at Arab Center Washington DC. Her research focuses on the intersection of technology and human rights and democracy in the Middle East and North Africa. She publishes research and policy analysis papers and editorials exploring the role of media and communication technology in the political process, including issues of digital authoritarianism and repression, disinformation and information environments, cyber power and geopolitics, surveillance technologies, propaganda and media representation, identity politics online, artificial intelligence and autonomous weapons, and digital rights, in addition to research on Palestine/Israel and US policy there. Kharroub holds a PhD from Indiana University Bloomington and an MA from the University of Westminster, and is the recipient of several awards and fellowships, including a Fulbright.

Lina Khatib is Director of the SOAS Middle East Institute and MBI Al Jaber Chair in Middle East Studies, as well as Professor of Practice at the Department of Politics and International Studies at SOAS University of London. Prior to this, she served as director of the Middle East and North Africa program at Chatham House and as director of the Carnegie Middle East Center at the Carnegie Endowment for International Peace. Dr. Khatib also co-founded and led the Program on Arab Reform and Democracy at Stanford University's Center on Democracy, Development, and the Rule of Law and was a senior associate at the Arab Reform Initiative. She has published several books and is a frequent writer and commentator on current affairs in the Middle East.

Rami George Khouri has reported and published op-eds and analyses on the Arab region and its global relations since 1968. His last post was Journalist-in-Residence and Co-director of Global Engagement at the American University of Beirut, where he established the Issam Fares Institute for Public Policy and International Affairs. He has edited the *Daily Star* (Beirut) and *Jordan Times* newspapers, and received the Pax Christi International Peace Prize for 2006. He has taught or been a visiting scholar at the American University of Beirut, Northeastern University, Harvard, Mount Holyoke, Princeton, Syracuse, Villanova, Oklahoma, and Stanford, and is a Joint Advisory Board member at the Northwestern University Journalism School in Qatar. He was general manager of Al Kutba Publishers, in Amman, Jordan, where he wrote books and hosted a radio show on Jordanian archaeology. He has BA and MSc degrees in political science and mass communications, respectively, from Syracuse University.

Nabeel Khoury is a Non-resident Senior Fellow with Arab Center Washington DC. After 12 years in the Foreign Service, Dr. Khoury retired from the US Department of State in 2013 with the rank of minister counselor. He taught Middle East and US strategy courses at the National Defense University and Northwestern University. In his last overseas posting, Khoury served as deputy chief of mission at the US Embassy in Yemen (2004-2007). In 2003, during the Iraq War, he served as department spokesperson at US Central Command in Doha and in Baghdad. In his last posting in Washington before retirement he served as director of the office of Near East and South Asia at the Bureau of Intelligence and Research.

Yousef Munayyer is Head of the Palestine/Israel Program and a Senior Fellow at Arab Center Washington DC. He also serves as a member of the editorial committee of the *Journal of Palestine Studies* and was previously executive director of the US Campaign for Palestinian Rights. Some of his published articles can be found in *The New York Times, The Washington Post, The Nation, Boston Globe, Foreign Policy, Journal of Palestine Studies, Middle East Policy*, and others. Dr. Munayyer holds a PhD in International Relations and Comparative Politics from the University of Maryland.

Mahsa Rouhi is a Research Fellow at the Center for Strategic Research at the Institute for National Strategic Studies at National Defense University. Her research and expertise focus on nuclear policy and security strategy in the Middle East, particularly Iran. Prior to joining INSS, Rouhi was a research fellow in the Non-proliferation and Nuclear Policy program at the International Institute for Strategic Studies, where she co-directed a track two project on geopolitics and nuclear issues in the Middle East and continues to engage as an associate. She was a post-doctoral fellow at the Belfer Center from 2016 to 2018 and a visiting assistant professor from 2014 to 2016 at the University of Miami. She received her PhD from King's College, University of Cambridge, UK. Rouhi's analysis and commentary has been published by *Foreign Policy, The New York Times, The Guardian, Boston Globe, The National Interest*, and other academic and policy journals.

Yun Sun is a Senior Fellow and Co-Director of the East Asia Program and Director of the China Program at the Stimson Center. Her expertise is in Chinese foreign policy, US-China relations, and China's relations with neighboring countries and authoritarian regimes. From 2011 to early 2014, she was a visiting fellow at the Brookings Institution, where she focused on Chinese national security decision-making processes and China-Africa relations. From 2008 to 2011, Yun was the China analyst for the International Crisis Group based in Beijing, specializing in China's foreign policy toward conflict countries and the developing world. Prior to ICG, she worked on US-Asia relations in Washington, DC for five years. Yun earned her master's degree in international policy and practice from George Washington University, as well as an MA in Asia Pacific studies and a BA in international relations from Foreign Affairs College in Beijing.

Sarah Leah Whitson is Executive Director of Democracy for the Arab World Now (DAWN). Previously, she served as executive director of Human Rights Watch's Middle East and North Africa Division from 2004 to 2020, overseeing the work of the division in 19 countries, with staff located in 10 countries. Whitson has led dozens of advocacy and investigative missions throughout the region, focusing on issues of armed conflict, accountability, legal reform, migrant workers, and human rights. She has published widely on human rights and foreign policy in the Middle East in international and regional media, including *The New York Times*, *Foreign Affairs*, *The Washington Post*, *Foreign Policy*, *The Los Angeles Times*, and *CNN*, and appears regularly on *Al Jazeera*, *BBC*, *NPR*, and *MSNBC*. Whitson graduated from the University of California, Berkeley and Harvard Law School.

About Arab Center Washington DC

Mission
Arab Center Washington DC (ACW) is a nonprofit, independent, and nonpartisan research organization dedicated to furthering the political, economic, and social understanding of the Arab world in the United States and to providing insight on US policies and interests in the Middle East. As a Washington-based authoritative research center on the Arab world, ACW addresses fundamental aspects of US-Arab relations through timely and objective academic research, policy analysis, and educational exchange.

Areas of Study
- Perspectives on democratization, human rights, and justice in Arab countries
- Current events and US policies in a changing Arab world
- Cultural, historical, political, and social dimensions of US foreign policy
- US-Arab economic relations and strategic partnerships
- Regional conflicts and peacemaking efforts in the Middle East
- Role of the US Congress in Middle East foreign policy

Affiliation
ACW is affiliated with the Arab Center for Research and Policy Studies (ACRPS) and its network of research centers around the world. Headquartered in Doha, Qatar, ACRPS is one of the premier independent research institutes in the Arab region focusing on the social sciences, regional history, and geostrategic affairs. Its research, publications, projects, and events examine the important issues and challenges facing the contemporary Arab world.

Support
ACW relies on contributions from individual supporters, organizations, foundations, and corporations. Contributions to ACW—a 501(c)(3) tax-exempt organization—are deductible under Section 170 of the Internal Revenue Code.

Arab Center Washington DC
المركز العربي واشنطن دي سي